To Matt, £8 —

It's All Too Much

I hope you like my second book so looking forward to chatting about it with you,

Alison xxxxx

About the author

Allison Keating, aka @thepractical.psychologist, is a chartered psychologist. She is the author of *The Secret Lives of Adults*, a weekly relationship columnist for the *Irish Independent*, and a regular on *The Ray D'Arcy Show* and Ireland AM.

She has twenty-five years of therapeutic experience in relationships, overwhelm, anxiety, panic attacks, trauma and general mental health, and she also consults as a work and organisational psychologist. This dual perspective – from the therapy couch to the workplace and back home – provides her with unique insights into the juggling act of modern adulthood.

Her mission is to be a psychological disruptor, bringing the science of understanding your nervous system into your daily experience of life. She aims to start a soft revolution that values you, rest, and the everyday joy of enough, because so many have told her it's all too much. Allison wants to change this for us all.

It's All Too Much

PRACTICAL WAYS TO PAUSE PANIC ATTACKS,
REDUCE OVERWHELM AND ANXIETY,
AND REDISCOVER EVERYDAY JOY

ALLISON KEATING
THE PRACTICAL PSYCHOLOGIST

Gill Books

Gill Books
Hume Avenue
Park West
Dublin 12
www.gillbooks.ie

Gill Books is an imprint of M.H. Gill and Co.

© Allison Keating 2024

978 07171 9906 8

Illustrations by Niamh McArdle
Edited by Rachel Pierce
Design by Bartek Janczak
Typeset by Typo•glyphix
Printed and Bound in the UK by Clays Ltd, Elcograf S.p.A.
This book is typeset in 10.5 on 16pt, Minion Pro.

*The paper used in this book comes from the wood pulp
of sustainably managed forests.*

This book is not intended as a substitute for the medical advice of a physician. The reader should consult a doctor or mental health professional if they feel it necessary. The case studies and examples throughout the book are a composite of issues presented in therapy.

All rights reserved.
No part of this publication may be copied, reproduced or transmitted in any form or by any means, without written permission of the publishers.

A CIP catalogue record for this book is available from the British Library.

5 4 3 2 1

To the people who live in my heart, head and soul: Thomas, Alannah, Hayley and Brooke. My family and friends. And my clients.

This book is for you, with the deepest hope to heal and change the human race from feeling too much and never enough to a soft revolution of everyday joy.

Contents

INTRODUCTION: ARE YOU HAVING A HAPPY ADULTHOOD? 1
        How to use this book 3

Part 1   **Survival mode** 7

CHAPTER 1   **WHY IS IT ALL TOO MUCH?** 8
        Why is it all too much? 9
        Why do I feel the way I do? 9
        The First World anxiety epidemic 10
        Why am I constantly anxious? 12
        Why am I living like this? 17
        Life in survival mode 19
        Can I move out of survival mode? 20
        The Practical Psychology 21

CHAPTER 2   **WHAT IS ANXIETY AND HOW DOES IT BUILD IN THE BODY?** 25
        What is anxiety? 26
        What is generalised anxiety disorder? 26
        The polyvagal theory of anxiety 28
        The 4 Fs: Fight, Flight, Freeze, Fawn 36

Knowing your state: Your personal profile map 41
The SOS state switch 43
The window of tolerance 51
The language of safety 53
Building your SOS switch capabilities 56
What have we learned? 60
The Practical Psychology 62

CHAPTER 3 **HOW DOES EMOTIONAL ANXIETY FEEL FROM THE INSIDE?** 64

How do you know if you are emotionally dysregulated? 65
The 3 I's: Irritability, impatience and intolerance 67
How it feels: Overwhelm 68
The Practical Psychology 74
How it feels: Hyperarousal 76
Hypoarousal 79
Can I work my way out of emotional dysregulation? 79
Learning to self-regulate 83
The Practical Psychology 88

CHAPTER 4 **HOW DOES PSYCHOLOGICAL ANXIETY FEEL FROM THE INSIDE?** 90

How it feels: Trauma 92
How it feels: Perfectionism 96
The Practical Psychology 102
How it feels: Performing 104
How it feels: Pleasing 105
The Practical Psychology 113
The soft revolution: Polyvagal theory for perfectionism, performing and pleasing 115
The Practical Psychology 118

CHAPTER 5	**HOW DOES PHYSIOLOGICAL ANXIETY FEEL FROM THE INSIDE?** 119
	How it feels: Panic attacks 120
	How it feels: Panic disorder 125
	The 'usual suspects' of anxiety 126
	The Practical Psychology 130
	How it feels: High-functioning anxiety – burnout and exhaustion 132
	High-functioning anxiety in the workplace 135
	The cost of opportunity 136
	The Practical Psychology 139
CHAPTER 6	**WHY WOMEN EXPERIENCE TWICE AS MUCH ANXIETY AS MEN** 145
	Emotional labour 147
	The Practical Psychology 152
	Hormones and anxiety 153
	Postnatal anxiety 157
	The Practical Psychology 162
	Perimenopause: The next journey 164
	The Practical Psychology 172

Part 2   Revival mode 175

CHAPTER 7	**HOW TO LEAVE SURVIVAL MODE** 177
	It's not your fault 179
	Leaving survival mode 181
	Coming home to you 183
	The heart of the matter 187
	What will it be like to exit survival mode? 189
	The Practical Psychology 191

CHAPTER 8 **THE GREAT DISCONNECT: UNHEALTHY DEFENCE MECHANISMS** 192
    Stop deadheading your emotions 194
    Numbing out 195
    Pausing anxiety 202
    Flooding and information overload 202
    The Practical Psychology 205
    Why is it hard to stay focused? 210
    How does numbing out tie in with anxiety? 212
    Focus facts 214
    Reconnecting: Why you need to practise orienting 217
    Finding out why you are choosing numbness 218
    The Practical Psychology 220

CHAPTER 9 **HEALTHY COPING MECHANISMS FOR EMOTIONAL ANXIETY** 225
    How do I make the change? 226
    Emotional regulation 229
    The role of emotional agency in emotional regulation 233
    The Practical Psychology 237
    Boundaries 239
    The Practical Psychology 264

CHAPTER 10 **HEALTHY COPING MECHANISMS FOR PSYCHOLOGICAL ANXIETY** 266
    Your inner critic 268
    Conscious drinking 272
    Conscious socialising 275
    Cognitive behavioural therapy 276
    The Practical Psychology 277

CHAPTER 11   **HEALTHY COPING MECHANISMS FOR PHYSIOLOGICAL ANXIETY** 282
    Resting and relaxing 283
    Micro-moments 297
    Why you need to strive less and rest more 302
    The Practical Psychology 303

Part 3   From revival to finding the everyday joy of enough 307

CHAPTER 12   **THE NEW CULTURE OF ENOUGH** 309
    The review process 311
    What is an existential crisis? 313
    What is my meaning and purpose? 314
    The question of incongruence 316
    Finding the everyday joy of enough 318
    The Practical Psychology 323

YOUR PSYCHOLOGICAL CONTRACT 326
YOUR PSYCHOLOGICAL TOOLBOX 328
ACKNOWLEDGEMENTS 347
NOTES 351
BIBLIOGRAPHY 355

Introduction: Are you having a happy adulthood?

'How was your childhood?' is a question you could expect to be asked in therapy. Why? Because your childhood fundamentally shaped and influenced who and how you are today. But I wonder if anyone has ever asked, or if you have asked yourself, whether you are having a happy adulthood. From what I can see, there are a huge number of overwhelmed people around us, which suggests a lot of people are having a less-than-happy adulthood. I'm pretty sure many adults have frequently found this 'hood' a difficult place to navigate, often feeling lost, confused, frustrated, and as if you're going round in unending circles.

This book, born from the constant urgency of modern life, aims to be a transformative guide for those yearning for change. Let's face it, you don't have time to read this book, and I didn't have time to write it. Something is radically wrong with that. So, I'm saying 'enough'. It's all too much, and that needs to change. It is my intention to challenge what we've accepted in society as 'normal' and advocate for radically softer, more meaningful change.

In the words of entrepreneur Naval Ravikant, 'To write a great book, you must first become the book.' I want to 'become' this book for me, my family and my relationships so I can turn to you with full-hearted integrity and invite you to join me in questioning the sustainability of our current lifestyles and to make meaningful, purposeful change. Integrity matters, and I'm not trying to sell you a quick fix because we both know it doesn't exist.

The obsession with and inane bombardment around health and being healthy is inescapable, and yet it hasn't translated into us being healthier or happier. *I don't feel like myself* is a comment I hear on the couch every day. I know that so many people feel utterly lost, disconnected from themselves and others. As I see the overload of 'self-care', it leaves me feeling a little weary. Wellbeing seems to have become commercially weaponised, just another thing to add to your list of perceived failures.

It is poignant that these are the most common phrases my clients tell me: I feel so overwhelmed; I feel like I'm losing control; I worry all the time; I wake up feeling dread and anxiety; I'm scared I'll never feel normal or like myself again. As a psychologist with 25 years' experience, I stand firm in declaring, enough is enough. This is a rallying cry against the relentless push of do more, be more, have more. I am here as a psychological disruptor, not to provide more information, but to offer practical ways to help you embody how you want to feel in real life. Perhaps wellness has become superficial, with aesthetically pleasing but bland brands that may inspire yet ultimately leave you feeling inadequate as you multitask your way through each day. I advocate for sustainable health and an enjoyable life.

This book addresses the internal disconnection experienced in a society that treats the body, head and heart as separate entities. That encourages you to ignore your heart and push through your physical limits, leaving your head overwhelmed and anxious. My intention here is to take what my clients have told me and to let you know that the overwhelm you feel isn't just a 'you' problem, it is also a societal problem. We will delve into its scientific roots, and I will provide you with practical tools to learn how to self-regulate amid life's demands. We will explore strategies to restore a sense of calm so you can figure out how and what to let go of to reduce the overwhelming load.

This book serves as a physical, mental, and emotional GPS map of your nervous system. The aim is to bring you to an understanding of where you are and then guide you to where you would like to be. This isn't a one-way, straight-line trip; life is constantly in flux, so this isn't about worrying if you feel you are going the wrong way, it's about having a deep understanding that there is a reason why you feel the way you do and that there is a way back to you.

How to use this book

This book is an in-depth examination of anxiety and the effect it has on your life. It is divided into three parts: Part 1 looks at understanding why you go into survival mode; Part 2 is about revival and finding healthier ways to cope with anxiety; and Part 3 explores the practical magic of finding everyday joy. At the back you'll find the Psychological Toolbox – I love a toolbox! I am thrilled to share with you the resources I use with my clients that you can now use whenever you need them.

An important thing to note is that I have separated anxiety into emotional, psychological and physiological facets. This is not to say that anxiety operates in three different furrows, each being ploughed on its own. No – the fact is that the three are inextricably connected, and anxiety affects all three at the same time. However, I have chosen to split it up like this to bring clarity to the many different aspects of anxiety, and to allow you to identify its parts, and thereby to understand which parts are having the greatest impact on you. That's very useful information for you to have.

- **Part 1** explores what survival mode is, how you enter it and why you stay in it. It shows how many of us are living stuck in chronic survival mode, and why you need to know how to move in and out of it.
- **Part 2** takes us to revival mode, after you have learned how to exit survival mode when you need to. Here, we examine unhealthy defence mechanisms that may have you in their grip, then we look at healthy coping mechanisms. This equips you with knowledge about the nature and source of your own anxiety, and tools to allow you to cope with it as well as possible.
- **Part 3** is the culmination of all your hard work and reflection during the course of the book, where you are ready and want to move from merely surviving to recognising the everyday joy of enough. This brings us to a pivotal point in our lives where we question everything, not in a horrible self-doubting, identity-crisis way, but rather in the spirit of finding what it is that will bring us back to joy. We want to move away from the feeling of it being all too much and return to a self-connection and a connection with others that is grounded in everyday joy. We will work on articulating what your purpose is and what gives your life meaning. That will encourage a new way of living, one that aligns with your core values. Instead of an ending, it is a joyous new beginning.

Most chapters have a dedicated section called The Practical Psychology, which is where the real work begins. I am going to ask you to get a notebook for this specific purpose, and for this to be for your eyes only. Similar to therapy, we need to give you a safe space where you can work through, clarify, acknowledge, process and figure out the next best steps for you. That is your personal journey to navigate, and the log of it is yours alone, too.

I hope you are as excited as I am to be embarking on this book. My hopes are grounded in 25 years of therapeutic experience of how anxiety impacts people's lives. I can't wait to share with you what I have learned as a psychologist and to show you how you can change your relationship with yourself and come home to feeling like you again.

I will always be grateful for my first role as a trauma therapist for people fleeing persecution from war-torn countries, oppression and genocide. I had two job choices: one a safe, pensionable role as an organisational psychologist in a bank; the other in a newly established unit dealing with complex trauma and PTSD (post-traumatic stress disorder). Always fond of a challenge, I jumped at what others were calling the 'riskier' role, and I have never looked back. Good risk, that aligns with our core values, helps us to make bold and courageous changes, and in the same spirit I am asking you to courageously come on this journey with me.

As well as being a psychologist, I am a normal mum, wife, daughter, sister and friend, and I understand the trenches of modern life. This book is not just theoretical: it was very important to me that it also provide a compilation of practices that lead to a healthier life. I promise that I will not ask you to do anything I haven't practised myself first. I will bring my 3 Cs to each endeavour – to **C**hallenge with **C**ompassion and **C**uriosity – and I ask you to do the same.

My clients often express the desire to be more relaxed, in control and at peace. This book asks why we aren't and how to become that. Rooted in evidence-based research and delivered in a step-by-step guide, it aligns with the practical needs of those seeking tangible solutions. In the words of Harvard biologist E.O. Wilson, 'We are drowning in information, while starving for wisdom.' This book promises not to contribute to information overload, but to provide practical, realistic solutions. It's about finding ways to meet your needs, living on your terms, while questioning the societal norms that block you.

- I want to help you find practical and realistic ways to meet your needs.
- I want you to feel grounded, not ground down.

- I want you to live more the way you'd like to, rather than always being 'On' and in 'Go' mode.
- I want you to be productive but in a radically different way than is valued now.
- I want you to have more joy and to know how to find joy, to be able to notice it and create it.

You want to thrive, but you are stuck in survive. I hear you, and I agree; I think that modern life is setting everyone up to be in a constant state of survival. It isn't just you and you are not alone. I am here to disrupt this cycle of systemic pressure that is so bad for our collective health.

This is a book of hope and calm. It is about bringing the science of safety to nervous systems stuck in survival mode, to bring you back to safety in a practical and compassionate way.

Are you ready?

If so, let's dive in …

PART 1
Survival mode

CHAPTER 1

Why is it all too much?

I do not want to be remembered as a woman who was always exhausted.

I do not want to be remembered as a woman who was always stressed, always busy, always rushing, always holding herself together and pushing through. I would like to be remembered as a relaxed woman, a compassionate woman, a curious, joyful, pleasure-loving woman. A woman who works hard and rests deeply, who loves fiercely and lives peacefully. A woman who knows her worth and her power, who accepts her imperfections and her vulnerabilities, who embraces her limitations and her possibilities. A woman who laughs and cries and aches and loves and is enchanted by the mess and magic and mundaneness of this beautiful, shimmering life.
(Nicola Jane Hobbs)

Why is it all too much?

Imagine waking up every day feeling like the weight of the world is on your shoulders and your chest. And with such intensity that it takes your breath away, and not in a good way.

It is likely this won't require a great feat of imagination because this is the reality for so many of us in our fast-paced society. Our daily lives are a series of demands, often overlapping, all of which seem to require the same urgent attention. We are always going, always doing, always thinking, always tired and yet carrying on regardless and somehow, incredibly, it's still never enough. Our bodies send SOS signals and yet it can be so hard to hear them amidst all the oncoming mental traffic. The effect of this is a constant sense of being close to the edge of overwhelm, coupled with a permanent sense that we're fighting not to become completely overwhelmed. It's like a tightrope walk over a precipice – if we make one wrong step, if we lose our focus for one second, we'll plunge into the abyss and headlong into what feels like failure and a loss of self. It's a never-ending balancing act that isn't balanced. Some days, we feel we can never win, which takes a huge toll on us.

The question is: How long can we keep it up?

Why do I feel the way I do?

What makes this even harder is that we are often plagued by a sense that we should not feel this way, that there's something wrong with us for having these thoughts and difficulties. We get angry at ourselves, wondering: *Why do I feel the way I do?*

That is something I hear very regularly in the therapy room. One client, Marie, summed it up when she railed at herself: 'I shouldn't feel like this. This is so silly. Others have it so much worse than me. I have so much. I am so lucky.' These are the pained words of dread, fear, anxiety and utter panic, coupled with a deep sense of isolation and disconnection from herself and others. These are unforgiving words.

Why do you feel the way you do? There are many reasons. Some are external, in your environment, and often not within your control. Some are internal, within your body and mind, embedded in your experiences and memories. Some parts you can work on and change; others need to be challenged and changed within society.

Over the course of 25 years working as a therapist, I've come to wonder: *How are we not all anxious?* It actually makes sense that we feel this way. But what has contributed to this state of anxiety that is the daily experience for so many people? One of the external causes surrounds us every minute of every day. Long before the word 'pandemic' became part of our daily lives there was an anxiety epidemic that spread through society, specifically First World society.

The First World anxiety epidemic

We are all familiar with the hashtag #firstworldproblems used self-deprecatingly to highlight our over-privileged and trivial inconveniences, like responding with a frustrated eyeroll when the barista gives you an oat milk flat white when you asked for a coconut milk latte. There are 'real' problems in the world and yours isn't one of them.

And so it begins, the internal and external conflict to distinguish between the 'real' problems and our perceived 'silly' ones, what we are allowed to feel and think and what we are not allowed to feel and think. Yes, there are real and serious problems everywhere, but negatively comparing yours to others' won't change your experiences with anxiety or overwhelm. The #fwp narrative is like an antibiotic in that it kills the bad bacteria along with the good. It leads us to chronically ignore and blank out the direct messages coming from our minds and bodies that our lives and how we have been living them is not working for us.

In fact, we have a very real problem with large populations of adults, adolescents and children feeling overwrought and overwhelmed, the consequences of which are worthy of our full attention. As a psychologist, I come at this from the individual's experience of how all your external and internal experiences have shaped you and brought you to where you are today.

And so, my first question to you is: 'How are you feeling?' Then: 'How is your day-to-day life?'

Think about yourself as you are today. Everyone can see the outer you, your public persona. But the private inner you, including that inner child, holds so many formative experiences from your relationships with your siblings, parents, partners, friends and co-workers, all of which have left imprints that affect how you view the world and how you view yourself, as explored in my book *The Secret Lives of Adults*. How do you show up in all these relationships? Is it safe for you to be yourself? Or is part of the painful *Why do I feel the way I do?* linked to you not being able to authentically be yourself? Those accusations of 'silly' or 'ridiculous' or 'lucky' are the result of feelings that are suppressed and hidden, pushed deep down not only in your mind but also in your body. That creates a big problem for you. (Thankfully, as we will learn, there are solutions for that problem.)

I am interested in the relationship between the external world you occupy and your inner world because when these two collide, it can lead to huge friction and frustration. This is only made worse if you feel unable to allow yourself to feel what you are feeling and think what you are thinking. Along with 'overwhelmed', I hear the word 'guilt' every single day. *I feel so guilty even saying this.* How can anything change when you feel guilty or scared of how others will feel if you 'change'? Do you know who you'd like to be, but struggle to even allow yourself to be your authentic self? Let me tell you, you are far from alone.

From my perspective as a psychologist, I dislike, disagree with, and avoid the narrative that tries to tell you that you aren't coping well enough or you shouldn't let that bother you or you aren't resilient enough. That is a weaponisation of wellness and of resilience that pits you against yourself, and I have to say it makes my blood boil because it is making people sick as they push past their physical, emotional and mental limits. I feel it individualises a societal issue – and that means you end up getting the blame and society doesn't need to do anything to change. In truth, what I hear about people's private lives are often public issues. We need to challenge the status quo and not buy into it anymore.

Why am I constantly anxious?

Honestly, that's the wrong question. The correct question is: How could you *not* be anxious? When you ask 'why', you throw it back at yourself, as if you are the sole source of anxiety and stress in your life. Instead, ask yourself some other questions: How does anxiety come about? What causes you to feel anxious? When does it occur?

So, what causes anxiety? Let's look at that.

UNCERTAINTY

Uncertainty and anxiety go hand in hand. Why? Because anxiety is future-based and often starts with the words *What if?* We don't like uncertainty because it makes us feel out of control. The truth is, life is uncertain, things change and often not the way we want them to, and it is hard and becoming harder to tolerate discomfort, especially when there are so many pleasurable distractions at your fingertips.

LOSS OF CONTROL

When you are feeling unsure and unable to control how things will go (external events, your environment, life), it is natural to buy into the illusion that you can be in control by 'worrying' or 'over-thinking' and that doing so will prepare you for any future scenario. One truth I have learned as a psychologist is that life is hard, unfair and unpredictable – and I'm an optimist! When you look at your behaviour and understand that the driving motivator of your brain is always to protect, that brings a softness to the conversation.

DREAD

No one wants to feel out of control, especially not in front of others, and this leads directly to dread. Dread is heavy and it lingers. You can then become frustrated with yourself that you are dreading whatever it is in the first place. You may wake up with dread, go to sleep with dread and find that it wakes you at the same time every night. It isn't just a thought; it is a physical feeling. I'll let you in on a big secret: often what people dread, especially the 'firsts', which are usually the worst, is anticipatory dread. The anticipatory dread is often worse than the thing you've been dreading.

FEAR

If you have experienced anxiety, anxious thoughts and, most notably, panic attacks, then you are well acquainted with fear and will have experienced the 'fear of the fear'. Learning how to read fear and how to adjust your fear settings is integral to changing your relationship with anxiety.

ANTICIPATORY ANXIETY DUE TO PAST EXPERIENCES OF ANXIETY

The problem with experiencing anxiety is that once you have experienced it, your body and mind go into full protection mode, doing anything to avoid feeling like that again. Physical sensations you may never have noticed before now feel threatening: *My heart is beating too fast, I feel dizzy; My legs are shaking; Oh no, it's happening again, I need to get out of here.* The cycle of anxiety leads to safety behaviours, such as using avoidance as a coping mechanism, which unfortunately prolongs and increases anxiety.

IDENTITY CRISES

How many identity crises have you had? It's easy to laugh at the obvious ones, watching the red sports car whizz by, as someone tries to recapture a freedom they may have felt in their youth. But many find it harder to pinpoint other identity crises that come up, often unexpectedly, when you find you are questioning who you are, don't know who you are, and/or don't like who you are or have become. There's a deep frustration that comes when you are behaving in one way and feeling another way, such as short-tempered by day and then lying awake at night with guilt, thinking about how you will do it better tomorrow. That sort of disconnect between the heart, head and body is visceral and deeply felt.

MAJOR LIFE TRANSITIONS

Major life transitions can lead you into experiencing a *Who am I now?* identity crisis. Changes can often bring up unexpected emotions, especially when there is an internal and external expectation that you 'should' be happy. It can make you feel at odds with how you feel as others tell you how 'lucky' or 'happy' you 'should be'. This can happen around pregnancy, labour, becoming a mother, being a parent. There are so many natural life transitions that can shake the idea of who you thought you were when the experience jars with your reality. There are huge dynamic shifts within yourself and all your relationships through the effects of illness, bereavement, accidents, loss of job, of relationships, of friendships, divorce – all the ways in which life can pull the rug from underneath you. A big element that I have noticed is the internal struggle around what you've been told you 'should' be happy about. That inner disconnect can leave you doubting yourself for years, until it eventually presents as a panic attack or anxiety – and yet it feels hard to put your finger on why you feel the way you do.

TRAUMA

Psychologist and trauma expert Peter Levine describes trauma as 'too much, too soon, too fast for our nervous system to handle'. I will explain the difference between 'Big T' and 'small t' as we go through the book as it is integral to processing and working through what is coming up for you (see Chapter 4). You know Big T – war, abuse, violence. However, small t impacts who and how we are, but we often don't register it as a source of anxiety because we are too busy dismissing it as 'not a big deal'. Therefore, the anxiety it is causing is also dismissed, and avoidance can lead to other difficulties.

TOXIC CULTURE

Where do we start? Perhaps with the concept of a successful life, how capitalism impacts how you live your life, the individuation of self, ignoring and overriding your own needs to keep pushing forward, systems that keep many people stuck and overwhelmed and unable to access the help they need. Consumerism encourages you to believe you are what you do, what you wear or what car you drive. I see how this plays out aggressively within organisations, families, institutions and society.

This culture is toxic in its impact on your health and wellbeing. Toxic positivity steals your right to process your experiences and emotions as the 'good vibes only' attitude disconnects you from yourself. We must look at the environment we live in because no matter how much sleep, good food and exercise you get, if you live in a toxic environment no amount of positive thinking is going to change that. Understanding this will help you see how you need to advocate for yourself, and others, around boundaries and toxic resilience. We are not solely independent; we need the systems around us to work.

STUCK IN SURVIVAL MODE

You don't get stuck by choice or go into it on purpose. *I feel completely stuck. I don't even know where to start. I know what I should do, but even starting anything seems impossible right now.* What does survival mode feel like? It feels edgy, overwhelming and as if you are at full capacity every day. It feels immensely frustrating in our *Have you tried ... ?* information overflow lives. Know this, though: at one point, survival mode served a purpose. Most behaviours, even when they aren't working on the surface, arose originally with the intention of protecting you. But if you are stuck in always-on survival mode, it creates anxiety.

STUCK IN FROZEN MODE

I'm sure you've come across the term 'trauma-informed', but what does that mean? The purpose of this book is to help you find out why you have felt the way you have, why you do what you have been doing, and then gives you a detailed and compassionate guide on how to get out of those behaviours.

Think of the last time you froze. What happened? Did you get a shock, did something happen that you didn't expect? Did your life and world change in a moment, forever? We freeze when it is too much. We freeze as an instinctive survival response, like the way some animals play dead. You may have said nothing to avoid the approaching conflict. Clients are often most upset with themselves when they freeze in traumatic experiences: *Why didn't I fight back? Why didn't I say no?* But when they learn that their response may have saved them, it lands so differently. Understanding why you freeze, or fight, or try to run away is incredibly helpful information, not just to understand intellectually, but to integrate this information into your body, which then becomes a completely different and transformative experience.

What all these sources of anxiety have in common is their underlying emotion, which is fear. And now you can ask your 'why' question: *Why do you feel fear?*

Fear is both positive and negative: you feel fear when there is a perceived or real threat to your safety. This is positive because the function of fear is to protect you. If there is a threat, you need to register it, evaluate it and, if necessary, act on it. It is important that you react mentally and physically to a threat.

The negative part is when that fear is ongoing and you get stuck in fear-response mode, which is survival mode. Fear makes you take notice, but often in a loud and frightening way. It isn't a gentle nudge to pay attention, it is an urgent alarm, a 'react first, think later' response that kicks through with a burst of adrenaline.

Now we can start to connect the dots on why we feel it's all too much all the time: we live with the surround sound of constant crisis. Do you read the headlines on your phone just before you close your eyes to sleep at night? Do you read them again just when you have opened your eyes in the morning? Do you click on the radio to catch the latest news updates? When you do that, you hear and read a steady stream of crisis and fear: mental health crisis, health crisis, housing crisis, environmental crisis, war, Covid, cost of living crisis, endless breach of civic trust across every institution ... it goes on and on and on. We live with bad news endlessly filling our eyes and ears – senseless, terrible situations that often we can't do a whole lot about.

Alongside this are our own internal crises and calls to arms: Why do I feel out of control of my own life? Why am I dreading the day ahead? What if our home is burgled? Am I doing enough to keep my family safe? Is this the life I really wanted to live? Why do I feel so numb? Why can't I put that difficult memory away where it can no longer hurt me? Does anyone actually love me at all?

We carry all these burdens, and we are carrying them constantly. Quite simply, it's all too much.

Why am I living like this?

Clients often speak to me of feeling empty, numb and overwhelmed, which is quite a nasty trio. It means you feel lost and disconnected, but at the same time you feel that you're being assaulted by competing and incessant demands. Add to this the tyranny of choice and comparison and you are quickly robbed of the ability to experience any satisfaction in your everyday life. Throw in some guilt that you feel like this in the first place as 'so many have it worse', and you are stuck in the perpetual anxiety of survival mode.

The strange and unhelpful thing is that you quickly adapt to this constant hum of stress. It becomes your everyday reality and it feels 'right'. The buzz of stress or getting things done under pressure can feel like a strength: *I only work well under pressure.* That's when the stress hormone cortisol comes along, firing on all cylinders as your body adapts to living in chronic stress. Combined with decreasing levels of dopamine, the feel-good hormone, this creates a vicious cycle of stress, leaving you without the motivation to change.

There can be many other factors as well. For example, if you grew up in chaos, that became your body's norm and relaxation will feel anything but. For some it might even feel scary and threatening. Staying hypervigilant may be what makes you feel in control.

In answer to the question *Why am I living like this?*, it's because it feels uncomfortable when you are *not* stressed. Think about it: do you ever get stressed or anxious when you are *not* anxious? I know so many of you will be nodding right now – and there is a reason why. Even though logically or rationally you 'know' you 'should' feel happier that the anxious thoughts are not there, your nervous system has been stuck in stress mode for so long that no amount of intellectualising or reasoning will make the anxiety disappear or change.

We are addicted and tied to stress, whether we want to be or not. Internally, we feel we are in an unrelenting 'Always-On' mode as we try to cope with the external demands coming at us from every direction. But we characterise this as 'busyness', tell ourselves everyone is in the same boat, and we get so used to it that it becomes our norm. Think of your daily interactions; I bet they go something like this: *Hi, how are you? Fine, grand, busy, you? Same! Bye, see you tomorrow.*

This adds to the dismissal of your internal experiences. Headaches, clenched jaw, literally a pain in the neck and shoulder, tension that you may not even notice because it's there so often. Check yourself now: do you need to unclench your jaw, roll your shoulders? How is your neck?

If we stop feeling like this, there can be a sense of panic, as though you're wildly looking around for something you've forgotten. If you are not wearing your Busy badge, you must be missing something or failing or falling behind in some way.

I think you might recognise this; that along the way you lost your ability to relax, to turn off Always On for a time. Without ever meaning or wanting to, your default setting has become Stressed Busy – and you're no longer comfortable when you *don't* feel like that. So you live like this because you've come to believe that this is simply your way of living. That results in anxiety on top of anxiety – you are experiencing anxiety because of chronic stress, and you experience anxiety if you suspect your stress level has dropped. It's a pretty awful Catch-22 situation.

As a result, many of us aren't aware that we are experiencing anxiety. You might describe yourself as having a racing mind, persistent worry, frustration and being irritable, but isn't that very familiar to us all? This is the systemic normalisation of how we are living, and it leads us to dismiss our own internal messages, even when they are screaming at us. We shrug and say, *Sure everyone is stressed*, and then feel we aren't coping.

Life in survival mode

When you are living like this, your body and mind primed to survive, ready to fight or flee, cortisol flowing, you are in constant survival mode. And when you are in constant survival mode, you cannot grow as a person.

It is not only your mind and emotions that are affected; it's your body as well. Survival mode affects you on every level – emotional, psychological, physiological. It inhabits your body from head to toe and calls the shots, even as you deny its existence. That makes is so much harder to break the cycle of constant anxiety and constant reactivity.

We are going to explore survival mode as it shows up in the therapy room. It might walk in as anxiety, but I'd like to share with you here how it shows up emotionally, psychologically and physiologically in your body. If we are super clear, then you can identify when it is happening and how to prepare practically for when you know it's building or going to happen again. This is not a replacement for therapy, as that is such an integral part of the work, but I wrote this book because I want you to know how to do it.

Can I move out of survival mode?

Yes, you can move out of survival mode, which is what we are here to explore. But it's important to understand that this book revolves around two immensely powerful ideas: no amount of information, intellectualising and rational understanding about anxiety and its effects upon you will change how your body reacts when it feels threatened; and it's not normal to always be thriving. Survival mode does what it says on the tin; its job is to protect you. It's just not useful to stay in it.

What is particularly frustrating and disheartening is that many conscientious, hard-working, kind, intelligent people have attempted to think their way out of anxiety, and then felt they failed when that didn't work.

I need you to know that it won't work.

Dealing with anxiety is not mind over matter. It is not toxic positivity. Both of those are deeply frustrating and inhibit you from taking action or seeking support as you feel you 'should' be able to get over this yourself. What is needed is to step back, recognise your own anxiety sources and triggers, and learn how to guide yourself back to feeing safe in your own body. That is what you are going to explore and discover as you read the following chapters that describe what survival mode feels like and how it affects you.

This is all based on the body of work that I have employed and observed to change people's relationship with overwhelm, stress, anxiety, panic attacks and fear. It combines evidence-based theory with my first-hand experience in therapeutic sessions with clients.

The Practical Psychology

Throughout this book you will find 'The Practical Psychology' where I will ask you to stop, pause, reflect, and answer specific questions or practise specific exercises based on what you have read. What I love about my work is the process of seeing people's experience with anxiety change, and this is the work that precedes it. Please use the 3 Cs when answering all the questions I put to you: Challenge with Curiosity and Compassion. Be open and kind to yourself when thinking about yourself.

Please write down your answers, don't just think about them. I know everyone is time-poor, but the gap between thinking the answer and writing down the answer is where change happens. I'd recommend getting a notebook that is just for your eyes, and if that means hiding it, then do that.

The aim of this set of questions is to for you to understand how fear shows up in your everyday life and how to change your experience with fear from one of feeling controlled by it to being in control of your response.

YOUR EXPERIENCE OF FEAR

How does fear show up for you?

_____

What keeps you awake at night?

_____

What do you worry about?

_____

What fears do you hide?

_____

How long have you experienced anxiety? Before you answer, pause for a moment ... Now, answer.

_____

YOUR EXPERIENCE OF ANXIETY

Ask yourself when you first experienced anxiety.

_____

Can you identify any themes or triggers that seem to bring on dread, overwhelm, anxiety or panic?

_____

If you have experienced anxiety or panic attacks, there is nearly what I would consider a personal grieving for the person you once were and for the person you thought you were. In terms of who you thought you were, how did a situation or trigger change that for you?

What was that like for you? Was it shocking, confusing, upsetting?

_____

Who do you think you are now?

_____

What parts of this new identity are not working for you?

_____

Why do you want to go back to the old you?

_____

Are there some parts of that past version of you that were influencing and causing you anxiety?

―――――――――――――――――――――――――――――――

Is it an identity crisis, opportunity, or both?

―――――――――――――――――――――――――――――――

If you could be the person who truly feels like you, what would you do more of?

―――――――――――――――――――――――――――――――

What would you do less of?

―――――――――――――――――――――――――――――――

What are your change blockers, e.g. are you known as the helpful one, the dependable one, or …?

―――――――――――――――――――――――――――――――

To deepen this exploration, is the fear yours, or a fear of how you think others will respond to the new you?

―――――――――――――――――――――――――――――――

This is a big one, so process the exact fears that come up for you around what it would mean to have healthier boundaries and to have a better and healthier relationship with yourself.

I cringe when people say 'You've changed' in a negative way. It is such a change annihilator and people prefer to avoid the pain of disappointing others as they actively sacrifice and betray their own needs every day.

Has someone said 'You've changed' to you? If so, what impact did it have?

_____

Can you see how you have been betraying your own physical, mental, and emotional needs? And can you list the consequences to your health and wellbeing?

_____

CHAPTER 2

What is anxiety and how does it build in the body?

When you look in the mirror, you recognise who is looking back at you, although some mornings I'm not so sure. For all the talk about anxiety, you might be surprised how many people don't recognise that the way they have been feeling is, in fact, anxiety. In a time of information overload, I am at pains not to add to your mental load. There can be a lot of headline jargon that has become part of our everyday speech and in ways it may take away from your inner ability to identify your own experience, or to know when to seek the appropriate help. It can lead to a disconnection from your own self as you negatively compare yourself and conclude *I don't have it as bad as other people.*

The very Irish saying 'I've always been a bit of a worrier' raises an eyebrow for me. It is important to know that when you persistently and excessively worry about everyday things for more than two weeks, you are en route to asking if it might be GAD – generalised anxiety disorder. This can often arise when you conflate worrying with caring and it becomes embedded into your identity, making it hard to let go of that persistent worry and to see the grip it has in your daily life.

What is anxiety?

Psychologists tend to use the definitions provided by the US-based National Institute of Mental Health (NIMH). The NIMH is one of 27 institutes that make up the National Institute of Health (NIH) and is the largest research organisation in mental health in the world.

The NIMH lists five major types of anxiety:

1. Generalised anxiety disorder (GAD)
2. Obsessive compulsive disorder (OCD)
3. Panic disorder
4. Post-traumatic stress disorder (PTSD)
5. Social anxiety disorder (SAD)

You are probably familiar with types 1 to 4 and these likely receive the most public attention.

The anxiety types most relevant for us here, in the exploration of what anxiety is, are GAD and panic disorder. However, we don't need in-depth psychological definitions of the different types – that won't tell you what you need to know. Instead, we're going to look at how anxiety builds in your body and the physiological processes and responses that define and identify it. The anxiety responses share a profile, which is so helpful to know as it empowers you to recognise what is happening, and why it is happening.

What is generalised anxiety disorder?

Generalised anxiety disorder (GAD) is the most common anxiety disorder in the U.S. with 6.8 million adults affected.[1] In the evaluation of GAD, clinical professionals look for the following indicators:

1. The presence of excessive anxiety and worry about a variety of topics, events or activities. Worry occurs for at least six months and is clearly excessive.
2. The worry is experienced as very challenging to control. The worry in both adults and children may easily shift from one topic to another.
3. The anxiety and worry are accompanied by at least three of the following physical or cognitive symptoms:
   - edginess or restlessness
   - tiring easily, more fatigued than usual
   - impaired concentration or feeling as though the mind goes blank
   - irritability (which may or may not be observable to others)
   - increased muscle aches or soreness
   - difficulty sleeping (due to trouble falling asleep or staying asleep, restlessness at night, or unsatisfying sleep).

I have a feeling that you might feel a jolt of recognition. However, many people minimise what they are feeling, describing it as an embarrassing case of 'over-worrying'. They'll laugh apologetically and say: *I've always been a bit of a worrier. I know it's silly.* That reaction means they don't seek or get the right treatment for GAD. They live with it.

But the fact is that the excessive and persistent worry of GAD has a big impact on your life. You might be living with it, but it's only a form of living – you're certainly not feeling wonderful and filled with energy and optimism. Far from it, and yet you accept this hollow version of yourself and keep soldiering on. From my own clinical experience, it would seem that the main reason people dismiss it is the absence of panic attacks. If there is no 'big' event that looks like extreme anxiety, then it can't be anxiety – right?

Wrong.

You can experience all the symptoms of GAD and the physical effects it brings without ever having a major traumatic episode that makes you realise it – or, at least, it can take a long time for that realisation to occur. In the meantime, you are struggling under the burden of anxiety and your mind and body and confidence are being depleted by it.

The polyvagal theory of anxiety

I love working with anxiety. All of it. To be honest, I feel like a mixologist, interweaving and adapting what I bring to the person in front of me in the therapy room according to what they need. I have never understood just using one methodology as people and their unique experiences don't fit into neatly formulated therapies.

I always knew the root is in the body, which may sound ironic coming from a psychologist. I knew that people arrived at therapy to find their 'why' – *Why do I feel the way I do* or *Why do I do what I do?* The thing is, this striving to intellectualise your felt experiences can disconnect you from the answer, which is in your body.

So, when I came across polyvagal theory, I was like, *Yes, here it is! Thank you.*

Note: The rest of this section on survival mode explains how I work with clients. The following chapters on polyvagal theory are complex and technical. I ask you to lean into it and trust me and the process. You don't need to be an expert, but having an awareness of your nervous system is the part you have been missing.

WHAT IS POLYVAGAL THEORY?

Polyvagal theory focuses on how your body's autonomic nervous system, particularly the vagus nerve, regulates both your physical wellbeing and your behaviour. It was developed in 1995 by Stephen Porges, a neuroscientist and professor of psychiatry at the University of North Carolina. It is a complex theory as it explores the core of who we are and how we are and what it means to be human in our body and mind; that is, our somatic (physical body) experience and our psychological (mind) experience and how those two experiences intertwine and affect each other.

I love the saying 'The way to the heart is through the stomach,' but I think it's actually through the nervous system. (Bet you can't wait to get your hands on my romantic Valentine's Day cards!) The truth is that the health of your nervous system is the key to your relationships and quality of life.

You will have heard of 'survival of the fittest' – our innate evolutionary drive to adapt to survive. Our autonomic nervous system (ANS) is divided into two states: one to calm us down (the parasympathetic system) – think of it as the brakes in the car; and the other to activate us to move (the sympathetic system) – the foot on the pedal. Polyvagal theory proposes a third response called the social engagement system, where we assess if it is safe to be open and engage with others or if there is any threat or danger present. Your ANS is your internal safety and security system, and that system's sensitivity will be shaped by your history and experiences, especially trauma, and that includes Big Trauma and small trauma (see Chapter 4 for more on this).

In a nutshell, polyvagal theory is the science of feeling safe. It is about cultivating an understanding of how your body and nervous system are constantly scanning every face, interaction and environment to determine whether it is safe, or if there is a threat or danger, which in turn will influence how you interact, connect and behave. With that understanding you can learn how to change the state of your body (physiology) and mind (psychology) to have better emotional and physical health and to feel safe and connected in your relationships with yourself and others.

Polyvagal theory is a way of understanding how our nervous system responds to different situations, such as stress, danger or safety. The really good thing is that it is about becoming still, tuning in, doing less. It is the opposite of grind culture. It's about taking small moments to lie on the grass, to know that you do enough and that you need to rest.

So put aside any ideas of hardship or grind. It is about coming home to yourself. Learning how to navigate your own way through how you experience your body, emotions and relationships is, in my opinion, one of the most important investments in yourself and your whole life.

WHAT IS THE VAGUS NERVE?

The vagus nerve is a crucial part of our body's nervous system. It is the longest cranial nerve, extending from the brainstem down through the heart and abdomen. It communicates bi-directionally from the brain to the body and back via vagal pathways and is thought of as the mind–body highway. For all the information we are constantly flooded with, knowing how to stimulate your vagus nerve is something everyone needs to know.

What you need to know:

- The vagus nerve is the longest cranial nerve in the body.
- It is called the wandering nerve (in Latin, *vagus* means 'to wander') because along its length it impacts most organs in the body, from your heart, digestive system and lungs, to your liver, kidneys, and large and small intestine.
- It is bi-directional, meaning it passes information to and from your brain through vagal pathways. It is known as the mind–body superhighway because of its extensive branches of communication.
- It is also a surveillance system that works away without your conscious knowledge, 'constantly broadcasting and receiving messages of welcome and warning' away from threat and towards safety and connection.

Think of two people who are about to set their house alarm at night. Let's imagine Jake, who has never experienced a threat to his safety, fear or trauma. He sets his alarm, walks up the stairs in the dark, thinking only of his bed that he is looking forward to getting into – these are 'messages of welcome'. Let's imagine Jane, who has always felt uncomfortable at night, so she looks over her shoulder and jumps as her cat rubs against her ankle, she feels her heart quicken and that nasty rush of adrenaline fly up her legs, *Blinking cat. Calm down, Jane*, leading to mixed messages of warning and 24/7 hypervigilance.

Think of your own life. Is there trust or do you feel you are always monitoring and scanning incoming messages from your environment and how your body is reacting for any potential threat? Do you marvel at friends who never see the potential pitfalls and/or catastrophise about situations, people or things? Wouldn't it be a different daily experience to know how to navigate your thoughts and your body's responses to these messages of warning and to work towards living a more open, connected and freer existence? While we may not have tigers lurking in the bushes, we have urgency, deadlines and lives that prioritise doing over being. This is why polyvagal theory needs to be the foundation on which you build your life, learning to use the vagus nerve to notice when it has wandered into survival mode, with the intention of teaching your body how to feel safe and return home.

It doesn't need to be either/or; it's about learning how to adapt with flexibility in the moment. Calmness and peace aren't the only answer. Sometimes you need to brake, other times you need to be activated to run and to learn to take the risk of sharing how you really feel. It's about challenging this notion of perpetual peace and happiness and understanding that life is messy, and that the trick is to not get stuck in survival mode.

It might be the case that you struggle to share your emotions with others because you did not feel safe sharing your emotions with your parent or primary caregiver. If they were unable or not equipped to deal with what was going on for you, they may have left you to deal with it alone. As a result, you might find it very difficult to break the habit of a lifetime because you have a deep-seated belief that if you ask, help will not be given.

Now this is not to blame the adults in your life as a child. They did not know about emotional regulation or the function of emotions. In the past there were rigid ideas about how children 'should' behave, and their own parents may have had even less understanding. While being aware that abusive behaviour is never acceptable, compassionate historical context is exceptionally important to keep in mind and is also healing.

Through this discussion of polyvagal theory and how you can use it, I want you to:

- Learn how to trust yourself
- Learn when to challenge yourself
- Begin to notice (without judgement)
- Become aware, understand and to then take action to return to safety and connection.

The three key principles of polyvagal theory are:

1. Autonomic hierarchy
2. Neuroception
3. Co-regulation.

PRINCIPLE 1: AUTONOMIC HIERARCHY

The autonomic nervous system (ANS) is like your body's automatic control centre. It is a network of nerves throughout your body that control unconscious processes, such as breathing and your heartbeat, without you having to think about them to keep you functioning well and safe. The ANS has three pathways, each with predictable responses in terms of how you think, respond, feel and behave. The word to notice is *predictable*. When you begin to notice how you respond and notice what triggers you, it places conscious control back with you, allowing you to make changes and to choose the best response, because an old survival response may not be what you need in your present moment.

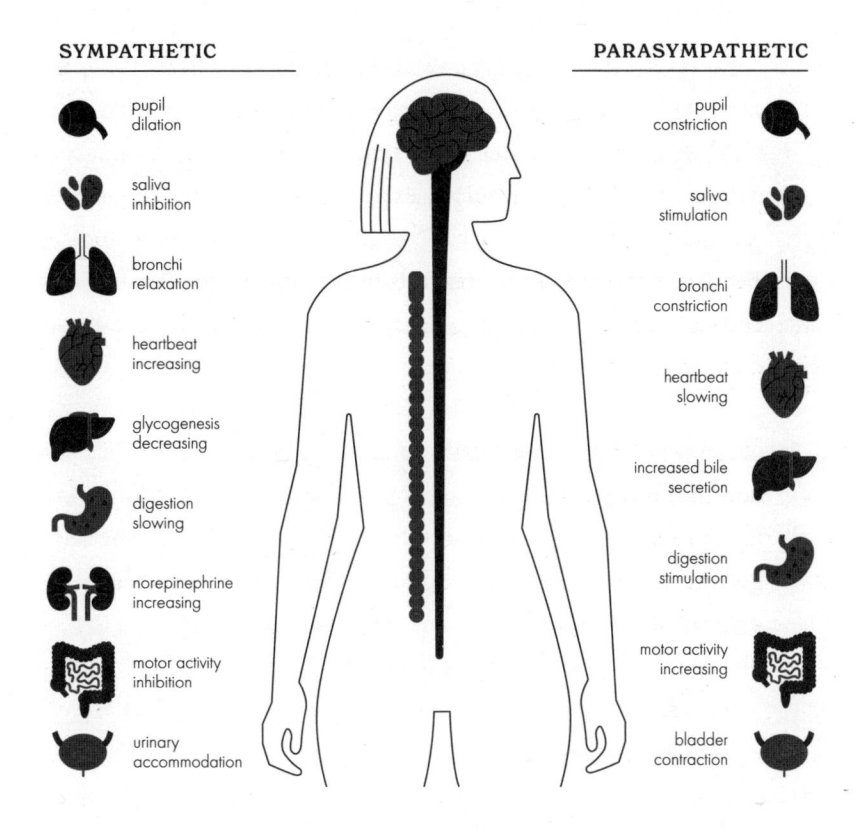

SYMPATHETIC	PARASYMPATHETIC
pupil dilation	pupil constriction
saliva inhibition	saliva stimulation
bronchi relaxation	bronchi constriction
heartbeat increasing	heartbeat slowing
glycogenesis decreasing	increased bile secretion
digestion slowing	digestion stimulation
norepinephrine increasing	motor activity increasing
motor activity inhibition	bladder contraction
urinary accommodation	

The three pathways of response of the ANS are:

- **The ventral vagal system** – the pathway to safety. This system fosters connection and is crucial for sustaining your health and overall wellness. When activated, we feel competent, clear-headed and grounded in hope, able to engage with ourselves and others. It engenders feelings of safety, connection, equilibrium and ease within our thoughts, emotions and physical sensations.

- **The sympathetic system** – protects with Fight and Flight. The sympathetic system safeguards you through the fight or flight response, regulating your breathing, heartbeat and energy distribution to

support your daily activities. When you perceive a threat, it propels you into action, often manifesting as feelings of anger or anxiety. Physically, it redistributes blood flow to your muscles so you can respond quickly, and it increases your heart rate and the size of your pupils.
- **The dorsal vagal system** – protects by immobilisation: Freeze. The dorsal vagal system is associated with the freeze response. Its everyday role is to regulate digestion, supporting our daily lives. When confronted with overwhelming danger, this system induces a state of immobilisation, commonly perceived as numbness or dissociation, and you experience shutdown. It slows down bodily functions to preserve energy, serving as a final defence mechanism against potential harm. When activated, it will leave you feeling exhausted, despondent, with no energy, and you pull back, leading you to feel disconnected from yourself and others.

Understanding these three principles of the ANS can help you to recognise and interpret your body's responses in different situations, empowering you to navigate through life's challenges more effectively.

PRINCIPLE 2: NEUROCEPTION

The word 'neuroception' was coined by Stephen Porges to describe our body's inbuilt survival radar. This is a 24-hour subconscious surveillance system that enables your nervous system to automatically and continually scan your environment for signs of safety, danger, or social connection. This happens without you even being consciously aware of it. It notes any threats or triggers and helps your body to decide how to react in different situations.

Cue: *It is safe, okay, good, I can relax.*
Signal: I feel safe – ventral state.

Cue: *Something seems off, I need to stay alert.*
Signal: I feel scared and fearful. Do I need to run away or fight? – sympathetic state.

Cue: *What just happened, what is happening? I feel in danger, I need to protect myself.*
Signal: I feel frozen, like I am watching/observing what is happening to me right now outside myself – dorsal state.

These cues are a combination of internal cues inside your body, external cues from your environment and messages between your nervous systems.

PRINCIPLE 3: CO-REGULATION

Co-regulation starts as soon as you are born, as two arms wrap around you providing the warmth, security and emotional nourishment on which your survival depends. To move to growth, co-regulation is a process where two or more people, often in a relationship, help each other to co-regulate each other's emotions, physical state and behaviour. The beauty of the practice is that it comes from warm hugs, gentle eyes providing reassurance, soft touch, gentle tone, and words that soothe upset nervous systems. It isn't about fixing; it is about sitting side by side in a supportive, empathetic way. When you co-regulate, you bring softness and compassion to the hard times.

This is crucial in anchoring yourself back to feeling safe, warm and connected. In a society that celebrates individuality, co-regulation is the antidote to isolation. Starting from the moment you are born, your mother's touch and voice made you feel safe in a strange, cold, new environment. That intimate connection moved you from fear to a place of safety, where you could feel calm.

In this way, we are biologically wired to connect with each other, to feel that we belong and matter to each other over our whole life span. This is an extremely powerful psychological need and when we receive it, the impact can be equally powerful. Co-regulation is a dance of reciprocity as we support, connect and trust in each other in our everyday lives, through the good times and the bad. If we can build trust in ourselves and in others, that allows us to grow and learn and be resilient.

You can see now that the vagus nerve is like our personal security, scouting out the environment, searching for potential threats and dangers, trying to react quickly and effectively when a trigger is set off, be it physical or emotional. When it feels the threat warrants a reaction, it has four reactions, or coping mechanisms, that it can call on, known as the 4 Fs.

The 4 Fs: Fight, Flight, Freeze, Fawn

When the vagus nerve kick-starts a protective course of action in the face of a threat of any kind, it can roar at you to fight, urge you to flee, warn you to freeze, or plead with you to fawn. The job of the 4 Fs is that they quickly adapt to protect you from real or perceived threats to your safety. Understanding that the function of the 4 Fs is to protect you, rather than make your life difficult, eases the discomfort of feeling immobilised by fear, overwhelmed by anger, or numb. They are the reason why your heart beats faster when you feel scared going into that presentation you have been dreading and why those unpleasant butterflies flutter in your stomach before that hard conversation that has to be had.

When in a 4 F state, ask yourself what threat (perceived or real) each F is looking for protection from:

- **Fight:** When you feel unsafe, you may try to self-protect by mobilising conflict.
- **Flight:** When you feel unsafe, you may try to self-protect by running away or escaping.

- **Freeze:** When you feel unsafe, you may try to self-protect by shutting down, immobilising and disconnecting.
- **Fawn:** When you feel unsafe, you may try to self-protect by people-pleasing.

The coping mechanism chosen will depend on the threat, how it has triggered you, and your past experiences of dealing with this threat. If one of these options seemed to work before, it will be used again. That's how you can get stuck in cycles of behaviour.

Let's take an example from a client. Janet began to identify that her people-pleasing wasn't part of her identity as she thought but was a result of growing up in a dysfunctional house where one parent would go into rages of anger, often over what seemed like nothing. She started noticing how she betrayed her own emotional and physical needs and pushed down how she really felt, rather than expressing it. This was because when she used to express her emotions, it often unleashed huge anger from her parent. She learned to please and be as perfect as she could to avoid the conflict. However, the constant dread, angst and fear of doing anything wrong led to a complete disconnection from herself and exhaustion and burnout in her marriage, as a parent and with her job.

The deeper problem arises when those states are constantly activated – where you are in threat response mode all the time because you are feeling anxious. The question I'd be more interested in is: 'Why are you feeling anxious so often?' This is a curious and compassionate *why?* The tone you use to question yourself is so important – instead of *What is wrong with me? Why do I always react like this? I never change*, allow your curiosity to lead you: *That's interesting – my body and thoughts are reacting strongly to that criticism. I've noticed this happens each time; I wonder what is under that hurt?*

What are the long-term consequences of constant activation?

An 'Always On' Fight stress response has specific health issues, starting with exhaustion from always being ready to fight perceived threats. This is a state of hyperarousal, which might sound good, but I'm afraid it's not. Health issues it induces include muscle tension, headaches, tight jaw, high blood pressure, cardiovascular issues, digestion issues and an impact on the immune system. It can cause difficulty with sleep, adding to more difficulty managing emotions, stress, anxiety and mental health. Cognitive impairment follows, with concentration and memory being affected, as well as your ability to make decisions. As we noted in Chapter 1, the state of being constantly stressed can come to feel normal and relaxing can become quite uncomfortable.

An 'Always On' Flight response is also hyperarousal and may appear in the form of chronic stress, exhaustion from constant readiness to flee, constant busyness, and over-working to avoid the pain of thinking or processing pain. Sleep issues include difficulty falling asleep, staying asleep or waking up not feeling rested. There's an impact on the immune system and heart, and difficulty regulating your emotions. Relationship difficulties can arise because you aren't really present as you constantly scan for threat and can't relax.

An 'Always On' Freeze stress response can feel like you are stuck, numb, unable to start a task or make a decision, heaviness in energy, physical, mental and physical exhaustion, withdrawal and feeling detached from people and places. Chronic freeze can lead to it being hard to know how to unfreeze and feeling overwhelmed even thinking about it, leading to a vicious cycle of feeling persistently stuck. Freeze and fawn are states of hypoarousal.

An 'Always On' Fawn stress response can feel like an inability to say no, difficulty setting boundaries in your relationships, burnout, exhaustion and resentment, looking for others to give you external validation, causing issues and strain across all your relationships and roles; not knowing who you are or what you like or want; and chronic stress on your overall wellbeing and physical health.

We have mentioned two key words: hyperarousal and hypoarousal. These are states of dysregulation in the nervous system and you can fluctuate between them.

- **Hyperarousal** is when your nervous system is in a state of heightened arousal and alertness, making it overactive. Think of how you are, physically, mentally and emotionally, when you perceive a threat (this could even be your boss asking, 'Can we have a chat tomorrow?') Cue increase in heart rate; you notice your heart thumping; you are breathing faster and shallower; noise, heat and other external factors may feel amplified. You might feel agitated, anxious, and definitely not relaxed.
- **Hypoarousal** is when your nervous system is underactive. You might feel as though you are stuck in the Freeze mode and as if you have no energy, feel numb and detached, and miss certain things because you feel a bit spaced out. You can become withdrawn and seek to avoid people, places, or things you normally manage well. You can find it challenging to concentrate on what you are doing. With the Fawn response, this can present as a detachment from your own emotions and needs in order to appease conflict from others or to please them.

These are not either/or experiences; many factors will influence how you feel depending on your history, and current or past stress or trauma. The key is to be able to notice, identify and become aware of when you are about to go into these states and to know how to get out of them when you are in them. This is a crucial piece of information: it isn't about never experiencing these symptoms but about identifying, without judgement, *Ah, I'm in a hypervigilant state. What do I need to do next to help my nervous system regulate again?* You may think it's a bit silly to even talk to yourself like this, but learning how to regulate your nervous system is life-changing.

DECODING THE 4 FS

All behaviour communicates. The ability to see beneath challenging behaviour, both yours and others', demands emotional maturity.

I once saw an image that communicated this idea, of a child wearing a shark fin in the water. Its intention was to help parents see beyond what looks like a kid acting out: to being able to identify what was going on below the surface. It resonated with me because it showed that even during their most challenging behaviour (the 'shark attack'), they are, in fact, seeking connection with you. That post-school restraint collapse that you might be familiar with happens because they are home and safe to express with you how they really feel. Sometimes we push at the boundaries with those we trust just to make sure they are there and holding us tight, which builds their sense of safety. I find that a helpful reminder when my own children's behaviour may seem like a 'shark in the water' attack. It helps me keep my cool as I know the real emotion is hidden under the surface and my job is to regulate myself so we can co-regulate together.

Adults are no different. It is hard to ask for what you really need when you are feeling angry and overwhelmed. But if we don't look below the surface of the anger, or outbursts, we miss the real needs: the desire for protection and connection.

That provides a simple understanding of what the 4 Fs are – and no doubt you can recognise them in your life – but what is really useful in a discussion of anxiety is learning how to know which state you are in and why. There is so much potential and power in being able to know, *Oh, this is why I reacted like that – it hit an old nerve of feeling not good enough*, or *I felt embarrassed*. When you can do that, you can manage your triggers and your reactions much more effectively.

Knowing your state: Your personal profile map

Deb Dana describes how we 'map' as a means of 'wayfinding' our way through our very personal experiences of our different reaction states.[2] Your personal profile map is a framework created by Dana to help you understand yourself and find your way through different situations and environments. When you know where you are going, you feel safer and more comfortable. When you feel lost, the world, and your experience of it, can feel much more threatening.

Your personal profile is a map to help you be aware of your unique patterns that regulate or dysregulate you in your autonomic nervous system. It helps you to identify bumps in the road that have been triggers before, to provide insight before you take that old familiar route. By drawing a map of yourself in this way, you achieve three helpful things:

1. You know where you are.
2. You know where you want to go.
3. You know how to get there.

This sounds like a solid plan to me.

HOW TO MAP AND TRACK YOUR NERVOUS SYSTEM
Hyperarousal

Gently recall a time when you moved into 'Fight or Flight'. I don't want you to feel triggered by the memory, so just gently recall the situation without letting the emotions associated with it take over. If it's helpful, imagine watching it from a distance on a screen in front of you.

As you think about what feelings may have been raised, such as anxiety, irritation, anger or quick reaction, answer the following questions to give yourself a view of how you feel about yourself and the world when you have been activated into fight or flight:

- What is that like for you?
- What does that feel like (a) in your thoughts and (b) in your body?
- What do you do, or say?
- What is your energy like? For example, do you feel agitated, fearful, angry, jumpy, defeated?
- Does it affect your sleep or appetite, or do you reach for other substances?
- Describe yourself in this state: *I am …*
- Describe how the world looks to you in this state: *The world is …*

Ventral state

This is the state where we feel open, curious, hopeful, safe, connected and engaged. Can you pull up a memory of a time you felt like this?

Don't feel pressure if this is a state you haven't frequented too much.

- What is that like for you?
- What does that feel like (a) in your thoughts and (b) in your body?
- What do you do, or say?
- What is your energy like?
- Does it affect your sleep or appetite, or do you reach for other substances?
- Describe how you look to yourself in this state: *I am …*
- Describe how the world looks to you in this state: *The world is …*

Hypoarousal

In nature, a state of hypoarousal is characterised by an animal 'playing dead' to put a predator off attacking them. However, it is often bad timing in modern life, when too much can lead you to shut down, procrastinate and then feel bad that you aren't doing what you are 'supposed' to be doing.

So can you think of a time when you reacted to a situation by feeling exhausted and that led you to socially withdraw?

- What is that like for you?
- What does that feel like (a) in your thoughts and (b) in your body?
- What do you do, or say?
- What is your energy like?
- Does it affect your sleep or appetite, or do you reach for other substances?
- Describe how you look to yourself in this state: *I am …*
- Describe how the world looks to you in this state: *The world is …*

The SOS state switch

Now you have your own personal profile mapped for each state. This will help you to recognise it when it happens and how to switch from survival to safety. Be mindful that these evolutionary states are there to protect, while knowing there is a way out. Of course, the question then is: *What do I do if I realise that I'm in one of the 4 F states?*

The answer is that you need to ground yourself back to the ventral vagal state, where you feel safe and connected. As we have learned, the vagus nerve influences three different physiological states in the body:

1. Ventral vagal state – a steady sense of safety, control, and calmness.
2. Sympathetic state – a state of readiness in response to a perceived or real threat.
3. Dorsal state – a state of disconnection in response to a perceived or real threat that feels overwhelming or life-threatening.

1. VENTRAL VAGAL STATE

When you are in this state of safety you feel a sense of connection and social engagement. You feel:

- open
- calm

- energised
- curious
- grounded
- able to learn

2. SYMPATHETIC STATE

When you are in this state and feel a threat or danger (real or perceived), your Fight or Flight responses have been activated and you are primed to react.

In Fight response you feel:

- ready to fight
- conflict-seeking
- energised
- anxious and agitated
- angry
- irritated
- frustrated

In Flight response you feel:

- worried
- anxious
- fearful
- panic-stricken
- stuck

3. DORSAL STATE

When you are in this state and feel a threat or danger (real or perceived), your Freeze or Fawn responses have been activated.

In Freeze response you feel:

- shut-down
- numb
- withdrawn
- frozen
- unreal
- dissociated

In Fawn response you feel:

- overwhelmed
- disconnected from your own needs and feelings
- numb
- compliant
- anxious
- conflict-avoidant

And you:

- prioritise everyone else's needs above your own
- have difficulty saying no
- have difficulty creating and maintaining boundaries
- feel pressure to be liked
- ignore and suppress your own opinions and needs.

There can be a huge difference between how your response manifests on the outside – your behaviour – and how it feels on the inside – your emotional reaction. This can lead to that 'shark attack' situation when people think they see the whole behaviour, but the real emotions are hidden below the surface, masked by your outward reaction. Often, people might respond by saying crossly, 'Calm down, what is up with you?' when what you really need is understanding and help to self-regulate and co-regulate your nervous system. Without this support from self or others, the outward 'over-reaction' doesn't get internally resolved.

This is where you can use your SOS switch to bring yourself from dorsal or sympathetic state back to ventral vagal state. In layman's terms, it means noticing your reaction, regulating and cooling your emotions down to manageable levels so that you can think straight, and choosing a different response and behaviour.

There are useful SOS switches for each reaction:[3]

FIGHT (MOVING TOWARDS)
What we see on the outside
- shouting
- anger
- rage
- blaming
- confrontation
- giving out
- high energy

What you are feeling on the inside
- fear
- frustration
- anxiety
- embarrassment
- shame

How to do the Fight SOS switch
- Shake it out (see Your Psychological Toolbox, page 328).
- Go for a fast walk.
- Furiously write out how you feel and why (should be scrawly, written with speed, with lots of WTAF).
- Punch a pillow.

- Scream (best when no one can hear you).
- If screaming out loud isn't appropriate, try a silent scream (same as a normal scream but whispered, without using your voice). Shaking your hands can also be a good accompaniment.
- Cool down (take some clothes off, run your wrists under the cold tap or splash your face).
- Take off your shoes and stand on the grass.
- Ask *What am I feeling now and why?* Write the answer down, now close your eyes and connect to where you feel this in your body. Put your hand on the part of your body that is feeling it the most. Describe what it is like (heart pounding, racing thoughts, highly activated, restless, agitated …).
- Try the 'Ha!' breath: stand with legs apart and knees slightly bent, make two fists, and as you exhale say 'Ha!' as your fists come down to your knees. Repeat until you feel a release of the pent-up feeling.
- Push against a wall – press your palms flat against the wall with outstretched arms and push. Keep your legs shoulder-width apart.
- Slow it down, breathe in, and as you breathe out ask, *What do I need right now?*
- Place one hand on your forehead and the other at the nape of your neck. Imagine breathing in space to help your thoughts have more room and to cool down the heat of the thoughts.

FLIGHT (MOVING AWAY FROM)
What we see on the outside
- always on the go
- avoidance
- procrastinating
- inability to concentrate or focus
- high energy
- over-working

What you are feeling on the inside
- panic
- anxiety
- worry
- fear
- no rest time – don't feel safe to rest
- overwhelmed – don't know where to start
- constant busyness to avoid feeling
- find sitting still difficult
- overstimulated

How to do the Flight SOS switch
- Tune into your body. This can be done while walking if sitting is too much at first. Gently ask: *What am I avoiding?*
- If it feels safe, ask, *Why?* (If you feel unsure of how you will respond, consider working through it with a therapist.)
- Start practising daily micro-moments of staying in the present. Start with a warm or cold drink – feel it in your hand, feel your body in the chair, breathe in and out. Notice when your mind feels the urge to check your phone or do anything else, but be in the moment.
- Connect with your body through the butterfly hug or a pat down (see the Psychological Toolbox, page 339).
- Heel drops (see Toolbox, page 330).

FREEZE
What we see on the outside
- stuck
- zoned out – dissociating
- daydreaming
- immobilised
- self-isolating

- shut down
- silent treatment: 'freezing you out'
- low energy

What you are feeling on the inside
- frozen
- numb
- despair
- hopelessness
- fear of the threat(s)
- terror

How to do the Freeze SOS switch
Ask yourself:

- What would make it safe to move out of freeze?
- Why am I frozen?
- What needs to be acknowledged?
- What am I terrified of?
- What would bring some hope?

If you froze in a threatening experience in the past, know that the freeze response is a physiological instinct to protect and that is why you didn't shout, or scream or say 'stop'. You need to heal from that and understand it was not your fault.

When you feel frozen:

- Move your eyes left, right, up, down. Stretch one arm out straight in front of you and hold a pen. Focus on the pen and then focus beyond the pen, then bring your focus back to the pen. This is a gentle way to bring you back into your body.
- Stand up and stamp your feet.

- Pat down your body (see Toolbox, page 340).
- Smell – find and have comforting smells to hand that bring you back into your body.
- Use the 5–4–3–2–1 method to refocus and recentre: name 5 things you can see, 4 things you can hear, 3 things you can touch, 2 things you can smell, 1 thing you can taste.

FAWN (PLEASING, PLACATING)
What we see on the outside
- people-pleasing
- lack of boundaries
- over-explaining
- over-apologising
- difficulty saying 'no'
- difficulty expressing how you really feel
- over-agreeableness (down to everyday decisions like deciding where to go to eat)
- low energy

What you are feeling on the inside
- Trauma response of appeasing others to stop or avoid conflict, criticism, or disapproval
- Moving closer to the person causing distress to placate them in order to avoid confrontation
- Abandoning own needs
- Putting others first

… which can leave you with an identity crisis when you realise you have been doing this.

How to do the Fawn SOS switch

- When you're asked to do something, STOP! ... tune into your body ... ask yourself: *Do I want to? Do I have the energy and/or time?* And please note that you still have permission to say no even if you do have the energy and time. Ask yourself: *Do I want to do it and why?* Why is it important – check your motives to clarify the motivation behind your answer.
- Keep practising this and it will get easier to think of yourself. Start small, even if only to change a wrong coffee order – speak up for yourself.

The window of tolerance

The term 'window of tolerance' was first coined by Dan Siegel in his book *The Developing Mind*,[4] which explores what it is like when we are in our emotional comfort zone and the imbalance we feel when we are outside it.

Think of you on a good day: your thoughts are clear, you make decisions easily and feel connected with yourself and others. You feel comfortable in your own skin, your mind and heart. There's an optimal sense of ease and openness. This is the Goldilocks zone of life, with an emotional bandwidth that is not too high, not too low, but just right when it comes to navigating your busy daily life. That is your window of tolerance.

When you move out of that zone, that's when you begin to feel overwhelmed. What pushes you out of this zone? Knowing this is very helpful as it allows you to tune in to when your mood or energy shifted, to understand that trigger, and then work on being able to emotionally boomerang back to a more enjoyable and optimal window of tolerance.

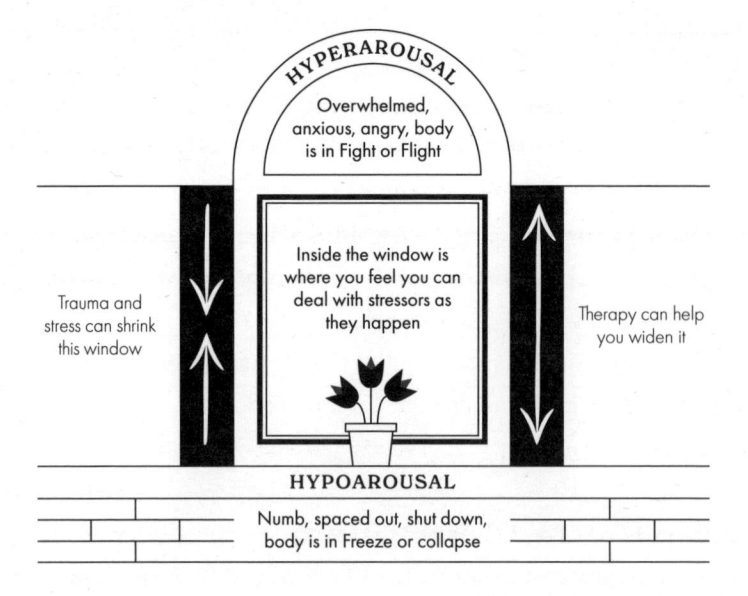

HYPERAROUSAL
Overwhelmed, anxious, angry, body is in Fight or Flight

Trauma and stress can shrink this window

Inside the window is where you feel you can deal with stressors as they happen

Therapy can help you widen it

HYPOAROUSAL
Numb, spaced out, shut down, body is in Freeze or collapse

The goal is not to be in a constant state of nonchalance or blissed-out Zen. Let's be real here. What we want is more moments, even micro-moments, when we feel good, I'd even say neutral. It's not an extreme ambition, but it is a new and pleasant way to be – less chronic chaos and more everyday calm. Modern-day chill vibes that actually work for normal busy people. Bliss within the mess.

I often say to clients when they are talking through something that upset them, say an argument with their mother, partner or boss, to notice *when* their mood changed. This is a helpful way to pin down when you emotionally moved. Each person's window of tolerance will have been shaped by their history, genetics, past and present life circumstances, to name but a few factors. That's why being trauma-informed is so important in a world that incorrectly measures how a person is or behaves at a surface level. One of my favourite parts of my work is the compassion piece; it's like being a compassionate investigator when you ask lots of questions and even the client is surprised by their own answers, revealing answers that make perfect sense when you have the whole story and not some generic, one-size-fits-all idea of how we 'should' be.

I know that stress, anxiety, and trauma narrow your window of tolerance and take you out of the Goldilocks zone, so it is my mission for you to understand this, with compassion, and to keep doing what helps you. And a lot of the time that will mean doing less, saying no, protecting your time and energy. More isn't the answer. This toxic norm isn't working for you, and it certainly isn't working for your nervous system.

The language of safety

I love language, I love words, their meanings, how the meaning changes according to how and whom they are expressed, and the relationship between those words and people. I have to say very tough things to clients, but they know they are safe, and my intention is always for their safety and wellbeing. I communicate this through the language of safety, which from a polyvagal perspective comes from my words, tone, facial expression and body language. This is how our nervous system communicates feelings of safety. So, in a non-threatening, soothing situation like therapy, your breathing and heartbeat may feel calm and you may even mirror each other's body language. Whereas when your body responds to cues of danger, it lets you know as well. This is the language of safety, letting you know how to respond if you feel safe and comfortable or if your body is telling a different story of red flags and caution.

There are three essential phrases to get to know and practise in the language of safety: vagal tone, vagal flexibility, and the vagal brake. We will meet these again in Chapter 3, but let's introduce them now.

VAGAL TONE

We all know what tone is in terms of exercise: as we work out and become fitter, we create more physical toning. With vagal tone, it is about how strong the vagus nerve's activity is and what level of fitness it is at. The fitter it is, the more efficiently it can regulate your heart rate, digestion and breathing, which in turns helps you to manage your stress more efficiently.

Vagal tone reflects the vagal tone of the heart – it is the balance between sympathetic and parasympathetic (vagal) activity measured by heart rate variability. You can change your vagal tone by the emotional regulation practices outlined in Chapter 9 and the Psychological Toolbox.

- **The good bit:** They are accessible to all, free and easy, e.g. humming, gargling or cold exposure (see page 332).
- **The working goal:** To train and work towards good vagal tone; to practise and engage in activities that help you return to safety and recover more quickly after stress or difficulty. This is how resilience is built, along with flexibility.

VAGAL FLEXIBILITY

Vagal flexibility is about the adaptability of the vagus nerve to respond efficiently to situations as they arise. This is a core skill I help clients to work on specifically in relation to anxiety and panic attacks. Rather than fearing the past experience of how you reacted and negatively anticipating future fears, you actively increase your nervous system's adaptability to the point where you can trust that you can switch from being relaxed to moving out of the way of danger as it presents itself.

Flexibility and resilience understood through the lens of your autonomic system is a pairing that recognises that the goal is not to be always in regulation, but rather to know when you are stuck and how to return to safety. You do this by mapping your personal profile – as you did earlier in the chapter. This allows you to track your reactions and to identify your triggers and how you respond to them. This in turn allows you to work on recognising quickly when you have moved to dorsal (Freeze/Fawn) or sympathetic (Fight/Flight) states, reducing the level of impact of that state on you and shortening the length of time you remain in that state. We're back to the SOS switch (survival to safety)– it means you can work back to that steady, calm ventral vagal state.

- **The good bit:** Learning how to bring flexibility, options and choices changes your relationship with yourself and others. It gives you space to breathe, think about things in a different way and behave in a way that will feel better inside your body.
- **The working goal:** Vagal flexibility means forgiving yourself for being human, expecting things to go off course at times and to allow your normal reaction to often abnormal situations; giving yourself the grace of being angry or sad and to not see these as blockers to emotional regulation; and perhaps noting that those reactions are key markers of past physiological stress and to give yourself a few more options for how you want to respond in the future. Listen to the emotions that are present; they have a lot of helpful insights to offer.

VAGAL BRAKE

The vagal brake means knowing when you need to stop and slow down. This is an exceptionally useful tool at the disposal of your nervous system. It means you don't jump straight into a reaction; instead, you pause, you think, you digest the information, and then you make a decision. This allows you to recognise if you are about to betray your own needs or trample your own boundaries. It's simple, but effective.

- **The good bit:** You will learn the difference between when your system is telling you that you are not in danger and when it is warning you to pay attention. This in turn will give you a sense of autonomy, control and confidence in your decisions and actions.
- **The working goal:** To feel more in control. To become confident in your assessment of when you need to stop, pause, or go.

Building your SOS switch capabilities

It's not an easy matter to catch hold of yourself and calm down when you are going nuclear with frustrated rage, or to understand the perspective of someone else when they are driving you around the twist, or to take a deep breath and state what you do and do not want to do. If you've had a lifetime of not doing these things, you might find it really difficult to flip that SOS switch. There are two techniques that can help you: hitting the Pause button; and anchoring safety.

HITTING THE PAUSE BUTTON

The ability to hit the Pause button is wildly underestimated. It's a tool I use regularly myself. I got the idea from my daughter: she'd go around with the remote control, and when she hit Pause we'd have to freeze. I need that Pause button when I'm just about to betray my own needs again and fall prey to the well-worn path of people-pleasing and perfectionism. I know you need that button too as, unfortunately, many of us seem to share this resistance to putting our own needs first.

This got me thinking about the non-biological traits we inherit, like conditioned norms that get passed down the generational line wrapped up as 'traditions' or 'the way we've always done it', but these legacies might not always fit with you and what you want. You can end up feeling you are on remote control, not in control. I bet you have at some time said, *They know how to press all my buttons* – but what if you had buttons that would bring more control and regulation into your life? What if, rather than feeling that remote control of someone pressing your buttons and controlling you, instead you felt the wonderful feeling of being in control?

The Pause button is essential, but to that I would add the Stop button and the Play button. This is a way to visualise the change you would like to make in your life.

The next time you need to use one of these life controls, imagine pressing the button you want to bring about the action or behaviour you need:

What do you need or want to **STOP** *in your life?* ⏹

_____

When and where would having a **PAUSE** *button work for you?* ⏸

_____

What and when are you going to **PLAY**? ▶

_____

_____

Here are a few examples, from the therapy room, of what you may want to Stop, Pause or Play.

> **STOP**
> Samantha made the same New Year's resolution every year – to stop losing her cool and speaking in anger – and it usually lasted about a week. After we explored the triggers, she found some definite patterns that we began to put into her personal profile map of when and what sent her into Fight mode and into a state of hyperarousal. She recognised some of the usual suspects of anxiety, such as her wish to do things perfectly, cue Christmas and family expectations – theirs and hers – tying in with a lack of her own boundaries and need to please everyone but herself. The result was a lot of unexpressed feelings and the steady two-month-long build towards resentment. The tangled Christmas lights may have been the final trigger, but the feelings were lit way before.

Before she could stop the anger, Samantha needed to accept that if she continued as she was, it would hurt her health and relationships. It was a challenge, but she began to stop herself before the pattern had a chance to build. This meant doing some deep work on relinquishing her need to control how everything was done and ask for help. The best gift she could give next year was not to be the burned-out resentful person she didn't want to be. Learning how to stop a behaviour isn't a once-off action, it is an ongoing process and effort.

> **PAUSE**
> 'I wish I had a Pause button,' Louise said.
> 'What do you mean?' I asked.
> 'I am sick of how I respond the same way every single time. It's like I walk towards this destructive cycle that trips me up every time without fail. What annoys me most is I can see it coming at me in slow motion. It starts by me getting excited about doing something, even though that familiar niggle is there telling me, "Say no – you have too much on already." I shush the niggle and say, "Oh yes, that will be fine, I can do that." The niggle knows I can't. I wish I just could pause for a second before I say yes.'

The next time you find yourself about to say yes, imagine you are pressing Pause on the remote. Then notice the strong urge that comes up as every bit of you is telling you to say yes. Then tolerate the discomfort of 'letting someone down' or disappointing them.

Breathe in and repeat, 'I am allowed to say no, it is safe for me to mind myself, I can't say no to me anymore.'

Use the Pause button to give you the moment to remember what it feels like when you want to please but end up exhausted. You now have this tool to hand for the rest of your life.

PLAY

'What do you mean I need to play more?' Mairead asked. Children play because it is fun. While we know it is good for their development, this is not why they play. It's for the fun and the laughter and the movement. Adults often pull back from playing because they may have been scolded – *Grow up and stop being so childish*. But I think when you lose the ability to be childlike and have wonder and awe about the world, you lose a core aspect of yourself. You have been saying that you feel stuck, Mairead, in a constant loop of tidying and keeping up appearances and, let's face it, there is no joy in that. I am asking you to start noticing where and what brings joy into your life. I want you plan when you are going to play, not spontaneous I know, but otherwise nothing changes, and you just continue picking up people's shoes whilst grunting under your breath. Stop waiting for someone to give you permission to play. Just do it. Build in time in the day for your joy.

ANCHORING SAFETY

Here is a technique created by Deb Dana to anchor you back to feeling safe and connected. This is a practice I show clients so they know how to anchor themselves back when they are feeling anything from anxiety to panic and everything in between.

I ask them to close their eyes, if that feels safe, take a deep breath, and release it, and to think of a place that makes them feel safe. People often say their bedroom is a safe space. I then ask them to describe what they like about their bedroom and what they are wearing, for example: 'I am lying on my bed, not in my bed, I am wearing a soft tracksuit, it's super comfy, and fluffy socks. My hair is tied up and it is quiet. My room is peaceful, and I have a nice picture in front of me that helps me feel relaxed.'

This is what I call 'soft clothes activated', when you come home and you get into something comfy. I then ask them to anchor the moment by pressing their index finger into their thumb, creating a neural pathway that is safe and comfortable.

This practice is so powerful, and I would recommend you try it throughout the day to build up this connection point when you go into Fight or Flight, Freeze or Fawn.

What have we learned?

We have covered quite a bit in this chapter, and much of it might have been new to you, so let's pause for a quick recap on the key points:

- Our nervous system is always trying to protect us.
- What might have helped in the past could have now become a maladaptive coping mechanism.
- Looking at this through a compassionate lens may help you to change what you need to change without any judgement or shame.
- The autonomic nervous system is affected by trauma, which helps you to wholly understand how trauma impacts your mind and body.
- These realisations and insights only come when we allow ourselves the space to listen to what our bodies are telling us.
- We need to track where and how we are and then actively engage in practices that will help broaden our distress tolerance.
- You can be in sympathetic dominance (hyperarousal) when you have experienced trauma and anxiety disorders, and you can be in parasympathetic dominance (hypoarousal) as a result of many factors, such as overwhelming stress, trauma, depression, chronic pain, low energy and slow wound healing. Either can lead to your system's survival activation becoming stuck, because you have been chronically in overdrive/Fight or Freeze for too long.

- Chronic dysregulation can occur as a result of trauma, PTSD, complex PTSD (CPTSD), anxiety disorder, depression, psychiatric or long-term physical and/or mental health issues, socio-economic factors, intergenerational trauma, modern life and toxic norms from consumerism to hyper-productivity to misplaced ideas of success.
- As you explore your personal profile map, it offers a pathway of hope where you can manoeuvre in ways that suit you to live a life that moves away from vigilant protection towards a life of connection.

In wrapping up, we've delved into the intricacies of survival mode and how easily you can find yourself entrenched in it to the detriment of your mental and physical wellbeing. You understand the protective evolutionary purpose and how to move in and out of it. When your survival reactions are constantly activated, the vagus nerve sends signals of threat, triggering one of the 4 Fs – Fight, Flight, Freeze or Fawn – and your body can become stuck in that response. This can be hard to spot as it can persist beneath our conscious awareness, so you might not be aware of it or characterise it like that, but its physical repercussions are certainly felt and are unmistakable. Whether you find yourself in a heightened state of hyperarousal or a subdued state of hypoarousal, both extremes exact a toll on your mind and body. But learning to recognise these states and developing the ability to adapt flexibly allows you to reclaim agency over your health and resilience.

Now that we understand what survival mode is, in the following chapters we are going to look at how it manifests in particular states of anxiety and how that feels inside the body. This will allow you to explore how you feel and identify where you fall along the spectrum. Understanding is the first step – and then we can move on in Part 2 to how you can manage anxiety effectively.

The Practical Psychology

As you reflect on this chapter, please answer these questions:

Who did you have to become to survive?
_____

What were the consequences for you?
_____

Does it feel unsettling to be who you want to be when everyone knows you as you have been?
_____

What parts of you are you grieving for?
_____

What opportunities or experiences do you feel you missed out on?
_____

Does it feel safe to 'be' you as opposed to who you think you 'should' be?
_____

Write out what the authentic you looks like:
_____

What is in your day, week, month that makes you feel like you?
_____

What would you say would be a life well lived? Think about it and when you are ready write down what that would look like:

A life well lived would be ...
_____

Now, can I gently ask, what are you doing in your daily life to bring some of that in now? That question isn't to make you feel bad or guilty, I know there are so many reasons why you are not doing this, but something has to change.

What one change would help you as you are right now?
_____

CHAPTER 3

How does emotional anxiety feel from the inside?

Emotional anxiety is linked to emotional dysregulation. This refers to a constant restlessness and discomfort within and an inability to let go and relax. As I look around, I feel we are consumed by lives that are chasing and chaotic and no one is escaping it, not children, women, men or grandparents. How we are living, in a constant state of survival, is toxic. The antidote to this is a learned practice that allows us to live a more considered life. Noticing and becoming aware are essential tools in this regard, and ones that we will be practising throughout this book. It can be easy to bypass a sentence like that, but the simple tools are often the most effective ones.

When you are dysregulated, your body and nervous system are out of balance, which can impact your ability to cope with stress, to regulate your emotions and to engage in healthy social interactions. You likely don't feel at home in your own body, don't know who you are or where you belong. You want to return 'home' to a place that feels safe and secure, but you don't know which way to turn to find it. However, knowing or feeling you are lost is the first step towards finding your way. Over the past twenty-five years I have listened as clients have tried to put those feelings into words. They have told me:

- 'I feel stuck.'
- 'I feel so frustrated with myself.'
- 'I feel like I'm always busy and yet constantly behind.'
- 'Even though I am exhausted I don't know how to rest or relax.'
- 'I feel others have it so much worse than me, I shouldn't feel this way and should be grateful for everything I have.'
- 'I feel so lost.'
- 'I don't know who I am.'
- 'I feel overwhelmed.'
- 'I feel angry and constantly irritable, and it makes me feel so bad.'
- 'I feel so anxious and worry all the time.'
- 'I think I'm losing it.'

Do you relate to any of these? If you do, what does that mean for you? It means that you, and too many others, are caught by and enmeshed in modern-day systems that are keeping you stuck in a state of chronic frustration and disconnection from yourself and others. The silent danger is accepting this norm. Be aware – just because something has become normalised doesn't make it normal.

How do you know if you are emotionally dysregulated?

You know when you just feel 'off'? This comes from being in a dysregulated state where there can be a disruption to your physical and psychological processes. You may find it harder to think clearly, you may feel overwhelmed, and this can have a domino effect into finding it more than challenging to regulate your emotions or to shift out of Fight, Flight, Freeze or Fawn, which then impacts the ability to regulate behaviour.

- You may feel constantly on edge, overwhelmed, or on the verge of feeling out of control.
- You may have difficulty relaxing even when you 'can'.
- You often feel agitated, frustrated, quick to anger and reactive.
- The 3 I's – irritability, impatience, and intolerance – will be loud and present. These are red flags that are very easy to ignore (see opposite page for more on this).
- There can be a sense of time urgency, where everything feels sped up, everything is a priority, you are always busy, always behind and time seems to disappear continuously into a deep vacuum.
- You may feel sensitivity to noise, textures (clothes), heat, smells, other people's moods, crowds. People may have called you over-sensitive.
- You may have gut and digestive and/or skin issues.
- You may experience pain more deeply.
- You may experience major shifts with your hormonal or immune systems.
- You may experience chronic pain or illness even though you 'do all the right things'.
- You may feel exhausted during the day and then you can't fall asleep at night as you experience sleep onset insomnia. Tossing and turning, finding it impossible to physically and mentally relax as your thoughts seem to be in the ultimate late-night race.
- Or you have difficulty staying asleep and wake up frequently during the night. This is called sleep maintenance insomnia, when you wake and have great difficulty falling back asleep.
- Or you wake early in the morning and cannot go back to sleep. You're just wide awake. But you don't feel refreshed from the sleep you had.

- Or you can experience all three types of insomnia on different nights, a combination that leaves you exhausted.
- Switching off may be immensely challenging, which can also impact on your ability to focus and concentrate.

The 3 I's: Irritability, impatience and intolerance

I'd like to look at these in a little more detail before we continue because, as I said above, they are really helpful flags, but we often dismiss them or don't notice them at all – at least, we don't until they get our attention by escalating to a panic attack. They are Irritability, Impatience and Intolerance.

Remember the 'shark attack' I mentioned earlier, the bit of the behaviour everyone sees that might show obvious irritability, impatience and intolerance? What's important to note is why those emotions and behaviours are present and, more important, what led to them and what was underneath them.

Anyone who is completely shocked by their 'sudden' panic attack will confirm, when I gently ask, that the 3 I's were most definitely present for months beforehand. They knew they were being irritable and less tolerant with their family, colleagues, and kids. They knew that everyone couldn't be as annoying as they seemed and they knew that things, people, and situations that normally wouldn't cause a flutter were creating quite the physical internal rage. When the 3 I's are present it doesn't feel great, you don't feel great, you don't like or feel like yourself and, to add insult to injury, others will have noticed and no doubt told you as well.

In a nutshell, emotional dysregulation is not a pleasant state. If you find yourself feeling chronically overwhelmed, irritable, impatient, and thinking *Why am I not coping well enough? Everyone else seems so resilient to this stuff of life. I need to do more but it is so hard as I'm so tired because I can't relax or sleep. I never stop and don't even know how or where to start* – you could be dysregulated. This means that your body and mind may be experiencing the relentless speed of constant overdrive. You are on the go relentlessly, then collapse with exhaustion and fall asleep on the couch each Friday night by 10 p.m., only to stare at the ceiling, wide awake, when your head finally hits the pillow. It is important to know that realising this is impacting who you are and how you function every single day, whether you consciously admit it or not, is a good thing. As mentioned earlier, recognising and becoming aware of it is the first step. There is hope in these two questions: *What is it?* and *What can I do?* The next step is not to blame yourself because there are various causes and factors.

Emotional dysregulation can have different sources, both external and internal, but part of it certainly comes from modern life, which I believe is pushing people into these dysregulated states. The pace and pressure of modern life is out of whack with how our nervous systems work. The most common effects of dysregulation (the main symptoms of it, if you like) are overwhelm and hyperarousal.

How it feels: Overwhelm

If I were to define overwhelm, it would be that it's the 'It's all too much' of the title of this book. It is a flooding of thoughts and emotions that you can also physically feel. It's a sense of frustration at knowing how much you have to do, knowing there isn't enough time and that it has already gone on too long, and you can't see how it will change. I'm not going to put in some simple and frankly quite annoying hack of 'If you just did this' – instead, I'm going to ask you to realistically look at your life and see what needs to change to reduce the perma-state of overwhelm. The truth about having good physical, mental and emotional health is that it takes thought, planning and feeling safe enough to do it, and that is hard to achieve given that you might be feeling unable to do what needs to be done, never mind having time to think about how to make changes. Even the thought of that might be overwhelming for you. In as much as overwhelm is systemic, so too are our lives, which means you can't just escape by changing your thoughts without giving consideration as to *why* you feel chronic overwhelm. My work is to show you how to switch from survival to safety and then your body and nervous system can learn how to respond differently, even if your circumstances don't change.

Overwhelm is a long time in the making, with many factors contributing to it, one of which is being chronically overstretched.

BEING OVERSTRETCHED

I feel overwhelmed when there is too much on and too many demands in my day or week. My way of dealing with it is to write it all down. When the To Do list is too long, which invariably it is, I rename it the 'unrealistic list' and make another, shorter one called the 'I can do this list'. I'm trying to trick my brain into feeling less worried and anxious by the sheer volume of all I have to do. But what happens is that my lists haunt and taunt me: 'You haven't done this', 'You still haven't signed up for that'. That constant drip, drip of criticism and striving to tick items off the list and the sense of annoyance at myself when I still have so many left unticked triggers feelings of anxiety. I know and recognise it, but it still happens. There is simply too much to be done, and only one of me to do it all. I'm constantly overstretched – trying to achieve what cannot be achieved in the time I have.

Familiar? Again, as we noted earlier, it's all too easy to just blame yourself for failing, to think that everyone else is coping beautifully and to castigate yourself for being lazy, for procrastinating, for not being a good enough time manager … there are any number of sticks to beat yourself with.

But there is another reason why we might accept living at the point of being overstretched all the time. What happens if we slow down? What happens if we are not so busy that we can actually hear our own thoughts? Could it be that you are actively suppressing, ignoring, and busying yourself to distraction? Has it got to the point where you are scared of *not* being overstretched because then you might have to hear the thoughts that are drowned out by your constant movement, on the go all day long? What's happening below the busyness – are you unhappy with your life? Or with your job? Is the routine dulling and boring you? Or are the bills making you a reluctant workaholic, trying to keep the head above water with the cost of living? Do you feel these are the life choices you wanted to make and that you want to live? These are really tough, sharp, uncomfortable questions and it's amazing the lengths we can go to in order to avoid asking them. Could that be in part what is feeding into your anxiety? Along with the uncomfortable reality about what can be done in any given day, every client I talk to, every person I meet, seemed stretched to breaking point, and it is too much. I think the systems are broken and are breaking people.

BECOMING OVERWHELMED

You can be overstretched for a long time before the moment comes when it escalates into a state of overwhelm. Something will snap – a change or crisis of some kind in your life – and it will finally become too much. The constant busyness, the pressing down of your thoughts and emotions so that you can stick rigidly to the routine and the To Do list, the ignoring of messages from your stressed body and mind – it all gives way and you are in freefall. Now you feel out of control and often deeply alone, ashamed, and secretly feeling you are going crazy – all things that have been said to me in the therapy room. It is likely that you have been thinking for some time that you must check in with the GP, check your bloods, find out why you're exhausted, talk to someone – and suddenly that 'I must' turns into '*I need* to talk with someone.' It becomes urgent and unavoidable because you realise that you need some help to work through this.

The crisis lands in the middle of your life, or the 'out-of-the-blue' panic attack steals your ability to function, you can't get on the train or bus, you are terrified to go to the meeting, you feel like you don't have the ability to meet any of the demands in your life, even the simplest task now feels like an enormous daunting mountain. The fear is gripping and it feels like it's taking over.

Remember: getting to overwhelmed took time. This isn't, in fact, out of the blue – it's out of all of the burdens you have been shouldering for so long. You were overstretched for so long that something had to give. And so you snap. The first way you'll snap will be those 3 I's – you'll become irritated, impatient, and intolerant, usually with your nearest and dearest. There's that lovely old Irish phrase: 'He/she is not him/herself at all.' That's how it feels – you are not yourself, you got lost somewhere along the way, you are struggling to recognise who you are now, and you don't know how to get back to yourself. It's a sense of disconnection from your own self, which naturally creates a deep anxiety.

Before you take out the self-flagellating stick and make yourself feel bad about why you didn't reach out for help sooner, ask yourself some significant questions first:

- Who taught you how to process these overwhelming emotions?
- More to the point, who taught you that it was safe and acceptable to express your emotions?

For many, the answer to the second question is 'No one'. What you learned instead, explicitly and implicitly, was to stop trusting the emotional information cues that came up for you. You may have been given out to or shamed as a child and adolescent for being 'too' anything – 'too angry', 'too sad', 'too emotional', 'too sensitive'. Maybe you were met with irritation and impatience and intolerance: 'Stop wallowing, it wasn't that bad', 'You have to get on with things', 'Stop worrying over something that's past', 'No use crying over spilt milk'. Shamed emotions become shy and regressive emotions if they are taught that 'they' or 'you' are too much.

But the thing is, these emotions don't disappear when they are suppressed. They are located in your body and pre-existing wounds are triggered in the now. That sounds healthy except you will quite likely express your hurt, frustration, or anger in a way that others won't like. Unfortunately, if you haven't learned how to recognise and accept the information cues that your emotions are providing, they will keep building and bubbling up ('I can't believe he said that', 'She knows how I feel about that'). To get that under control requires you to recognise that some of your hurt is old hurt and possibly not fully related to the argument you are having right now.

It's about keeping a psychological timeline in your head and noticing when you have a strong reaction or are triggered and to ask yourself: 'Is how I am feeling fully to do with this, or is a feeling that is familiar and deeply uncomfortable also present?' So, if your pattern is, for example, that you feel you are being taken for granted, you feel unseen and unvalued, this may be true in the present situation but it may also have older origins that you need to sit with. What I mean is that if you haven't learned or even seen modelled how to tolerate the discomfort of what is coming up for you, it's time to ask, 'How have I responded in the past?' and then to ask, 'How would I like my nervous system to respond differently?' When your nervous system is activated and mobilised into familiar Fight, Flight, Freeze or Fawn responses by allowing current and past wounds to be felt, processed and healed, this is the path to freedom and safety. What most of us do is a combination of suppressing uncomfortable emotions, ignoring them, or numbing them in destructive ways. Sitting with what is present is an embodied practice. It is not just thinking your way out of it.

Can you see how the cycle builds? You may react strongly to, say, an argument with your partner, children, or anyone, and they may call out your behaviour as excessive. Immediately, that shame you learned early on swoops in, along with the inner critical narrative of 'What is wrong with me? They're right, I am too sensitive' and then all that happens is that the emotional wounds are added to – not seen or healed. You haven't overstretched yourself out of an illogical desire to be busy. You have busied yourself to the point of utter exhaustion to avoid pain that didn't feel safe enough to feel in your body.

Pause for a moment and process that sentence.

Why are we filling up every second of our lives? We fill up our senses to the point of overwhelm from the moment we wake up until the moment we go to sleep and while it may be entertaining, it's a cheap and short-term dopamine hit to avoid feeling. You have been numbing out because the pain was too sharp, heavy and or painful and you didn't know where or how to start. But that feeling of not doing enough and of not being 'good enough' threatens how you feel and think about yourself.

THE SHAME OF OVERWHELM

Let's get one thing crystal clear: It's time to stop feeling guilty, stop self-blaming and stop self-shaming.

This is not easy to put into practice, however, as it seems everyone has an opinion on everything you do or don't do. Opinions are a short hop to judgements, and it can be very triggering to feel judged by others. Whether you work full-time or part-time or are 'just' a stay-at-home mum, whether you exercise enough or too much, whether you are seen as overly ambitious or not ambitious enough … whatever it is, someone will want to hand out unsolicited 'advice' around your choices. The voices of family, friends, people you know slightly, people online, can make it feel like you have 24/7 commentary pundits weighing up your life. The 'Comments' section isn't lost on me. And that doesn't even include your own inner voice, which can be merciless. It can all add up to you not trusting yourself and doubting every decision you make.

What intrigues and frustrates me around this is that no one, not even you, has the whole picture. Truly understanding yourself within how you are in public and in private, the unconscious part that drives a lot of your behaviour and is often shaped and carved out from a mixture of influences, conscious and unconscious, is a major blind spot for us all. The danger, and it is a danger, is that the messages you receive will lead you to take on more than is possible, leading ultimately to overwhelm. This is a cumulative process of overload. When a client says to me, 'I don't know where this anxiety or this panic attack came from, it came out of nowhere', I know – as you now know – that there is always a trail of breadcrumbs leading back to how and where it started.

Let's imagine overwhelm for a moment. I see it as a large glass container. It looks like there is lots of space in there and room and time, but when faced with a constant pouring in of stress, life, information, and no breaks, it fills up faster than we think.

Self-care won't fix chronic overwhelm. It might provide a temporary plaster, but it will not fix the root cause of the issue. It is necessary for you to do the work to find out what is going on beneath the surface, what is feeding into your actions and choices, what you need to change to ensure you are not overstretched and, if you are, that it doesn't build to the point of overwhelm; while remembering that a toxic culture is part of the problem. That's why I'm going to ask you to answer some questions now, to build a picture of how this is affecting you.

The Practical Psychology

If you took an overview of how anxiety or overwhelm affects you, can you answer the following?

Do you feel consumed by anxiety?

_____

Do you feel consumed by your thoughts and feelings and emotions?

_____

Do you feel consumed by external messages of how you 'should' look, be and behave?

_____

What are you a product of?

_____

Write down what overwhelms you:

_____

Why does it overwhelm you? (e.g. I know time can trigger overwhelm for me.)

_____

Can you bring compassion to what has led to the experience of overwhelm? Don't blame yourself, don't criticise yourself, just look at where you are at and accept it – and that you have the power to change it.

How does overwhelm show up for you?

_____

Do you feel overstretched?

_____

If so, write down what specifically overwhelms.

_____

What makes it worse?

_____

What would help?

_____

How it feels: Hyperarousal

We met hyperarousal in Chapter 1, where we learned this is when our nervous system is in a heightened, overactive state of physical and psychological arousal. You could think of hyperarousal being like the hare and hypoarousal being the tortoise.

How do you know you are in hyperarousal? Let's do a little body check. How are your neck, shoulders, and jaw when you are rushing from one thing to the next? How are your stomach and digestion? How are all those thoughts – are they dancing jerkily from one thing to the next? Does everything feel urgent and rushed, even your heartbeat?

Running in tandem with hyperarousal, you will find hypervigilance also hard at work. I tell clients that hypervigilance is the sniper in your head, alert, tensed, ready to fire. Even when you tell the sniper to relax and reassure them that everything is fine, they can't process that because they have never learned how to relax. They are in charge, in control, so stop annoying them when they are 'protecting' you 24/7. Your internal watch guard thinks it is protecting you by scanning, monitoring, and feeling in control. However, most of the things they are worried about have never happened and will never happen. The origin of this for many people is that something did once happen, and it may have been life-changing and not in a good way, and their body became stuck in a state of hypervigilance to 'never let anything like that happen again'.

When you understand why 'protect mode' is on and that being overactive is down to past events/experiences, this allows the grace of compassion to come in. You can then change the *What is wrong with me?* narrative to one of learning how to create safety in your body and to regulate your nervous system so that the sniper can be stood down.

One hugely difficult aspect of trauma is how it keeps showing up in the present. Thinking good thoughts isn't going to persuade hypervigilance to stand down. You must teach your body to trust again and to know that if something bad happens, you have the skills to adapt. That takes trust, time and practice. Can you see how easy it is to get stuck in survive? Can you see why hypervigilance, even though it seems robotic, thinks it is protecting you? But can you also see why it is time to find another way?

As part of hyperarousal, we also often find dread and despair, followed swiftly by a sense of doom. We've met your sniper – hypervigilance – but in the background, running the comms office, is hyperarousal.

Your emotions have very specific functions and work tirelessly to give you direct messages about how you feel. When you think 'I feel irritable and frustrated', that's your emotions giving you a heads-up on what's going on inside. But if those important internal cues are blocked and unheeded, that stops or inhibits the necessary external action that is needed to deal with those feelings. The fear builds as you tear yourself apart thinking, *Everyone else has their shit together, so what the hell is wrong with me?* The active denial of self and of how you feel in your mind and body isn't helping you. The emotion is stuck deep inside, not going away as you wish it would, or maybe as you tell yourself it has.

How many times have you wanted to say to yourself, *I wish I could just stop thinking about that*? It would be great if that worked, but it doesn't. You can push it from your conscious mind, but the problem is what happens next. The emotion gets stored in the body and it remembers what you are trying so hard to forget. This is particularly the case with traumatic experiences, but it applies to all the experiences that have left lasting imprints on your psyche, shaping the person you are today.

This aspect of how trauma can get stored in your body is explored in depth in *The Body Keeps the Score* by Bessel van der Kolk.[5] It describes how traumatic experiences can get stored in the body, leading to physical and emotional symptoms, often long after the incident, making it difficult to connect that experience in the past to how you are being triggered now. The rhetoric around how 'time is a healer' does not help here. Think of a fright or traumatic experience you've had. Can you remember the physical, emotional or psychological thoughts or sensations you had at the time? I'm drawn towards how Gabor Maté describes women as the shock-absorbers of society. Our bodies absorb the shock of difficult, challenging, traumatic experiences. If you do not sit with or process the pain or loss of self, the emotional ghosts are rattling around inside your mind and soul, tormenting you. It's not easy to face what we fear. It's understandable that you turn away in whatever way makes logical sense for you, but it will keep you stuck. Helping you acknowledge, validate and accept what happened is no easy feat. Neither is living with it.

So, to be super clear, if you think you have all the 'stuff' packed away in a Pandora's box in the back of your head that you 'just don't think about', your body never got the 'bury it' memo. This is why your anxiety has gotten worse 'out of nowhere'. It has been building and your body is often the one who acts upon it first – you fall ill, or you experience a panic attack, or you live with stress symptoms that drag you down mentally and physically. If the root cause is still not addressed, if you try to tackle it in other ways, with just medication, for example, or self-care routines, it becomes deeply frustrating when nothing you do seems to be working or changing and, if anything, it feels like it is getting worse. Unfortunately, instead of reaching out at this point, many people reverse back into themselves, shame telling them they are being 'stupid' and 'have nothing to complain about' … and on the cycle goes. Anxiety can be a deeply isolating experience.

In this way, you end up living inside hyperarousal. Consumed by it, drained by it, and also terrified to leave it because it is 'protecting' you. Courage and confidence are lovely words to say but are much harder to put into practice, especially when you feel your mind is racing from the moment you open your eyes until you fall asleep. Trite advice, like 'Relax, it will never happen', will only cause you to shut down and feel bad about yourself. The emotions of anxiety are nasty and pernicious. Self-doubt, loss of a sense of who you are, fear and loathing, feeling scattered and burned out. Deep frustration with yourself and a restlessness that is physical as well as in your thoughts. A driving fear that you will never feel like yourself again. You may be able to spot hyperarousal in someone you know well, but oftentimes it is so well hidden even the person themselves doesn't see how stuck they are. It's just so easy to shrug and say 'Everyone is stressed, what of it?'

Hypoarousal

We met hypoarousal earlier, and this is also a form of emotional dysregulation. The emotions may be largely the same, but they present differently in hypoarousal. Think how a tortoise retreats back into its shell: this is hypoarousal, where you withdraw from others and worry and ruminate. This adds to the feeling of being stuck or frozen in whatever issue(s) is spiralling around in your head, heart and body. Same source emotions, different visible outcome.

Can I work my way out of emotional dysregulation?

Yes, you can. Not only can you work your way out of emotional dysregulation, but it is also an exceptionally transformative process, one I want everyone to have access to and come to know. Easy? No. Fast? No. A once-off thing? Absolutely not. The quick, easy sell is part of the lie we've been sold so often in the shape of some product or gimmick that will leave you feeling like you are the one who failed. Learning how to work with your internal nervous system and the world around you is a new dance to learn. Change is possible, but here's the bit they don't tell you: your brain will resist it with every nerve fibre of its being to keep you within what is familiar to you. Change is scary because we don't know exactly what lies on the other side of it. Even if how you feel is anxious or bad, it is familiar to you.

This is called the homeostatic impulse, whereby we unconsciously strive to maintain the status quo, even if it's not good for us. The homeostatic impulse isn't just physical, it is also impacting your thoughts, belief systems and your emotions and will adapt to bring you back to what is familiar. That is fine if it brings you to a nice spot, but if chaos is more familiar, then it's vital to actively override and overcome this resistance to change. As Peter Levine has written, 'Trauma is a fact of life. It does not, however, have to be a life sentence.'[6]

TITRATION

Titration is a process of gradually introducing new ways to regulate the nervous system and make the necessary adjustments to support this process. It brings us back to the Goldilocks principle of 'not too much, not too little' and learning what is 'just right' for each unique situation and person. In relation to polyvagal theory, we use it to help emotional dysregulation by introducing incremental approaches to change.

Applying the concept of titration to your body, it means weaning your nervous system step by step. Think of it as being like weaning yourself off medication: you wouldn't jump from 75mg to 5mg in one go, and with good reason. In the same way, your body needs a slow and steady approach. It needs to learn that it can feel safe in small, attainable steps. Our bodies will return to what we know, to that state of homeostasis, even when it isn't good for us, because it is familiar and familiar feels safe. Obviously, this is where 'better the devil you know' came from, but it is much older than that and it is evolutionary in origin. This process helps you to build resilience, knowing you can tolerate the discomfort that will come from confronting what you may have been avoiding. This is particularly the case when working with a mental health therapist, psychologist or psychotherapist – because they are trauma-informed, they will safeguard you. It is a gentle, safe process of pacing the change. It is tough, yes, but done correctly it is not re-traumatising. When it comes to trauma, pacing is key. Here is a helpful working definition of trauma by Resmaa Menakem: 'When something happens to the body that is too much, too fast, or too soon, it overwhelms the body and can create trauma … Trauma is a wordless story our body tells itself about what is safe and what is a threat.'[7]

APPLYING THE BRAKES

In Chapter 2 we introduced the idea of the vagal nerve system and you met the term 'vagal brake'. This applies here, too, because it's a braking system that allows you to dial back your emotional levels in a manageable way. Rather than 'crashing' – which could be by losing your patience, feeling completely overwhelmed and unable to do what you need to do – you practise the skill of adjusting the shift between high and low states by verbalising them in real time, as it's happening: *I am going too fast here, my thoughts are too fast, I am trying to do too much, the back-to-back meetings, switches from work to home to work again.* Then you can use whatever you find works for you to pause, slow down and recentre, to put you back in control of the speed. You can do this through a simple visualisation technique.

Put a number on how you feel in the moment, then brake back to the speed you need:

Relaxed				Neutral			Out of control		
1	2	3	4	5	6	7	8	9	10

PUTTING THE BRAKES ON

I used this technique with a client, Sam, who was experiencing anxiety and panic attacks, and he was surprised by how well such a simple tool worked for him:

'I realised I was at 9 heading fast towards a 10. I imagined my foot on the vagal brake and saw the numbers on the dashboard going at a speed that felt out of control. I imagined my foot pressing the brake gently down and "saw" the numbers come down one by one, from 10 to 9 to 8 and so on. I breathed through each number, knowing the breath was sending a signal to my brain that I was safe, and the breath relayed this message to my body like we talked about. I sat with the uncomfortable sensations and reminded myself that I had experienced sensations like this before and even though it felt scary, that I had gotten through it before, that I had survived, and that it would pass.

'I felt upset and frustrated at myself for having another panic attack and it also felt it like a small win that I did feel more in control while feeling out of control. Imagining and practising using the vagal brake is helping not just with my day-to-day anxiety and panic attacks, but I am finding more space to respond in a different way when triggered in my relationships. It feels different, the panic is still there but I know I am driving it more in the right direction.'

(We'll look at panic attacks in detail in Chapter 5.)

'It's weird I had this idea and you know my primary goal in therapy was to never have a panic attack again and to get rid of my anxiety. I wanted to feel peace when what I needed was to uncover the roots of when I felt unsafe – a completely different experience. Even though it is hard, I do feel I have that inner GPS system as I understand that my anxiety is from the inside and out. You know, I wished just to go back to being myself, but I now see that wouldn't even be a good idea. I was running myself into the ground and so much came from this identity I had about myself being helpful, and assuming others' responsibilities even for how they felt. I was terrified to be in my own body and with my thoughts, it was a horrible place to be.'

The vagal brake isn't just there to slow things down when your emotions and physical sensations escalate. If it's more control that you want, purposely developing skills with the vagal brake and learning how you can drive it gives you an important sense of self-autonomy and builds confidence that you have the tools to manage your anxiety and emotions whenever and wherever you are.

Learning to self-regulate

Learning to self-regulate is the most important life skill you need to know and practise. People recover from anxiety and panic attacks and they learn how to regulate their nervous systems so they can manage those dysregulated states whenever they occur. That is very important to know.

While it is certainly challenging work, addressing the root causes of your anxiety, and processing grief, trauma and difficult experiences is profoundly cathartic. It is the means by which you can learn to regulate your nervous system. What I love about it is that not only do you heal yourself, but regulating your nervous system positively impacts everyone around you. The healing ripple effect spans across past, present and the future. This is another reason to learn how to regulate your nervous system. It has a positive impact right across your life.

When we speak of regulation, we are talking about developing the breadth of our emotional maturity. What does that mean? It is about cultivating our ability to tolerate the discomforts life throws at us and repurposing it in a way that stretches us, adding room for our nervous system to flex, move, adapt and grow. This is very much an ongoing process and I want you to be very aware that if you aren't making mistakes, it will be hard to learn. Taking risks, stepping outside your comfort zone, especially familiar emotional states, is deeply courageous, hard, and transformative. You will not get it right every time, so ditch the perfectionism and give yourself a break when you drop back into old habits. They are hard to break, but you are aware of them, and you are trying. That's good enough. When you feel dangerously in the red and the anger and frustration are about to tumble out of your mouth, you need something clear with immediate feedback to dial down those emotions. There is another simple visualisation trick that you can use to do this.

In Chapter 2 we talked about using our 'remote control buttons' as needed to Pause, Stop or Play and we're building on that now to talk about your traffic light system for self-regulation. If you pay attention to what you are feeling, you can notice when you are moving from green to amber to red – and you can take action to get back to green as quickly as possible. Personally, I like easily identifiable visuals that will work in the moment. I often say to my kids, 'I'm getting to red', as a warning that we need to bring it back to amber to deal with the situation at hand.

	How will it feel in my body?	How will it feel in my mind?
Green light (ventral state)	It will feel right, it will feel comfortable. You'll feel able to cope calmly with situations that arise.	It will feel authentic to your true self, a sense of ease.
Amber light	It will feel like you are not sure what to do: you may feel stuck or numb.	You may feel it doesn't matter what you think, you don't feel like you can affect change.
Red light	It will feel agitated, tense and like you need to do something quickly, like run away or fight back or be defensive.	That sense of urgency and needing to react fast is overriding other thoughts.

I think the traffic lights are clear indicators of how you can make progress with self-regulation. When you are in the full fury of the 4 Fs, this is the time to cool down your nervous system – and I mean that both literally and emotionally. If you are at home or in the office, go and run cold water on your hands and wrists. Take a few physiological sighs

– this is two short inhales and one long exhale (see Toolbox, page 329). Physically connect with how you are feeling by placing your hand on your body where it feels reactive, hurt, sad, frustrated or angry.

When you are at the red light, that is not the time for talking. Your brain has been hijacked by a cocktail of neurochemicals and powerful emotions and you are champing at the bit to say what you don't want to come out. The best thing to do when you realise the red light is lit up is to walk away. You can verbalise it as well: 'I am walking away as I am at red/angry and I need to cool down and then I'll be back.' You're pressing the Stop button for your own sake and everyone else's. That is a good way to deal with those engulfing emotions.

The 'I'll be back' isn't a Terminator slick thing to say; it will be helpful for the person you are arguing with if they have abandonment fears or worries. If you walk away with no explanation, it will be triggering for them and will probably escalate and add fuel to the fire. But that process of naming how you feel will help you feel more in control.

After you have soothed yourself using one of the techniques above, ask yourself: What is below the top emotion? Do you feel invisible, undervalued or taken for granted? Do you feel angry that you are allowing others to cross your boundaries and that you are stuck in this reactive cycle and when it is all finished all you are left with is guilt and a sense of failure?

Getting past that top emotion requires you to get to know yourself better, more authentically, to ditch avoidance and distractions and process what's actually going on for you. To be healthier in our mind and body, we need to be messier, to mess up, to make amends, to fumble and grumble and start again. Growth isn't beautiful, it's heavy, painful, isolating and vulnerable. Dare to be yourself. Show up in the mood you left the house in, tell your friend you are having a tough day, say with honesty 'It's just too much.' Listen to the signals and information cues coming from your body. If it is saying, *I am exhausted and have had enough and everyone is annoying* – that's red – take a genuinely productive day off, or the morning, or an hour, to rest. Start where you can.

Tune in to your whole self when your authentic self feels off. Listen. Spend time with yourself; even the smallest check-in with your heart as you awaken each day and at night as you close your eyes. Thank yourself for all you did, even if the day was hard, in fact especially if the day was hard. See the top note of your emotion as an invitation to explore the essence of what it is conveying to you and then ask, *Okay, that's it, I feel utterly spent, now what?* Now you can look at what you can or can't do about it and it opens the door to your own needs.

THE TOUGH CHOICE OF SELF-COMPASSION

Once you do notice and become aware and work on regulating yourself, the way to maintain this and make it work for you is to practise self-compassion. I know it may sound a bit uncomfortable, but then so is being in a constant state of dysregulation. The next step is to engage in a new and better relationship with your nervous system.

Can I ask you a question? Were you nice to yourself today?

I wasn't. I did something stupid, a silly mistake, probably out of pure tiredness, and I did not come back to myself with kindness. I quickly gave out to myself and said, 'You ... blinking eejit!' There were some Fs in there, but you get the picture. I came back with compassion a few minutes later, and that's okay, I needed to feel what I felt first. But I let it go quicker than I would have before, which I'm taking as progress.

Do you find when you make normal mistakes that you are super hard on yourself, but if a friend, colleague or loved one told you they had done the same thing you would be supportive, understanding and kind? Why is that?

In my experience with clients, what I see again and again is that we find it very difficult to practise self-compassion. We are hard on ourselves. It's a way of thinking that becomes very embedded. To practise self-compassion, you need to see and accept and be willing to act on the idea that *you are as important as everyone else*. The 'as' is the hard part, especially if you have been told otherwise: 'Don't be so selfish'; 'Stop always thinking of yourself first'; 'How could you say that to your mother/father, and all they do for you?'

Familiar? Then you'll have to work on that 'as' – you are *as* important *as* everyone else, so treat yourself that way. Start small but keep bringing self-compassion into everything that you do.

I find that clients' noses scrunch up when I 'introduce' compassion to them, they try so hard to hide the mini eyeroll. That tells a big story, the nose 'tell' shows me they have been admonished for being 'too sensitive, dramatic, soft', take your pick; or worse – someone saying, 'She really loves herself' is the ultimate Irish put-down. No wonder you run a mental mile when you hear the words, 'Now this week I'd like you to practise self-compassion.'

There are many reasons why self-compassion is tough. Often, rather than seeing it healthily modelled in your childhood, you were taught to admire being the martyr, that love was about giving every bit of yourself to everyone else. Do you see how it would be hard to then take consistent mini-breaks just for you, even a cup of tea in peace? *I never saw my mother sit down* and *My parents never fought* are two things I hear a lot. The problem is, if you never saw your mother relaxing and never saw your parents have healthy arguments to resolve issues, how do you know how to do it yourself? Introducing compassion offers you a distanced perspective, like a kind observer who would be kinder to you than perhaps you are to yourself. Notice where compassion is lacking in your life and see where you can add it in, bit by bit.

HOMECOMING

We noted above how emotional dysregulation and the sensation of being flooded with emotions can separate us from ourselves, make us feel disconnected, unsure of who we are and what we want. When you tackle the true underlying causes of your feelings and start to centre your own experience, it can be very powerful. The ability to self-regulate, which you can practise and make your own, delivers you back to yourself. It gives you a sense of autonomy and control that you may feel you have lost.

This is the positive aspect of emotional anxiety and its physical manifestations, like panic attacks. While they are horrible experiences, they do serve a purpose – those red flags signal your chance to stop, review and reset. They are giving you the direct message that you need to make changes, and they are giving you the opportunity to focus on making those changes.

I think it can be quite poignant to realise that this homecoming, this coming back to your authentic self, is often a return to the child you once were. I love children's honesty, whereas as adults we often strive to socially fit in and 'belong', and in doing so we lie and betray our inner selves. Seen this way, anxiety is a beacon, guiding you back to yourself, illuminating in the clearest way that you can't keep betraying and sacrificing yourself for others.

The Practical Psychology

Our body is full of lies that we believe about ourselves. Self-limiting narratives, endless criticism, and negativity, in an echo chamber of *You should have done this, said that.* Part of your belief system is often inherited; therefore, it is wise to question why you believe what you do and to ask, Do I really think that?

What beliefs do you hold that may not be aligned with your true self?

_____

This isn't about unravelling your sense of self; it's about questioning the beliefs that you hold about yourself and the world you live in. Our questions are always conducted by using the 3 Cs: Challenge with Curiosity and Compassion.

What inherited beliefs do you have that may not feel like 'you' anymore?

_____

What consequences have occurred when you voiced a difference from the accepted opinion?

_____

Did that silence you?

_____

What are some new beliefs that you now feel represent you more authentically?

_____

Anxiety is deeply integrated with your sense of self. Let these questions help you find yourself and come back to the person that you feel is the real you.

CHAPTER 4

How does psychological anxiety feel from the inside?

What is packaged as the ultimate indicator of success? It is happiness, or at least the continual pursuit of happiness. But guess what? It is the ultimate unattainable lie. Why? Because happiness isn't a constant or something that runs on a continuum. Not only is this not possible, but it also wouldn't even be good. If I switched you to a diet of your favourite treat for the rest of your life, what was once your most desired flavour would quickly turn to sickly sweet.

The notion of a constant straight line of happiness is the fallacy we are tripping over. It has created a generation of dopamine-seekers who can forget the nuance of difference, the reality of life, which is that … you are not in control. You have never been in control. Surrendering to this may be one of the most liberating things you can do in your life.

What has this got to do with psychological anxiety? Everything. I'm tired of the fairytale, the coy narrative of happily-ever-after. You and your life are complex and nuanced and constantly evolving. You may have got married and divorced. You may have wanted a family but for a host of reasons this didn't happen. You may have lost those who were your world. Moments in life can come in like tsunamis and crash down on your world and obliterate everything you thought you knew. Do you know what I see in the therapy room? Hearts that have been broken. Minds tormented by *What if?* and *How could that happen?* and *Why did this happen to me?* And bodies filled to the brim with aching pain that hasn't been processed. This is where anxiety grows and thrives.

There is another, connected problem as well. I think society is failing people by telling them what trauma is and what it isn't. Even now, you might be tempted to skip past this chapter because you feel what you have experienced, what you feel, doesn't qualify as 'trauma' or 'burnout' or 'psychological anxiety'. You might feel you've no right to think it might apply to you. And why is this? Because you might not know the definition of trauma or anxiety. Because you may have been misinformed when seeking out a definition. For any of these reasons you can end up thinking, *That doesn't relate to me, I'm not that bad*, and then you don't identify it in your life.

Anxiety may be a fear of the future, but it was often created in the past. You need to learn how to integrate what happened and what that meant to you. Through this, you forge a better and more authentic relationship with yourself. At the heart of anxiety, you will find an identity crisis – and the only way to end that crisis is to embrace your identity as you are, and not as how you think you 'should' be, which allows you to then make the changes you want. Acceptance of yourself must happen first before change can come in, and that is tricky. If you want to have a different relationship with anxiety, acknowledging and accepting what happened to you is the key.

How it feels: Trauma

Here is something that someone who hasn't experienced trauma won't recognise. Feeling safe and connected is part of the goal, but for someone who has never experienced that state of safety, it will not only feel alien, but it can also feel unsafe.

BIG T, SMALL T

Everyone experiences trauma. You may or may not have experienced the things that first come to mind when you think of the word trauma, but that doesn't mean you haven't experienced trauma in your life.

- **Big Trauma** or **Big T** is acute and chronic psychological trauma, such as the threat of or witnessing of violence, conflict, war, death, violence, abuse, major accidents.
- **Small trauma** or **small t** occurs from less identifiable psychological wounds that nonetheless can produce significant distress and have often been accumulating over years, which can make them harder to recognise.

Both types of trauma have an impact. This is crucial to say and to hear: what is traumatic for you does not have to conform to someone else's definition of trauma. An event that produces a stressful psychological impact on you is a trauma and can lead to anxiety. You don't need to compare yourself to others to find out if you are allowed to feel that way and to express it that way.

The two key takeaways regarding trauma are:

1. The comparison between what constitutes trauma in the way most understand it (war, abuse, PTSD, violence) breaks the connection with yourself and others in identifying what was traumatic for you.
2. This is a major inhibitory factor to living a healthy life, as people aren't seeking or getting the help they need. The health statistics

for the First World reflect this in our physical and mental health. Dismissing your internal cues, telling yourself it's not trauma, or listening to someone else telling you that, is a major blockage to regulating your nervous system and living your life in an integrated way.

Among many other things, therapy can offer clarity along with much-needed compassion. Emotional wounds hurt and need so much more than the ineffective concept of time somehow magically making it all go away. But coming at anxiety from the body first is still radical in the westernised perspective. The wounds of trauma are invisible, and yet their presence is felt daily in so many ways, showing up in how you feel about yourself, whether you feel safe, if you feel you can relax, your place in the world, in your relationships, how you process shame, guilt, why you push beyond your physical and emotional limits. Can you see the impact of unresolved trauma in your relationships? It can rob you of your experiences, leaving only self-doubt and alienation from yourself. The approach to processing trauma needs to be practical and there needs to be insight into *why*. When you can see what wounded you and why, it has a deeply profound impact on your ability to choose what are the next best steps for you.

I regularly see people who cannot see the role Big T and/or small t has played in the development of their anxiety or panic attacks. What happens then is that they look only at the presenting issue, with no understanding of their past experiences feeding into it. That cuts off the most vital information about their anxiety and its source because they do not have access to their own experiences, and that is because they do not know how to process what happened and integrate it with who and how they are today. It is the fundamental key to what is happening with your anxiety, and it has been within you all the time, but hidden, covered in shame, ridiculed and diminished. What you need is a space where you feel safe enough to share your experiences. I have found over the years that it is not just the trauma that causes suffering, but the secondary deep pain of others' reaction to those experiences. That is what decimates your place within yourself, your family, community and society. Valuing people, every person, and acknowledging their experiences is something we all need to work on. We can and we must do better.

Titration, which we first encountered on page 80, is part of the somatic experience of becoming aware of how your trauma shows up in your body and slowly introducing interventions, whereby you get to meet the emotional pain as it is and where you are now. A key skill in trauma recovery is being able to regulate and move from survival to safety in your own body and being able to understand and work within a window that is tolerable for you. This will be an ongoing step-by-step experience. It might be a case of 'one step forward and two back', but it is likely more a case of moving forward, and sideways, and falling down, and getting back up, and moving ahead again. The process will be hard and rewarding and frustrating, but I promise you it will not be linear. When the pain is too much, that is not healing; feeling pain for the sake of pain isn't cathartic and can cause secondary trauma. In your therapeutic process the relationship between you and your therapist and everyone and everything that supports and facilitates your healing will challenge you. Remember the compassion.

PSYCHOLOGICAL ANXIETY MANIFESTING AS THE 3 PS: PERFECTING, PLEASING, PERFORMING

I woke up with a beautifully clear thought the other morning. One of those thoughts that got me out of bed because, even though it was early, I knew I had to write it down in case it flittered away like a butterfly. Those early morning clear thoughts have a nearly magical quality to them, possibly because they are free of the thinking mind, and we get a gorgeous glimpse into our subconscious. What I thought was this: So many people tell me that they crave peace and yet I know, and they know, that silence terrifies them. Do you crave peace and yet simultaneously fear silence? Pause and read that line again. Is time on your own the silent enemy in all this? In the therapy room I often hear the words, 'I hate being by myself with my own thoughts', usually followed by a physical shudder.

When talking about this, what often becomes apparent is that you have been distracting yourself by relentlessly perfecting, pursuing and performing. You are utterly caught up in pleasing as many people as you can – except yourself. These are known as the 3 Ps: the need to perfect, to please and to perform.[8] These impulses can take over your mind and end up causing psychological anxiety as you struggle to be all things to all people all at once.

I think there's a good chance you will relate to people-pleasing; it's so widespread. What if I told you that it is part of the Fawn response and is a trauma response? *To what?*, you may ask, *I had a lovely childhood* – as said every client ever. Women are societally and relationally conditioned to be compliant, polite, pleasing, and to do it all as if it is effortless. But you and I know that everything takes effort, and yet we have bought into this soul-sucking impossibility. Again, the 'perfect childhood' narrative is the stuff of fairytales – how can we ever learn or have compassion for our parents knowing they also were doing the best they could at the time? (Please note that this does not include any form of abuse.)

The small t I speak of will have touched everyone; no one gets out of life alive. A lot of wounds are invisible yet keenly felt and continuing to have an impact. My wish for you is to be able to notice and identify what comes up, and if that means knowing that you are lost, that is totally fine, because then you can work on your personal profile map and find your way home to the real you.

The first step, as always, is an honest assessment to find out if you are trapped in this cycle of behaviour. We will look at each of the 3 Ps in turn – and how each feels from the inside.

How it feels: Perfectionism

In our relentless pursuit of perfection, our nervous system can become entrenched in a 'fight or flight' mode, perpetuating a cycle of stress and anxiety. Perfectionism is action, driven by relentless thoughts and unattainable expectations. The most insidious part of perfectionism is its integration into your sense of who you think you are and then into what you think others expect of you. It's crucial to recognise that, as polyvagal theory has shown us, perfectionism isn't just a psychological construct, it also has physiological implications for the body.

When in the activated mode of hyperarousal (Fight or Flight), you may feel hypervigilant to any perceived threat, such as making mistakes or getting something wrong. This may show itself through a fear of criticism. The idea of failure will drive a perfectionist to ignore their physical needs, skip meals, work late, and get it over the line regardless of their own needs. When we break down what is driving perfectionistic behaviour, it may have become a coping mechanism to avoid perceived failure and anxiety. This is the key to disrupting this behaviour because if you can understand what purpose it thinks it's serving, that makes it easier to break free.

Perfectionism can also show up in people-pleasing (Fawn) and in procrastination (Freeze), where to start the task feels impossible unless it is perfect. So you can see-saw sharply between underactive (hypoarousal) and over-active (hyperarousal), but both cause you anxiety.

When I start writing about perfectionism, the song 'Never Enough' from *The Greatest Showman* inevitably begins to play in my mind: 'Never, never, never enough, never enough'. Recently, I've come to realise that we've been playing a losing game, one where the odds are stacked against us. Society, or 'the house', is set up to relentlessly push the pursuit of having more and being more.

I read and loved Florence Scovel Shinn's book *The Game of Life and How to Play It*,[9] in which she noted that 'most people consider life a battle, but it is not a battle, it is a game'. From my perspective the 'game' of life is unfairly driven by commercial juggernauts that are devouring its consumers. We both consume and are being consumed. For many, everyday life feels like a battle due to the ever-increasing cost of living – and I would see that in terms of financial cost as well as psychological cost. As with any game there must be a winner and a loser, and many tell me they feel like they are the loser. They feel they are losing themselves, losing control, losing energy, all while desperately trying to maintain the unattainable and yet, no matter what they do, they feel like they are never 'doing' enough. Perfectionism's internal and external factors are interconnected in the game of life. When you are playing among relentless and unsustainable societal expectations and the stakes and costs keep getting higher and higher, it is easy to see how you can become trapped in a perpetual state of being a perfectionist.

The clients I work with are smart, kind, conscientious and brave, but they are also overwhelmed and often perfectionists. The biggest issue with perfectionism is that the eternal striving imposes a hefty personal cost on yourself and your relationships. I'd almost swap the word 'perfectionism' with 'relentlessness'. Here's the first-hand story of the inner world of a perfectionist.

AK: Tell me how perfectionism shows up for you?
A: I know what I'm doing. I understand how it impacts me, my husband, my kids. Yet, every single time I have to do it 'my way', or 'the right way'. I annoy me.
AK: What would it be like for you if it wasn't perfect?
A: Not okay, I'd feel so bad about myself, and guilty, the pressure seems year-round – perfect Christmas, present pressure – each year mounting, in delivering a more 'special' experience. For it to be magical and memorable, when all that happens is I blow a

fuse if something or someone doesn't go along with my expectations of how everything should be, look or taste. It is exhausting and I am exhausting. The worst part is, me being like this is my identity, the idea of not doing it the way I think it needs to be done terrifies me, like, to the core.

It would feel like I've been lying to everyone; they think I'm organised and calm and perfect. When the truth is that the effort it takes is so destructive. People always comment on how well I do everything, I feel I can't let that mask down.

There's no ease in my life. I can't let anyone into my house unless it's perfect, I have to get up early to put on my face and plan what I'll wear, to look like I haven't tried, but I have really tried. Everything is planned. I'm never present, I am planning what needs to happen next.

AK: But what would happen if you did things well or to a level of 'good enough'?

A: [Disgusted face at the thought of this.]

Could this be true, that you felt you had to be perfect to be lovable or to survive? If you feel that could be true for you, ask this: *Why did you feel that way? What led you to believe that?*

I'm not blaming social media, but we are so visually influenced and naturally engage in upward and downward social comparison. If you, like me, open your Instagram and see others have been achieving wonderful and worthwhile goals, it is only natural that rather than being inspired you feel not good enough. I'm going to be straight with you: changing perfectionism is no easy feat, and the very act of changing how you've always done things is going to feel horrible at first. Perfectionism is a nasty taskmaster, though, and it spills into so many aspects of your life. Why perfectionism? Asking why we do anything is a valuable question. I might rename it 'the kind why'. Think of the last time someone asked you why you did something and there's a high chance it was said in a somewhat accusatory way. Now, imagine if I *kindly* asked you why you did something. Your physical demeanour will change, you may let out a sigh, as if the permission slip has just been handed out.

I watched a brilliant series about comedians and the history of comedy. I had often noted that comedians would publicly say they struggled with their mental health and to me the psychology of comedy is their keen ability to observe our humanness and know their own. That relatability and connection is something I use in the therapy room. One poignant theme that spanned across the series was learning they had a gift to make their mother or father laugh. You could see they were hooked from that point. If their parent was struggling but they could change their mood, even for a moment, that was an addictive feeling. How does this relate to perfectionism? If you find something that gets your parents' attention, making you feel securely attached, loved, that you belong, that you are worthy of love, that you have value, that is also hugely addictive. However, if the source of that something lies outside you, then you must strive relentlessly for it. If the source is being 'a good girl', a high achiever, a reliable doer, then you strive relentlessly for that perfectionism, to keep getting those hits of love you need to survive. Can you see how this perfectionism can quickly morph into a maladaptive coping mechanism? Inside you, it takes control: *I am not good enough; therefore I must do more, be more, achieve more.*

Perfectionism lies at the root of many serious disorders, such as OCD, eating disorders, depression, anxiety and PTSD. It is the idea of perfection that seems so tantalising and yet it traps us in this pattern of exhausting behaviour. We have to crush the idea of perfection in every aspect of life – and especially within the growth narrative. We need to make room to be allowed to not get it right and to definitely get it wrong. We need to make room to learn, to grow, start again, to be allowed to be fed up. Look at it another way – see it as progress over perfection. This is the idea that you try, give up, try again and it is in that process that you learn the most; this is what allows you to make progress. Growing pains are painful, and this is a difficult thing to do. Can you have compassion for the reasons why you haven't made the changes you know you want to make? Can you see how you've been stuck because you were frozen with fear? Can you sit with the idea that if the whole or a large part of your identity was centred on being perfect, that it is so far from perfect that you are exhausted and burned out? (We'll talk about burnout on page 132.) Can we advocate for the reality of growth and keep reminding ourselves that change and growth are not located on a straight, continuous line?

This also links to the need to continuously assess and review yourself, to find out what you are feeling and what might need to change. I often see the idea of perfection seeping into therapy, whereby the client feels they ought to see me X times and then be 'fixed'. They should tackle the problem and solve it. All done and dusted! That's when I see the vulnerable look in their eyes when they have had to 'come back' to therapy. It puzzles me, and I explicitly say to them that they don't feel this way about their physical health – have you ever apologised to the doctor when you go back to the GP's surgery? Of course not. And yet the truth is that your mental health is much more vulnerable than your physical health when you consider the constant challenges that present themselves in your daily life. But somehow this perplexing stigma prevails that somehow you should 'just know' how to manage this present issue. You should face it and sort it quickly and move on. That's perfectionism at work right there. It happens whenever you don't give yourself the time and space to do whatever needs to be done when you rush yourself and demand too much of yourself. It's the idea of a 'perfect response' that underpins the impatience – and the embarrassment.

When you catch yourself doing this, remind yourself that you never received any guidance or instruction on how to operate adult life. You're learning on the job. It takes time. It takes learning from mistakes. It is anything but perfect. But at the same time, that's where the joy comes from. Remind yourself: chronological age does not equate to maturity. You do not magically become possessed of great wisdom at any age. It's work, and work in progress.

HOW DO YOU CHALLENGE PERFECTIONISM?

The first step is to acknowledge that this is an unhelpful coping behaviour. Then you need to work on building your inner acceptance, self-esteem, body image, self-worth and confidence.

1. Interrupt the thoughts.
2. Disrupt the behaviours.
3. Notice.
4. Then name it.
5. When you slip up, try again.
6. Soothe your nervous system, as it will kick up about this.
7. Be aware of and be prepared for the need to tolerate the disapproval and disappointment of some people.
8. Get support professionally, from your inner circle (family and friends), and at work.
9. Treat yourself with compassion and see this as part of your work in progress that will always require psychological flexibility.
10. You could own it by saying, 'I am a reformed perfectionist', to help you manage when things aren't exactly as you want them to be.

Following on from number 7 above, just a note on how others may receive you as a reformed perfectionist. Bringing a reality check in here; a lot of people won't like it. This will be challenging and may send you running back to your performing, people-pleasing and perfectionist traits. Please remember your Pause button, use it freely, along with the Stop button, to end conversations that aren't going anywhere. If you have been the organiser, planner and all-round perfect 'doer', you doing less means others will have to do more, or at least their fair share. You might encounter different reactions: some might applaud you and others might be appalled. But I am going to encourage you loudly to please keep going, tolerate the momentary discomfort of their annoyance or disappointment, and take note of the good guys who support your transition. (We'll talk more about boundaries on page 239.)

The Practical Psychology

Becoming a reformed perfectionist requires a lot of self-awareness and work. It asks you to notice each time you use the *I just have to do it this way* narrative and gently asks: *Why?*

In my work, I seldom see anxiety without an accompanying idea of perfection, of 'how I *ought* to be'. And I seldom see any self-compassion with regard to the origins of when and how you learned to become a perfectionist. This is where you need to start tackling your inner perfectionism – by finding out how and why it affects you in this way.

When did you learn or see that you had to be perfect?

_____

How has that impacted you?

_____

What holds you back from doing things differently?

_____

What are your perfectionist strengths?

_____

What parts of perfectionism cause you pain?

_____

What one small change could you make that would be helpful?

_____

If you stacked* another change on top, what would it look like?

_____

*Stacking is placing one thing, such as a habit, on top of another in a cohesive way. For example, if you have 'always' oversubscribed yourself and now you've taken yourself off one committee, then you could 'stack' the time you would have been there to do something for you, where you continue to give, but this time to yourself.

Imagine how that would feel if you made those two changes. What excites and freezes you as you think about this?

_____

Then hit the **Pause** button.

Pause and reflect for a moment, then ask yourself:

What are the consequences if I stay the same? Please put your answer in writing.

_____

Some examples of possible answers:
- Exhaustion – physical, mental and emotional
- Irritability, frustration, resentment, anger
- Anxiety, overwhelm, feeling lost
- Anger at yourself for repeating the same behaviours.

A final word: there will never be a right time for starting to change, so it's best to simply start now.

How it feels: Performing

Performing is directly linked to perfectionism: the desire for perfection drives the performance. We value perfection in the home, in our relationships and at work. We value being 'productive' and often invest in a misguided concept of 'success', seeing it as an external status and commodity-driven concept. When we value these things, we try to present them to the world as our traits, our values, our 'success'. In other words, we strive to seem perfect and perfectly together. When that isn't true – and the fact is it's never true because we're all just humans living unpredictable lives – we act the part, put on a performance to convince everyone else, and ourselves, that this is who we are. Just as we've seen with perfectionism, the base of this performative behaviour is fear – you are afraid that you are not good enough, that you are not worthy of other people's respect or love, and therefore you cover over your real self with this shiny, 'acceptable' self that you believe people will like and admire and want to be around. You are pulling on a mask that you think will protect you from being criticised or disliked. It's still about fear and self-protection and is often rooted in attachment needs that may have not been met. For more on this, see my book *The Secret Lives of Adults*.

But again, as we've seen with perfectionism, it leads to you feeling outside yourself, needing others' external approval for your acceptance, leaving you disconnected, resentful and hurt. You come to rely on the act, even unconsciously believing this is who you are, but you resent the actor – and if others think this is the real you, there is a real terror that if you don't continue this dizzying level of performance you will be caught out, so you relentlessly push past all your limits. It's a bag of very mixed painful emotions and reactions and it's easy to see why and how it would lead to a deep sense of anxiety.

How it feels: Pleasing

When we pare back what drives us as humans, the ultimate desire to be loved and to belong is at our core. We learn what is acceptable and unacceptable from an early age. You don't need to be an expert in body language to know if someone is happy or disapproving of what you have or haven't done. People's facial responses and our interpretation of those cues lead us to act in ways to try to secure more love and acceptance. Even if that means betraying our own needs.

Sit with that for a moment.

Do you override your physical and emotional needs in a perpetual 'others first' mode? This is called people-pleasing. It is a pattern of behaviour whereby you do things to gain approval, seek validation and avoid conflict by meeting what you think are their needs, often at the expense of your own. Do you say yes when you want to say no, over-commit and over-extend and do anything to avoid conflict, never want to 'let anyone down' so you sacrifice and betray your own needs? If you do, then people-pleasing is your coping mechanism. The fear underlying it can stem from a lack of self-belief and feelings of inferiority and not being good enough.

The way out of pleasing is to notice and change behaviours to move from the automatic *others first* mentality to *I am as important as* ... I'm not asking you to see yourself as more important or less important – I'm asking you to move to a position where you are *as* important as everyone in your life.

Why have you been unable to do this? If you voiced how you felt, said no (without the over-explanation), put boundaries on your time and energy, did you receive a cold response? If that was your experience, you may have internalised huge anxiety around the danger of that cold response becoming an accusation that you are 'selfish'.

Ask yourself why you wear yourself out and do things you don't want to do or don't have time to do. In that behaviour, can you see the fundamentals of how you have been coached, conditioned, cultured and corrected into being 'pleasing'? It has been inscribed like a tattoo on your brain and it's not easy to erase. Did anyone teach you that it was okay to say no? Or were you taught that 'no' is a dirty word? Has that become part of your belief system? If so, are you afraid that if you try to change it, the world as you know it and as you occupy it will fall apart? For the pleaser, that is a terrifying thought. You are panic-stricken, thinking: *Who will I be if I am not this person that everyone knows and has come to rely on?*

So the reason you have kept a pattern of behaviour that depletes you is because you are afraid. You are afraid of who you might become, and of how others will see you – and judge you. The idea of disapproval and disagreement paralyses you. That's why you maintain this 'lovely' person who is easy to like, non-confrontational, available – because the opposite of pleasing often involves the notion of someone being 'difficult'.

If you want to change your relationship with anxiety and how you live your everyday life, a big part of that is tolerating other people's disappointment with you. For the pleaser, this is very frightening. The words that might be directed at you are the stuff of nightmares: *You've changed*; *That is quite selfish of you*; *What about me?*; *Why are you saying/doing this?* When you boil it right down, this means shame has been one of the biggest blockers to your wellbeing and health.

The pleaser is threatened with an identity crisis if they change how they deal with others, and that threat creates huge anxiety and a physiological response in the body as one or more of the 4 Fs are kicked into action. The identity crisis looms:

- 'If I'm not doing everything seamlessly, then who am I?'
- 'I didn't expect to feel like this after becoming a mum. Who am I?'
- 'I don't recognise myself or feel like myself anymore. Who am I?'
- 'I never felt anxious or overwhelmed before. Who is this person looking back at me in the mirror?'
- 'If I don't do my job, who am I?'

- 'If I am "just" a mother, where are the other parts of me?'
- 'I can't do everything, but what option do I have?'

Think about this scenario and how you respond to it:

Boss: Hey Louise, can you get that report to me by 5.30 this evening at the latest?

Louise's boss knows (because it was agreed) that her workday ends at 4.30 p.m. and starts at 8.30 a.m. to facilitate a crèche pick-up at 5.30 p.m.

In that moment, Louise feels her heart beating a bit faster, her mind starts racing. *Bloody hell, he knows I leave at 4.30 and it drives him around the twist. He also knows I am going for the internal promotion that is really the job I'm doing right now. I know I could go to HR about this, but then they will look at my potential for the job that I am already doing in a negative way.*

Louise: I really wish I could, but I have to pick up Milo and Jill, and I'm already still on the other project you asked me to finish today. The crèche closes at 5.30 so I can't today. Sorry.'

Does the idea of speaking up like that make you feel sick with nerves? Do you admire Louise but feel you could never say that? How often do you speak your mind? People-pleasers are accommodating, but not with themselves. This will need to change. We are caught within the external, societal expectations placed upon us and also, if you are prone to pleasing, within the internal constant conflict between 'what I actually think' and 'what I actually do'. If you are continually damping down your true thoughts and desires and needs, you are living inside an anxiety that is affecting every part of your life.

How about this question: Would you consider yourself a 'good girl'? If you quickly answered no, go back to the question for a moment. The feminist in you may be screaming *Hell, no,* but how often do you effectively say no? And I also have terms and conditions with the 'no':

- Do you say no without over-explaining yourself?
- If you over-explain, what happens for you?

Why am I addressing women here? Because women are enculturated into a fixed idea of what it means to be female, including how to act, what is acceptable and unacceptable, what is rewarded and what is punished. I hear you thinking, *But that has changed, we have evolved.* Yet each International Women's Day I hear lots of talk of being a superwoman, doing it all gracefully. It seems difficulties are often shrouded in the cape of magical powers, without much interest in what goes on beneath it. Being a 'good girl' lines you up for people-pleasing, over-extending yourself, losing your identity and mirroring what you think others want. It breaks authentic self-connection and by avoiding conflict, you will have conflict. Boys and men have, in general, been socialised differently. I often tell women to admire how some men tend to their needs, be it exercise or resting when tired. The women need to take off the capes and also sit down.

FAWN RESPONSE

Chronic people-pleasing is part of the Fawn response and it is a trauma response. This means you learned to behave in a specific way in response to experiences that felt threatening when you were growing up. It is a survival strategy. If we take one of the core topics of my first book,[10] which centred on attachment, there is a similar working goal in polyvagal theory, which is to form early attachments that feel safe and secure. A number of factors can contribute to developing this Fawn response, such as a chaotic, abusive home life where you may have been parentified, meaning you, the child, had to mind the parent or put their needs before yours. You might have been pleasing to avoid any physical, mental or emotional repercussions. You were likely hypervigilant, knowing from how the key went in the door what the mood would be. You may have learned how to be the compliant, obedient, 'good' child to avoid conflict and protect yourself. You learned to play along. This came from major fears of being rejected or abandoned by a parent. You may have had the threat of a parent saying they would leave. That threat was internalised and brought into your future relationships.

This pattern of behaviour may show up as anxiety (often high-functioning anxiety), but when gently explored it reveals itself as a trauma response and may go back to a fear that being loved, lovable and accepted depended wholly on pleasing others, often within a fragmented childhood. This trauma response becomes an overwhelming urge to please and appease others, which can lead you to disconnect from your own needs and desires.

You might feel you cannot identify any trauma in your life that corresponds to this, but did any of the above sound familiar to you? Were you considered the 'easy' child? Did others comment upon how mature you were for your age, or was it trauma and that you had to grow up too soon? Do you find yourself saying 'yes' because you fear the anger or disappointment that might come back at you if you say no?

Chronic people-pleasers are most often women. From girlhood, women are taught not to display anger. We are praised for being nice and compliant and docile. You can probably remember some of the phrases shot at you: *Stop being so difficult*; *Stop overreacting*; *Stop being so sensitive*; *What is wrong with you*; *They didn't mean that*; *Don't upset your mother*. It's often subtle enough, but it puts down strong roots in your psyche.

The cost of this is that you lose an essential part of your internal navigation system – you. Your own feelings and thoughts are suppressed and/or repressed, leaving you voiceless. Who did you do that for? You did it for them because you thought that you had to be this affable, agreeable person to be loved and accepted, as opposed to feeling guilty, anxious having been told that you are selfish to not put others first.

- **Suppression** is when you intentionally try to push down unwanted thoughts and emotions from your conscious awareness.
- **Repression** is an unconscious act of pushing away unwanted thoughts or memories as a defence mechanism.

You quietened your voice and your needs and put others first. When you do this, repress or suppress yourself, it is painful. You are ignoring what is and is not okay, what will or will not work for you. This hurts you mentally, physically, and emotionally. It impacts you to the core of who you are because you actively betray and detach from your true self. I see the painful results of this in my work every day. One of the common traits of it is over-explaining.

Over-explaining

People-pleasers over-explain because they are at pains not to be misunderstood. This may have come from not being heard, or understood, or getting into trouble if you got it wrong.

As we know from polyvagal theory, the autonomic nervous system (ANS) plays a role in regulating how we respond, connect and behave socially, and this helps us understand why we may find ourselves over-explaining. A history of feeling misunderstood will drive a strong need to be accepted, liked and to belong. Over-explaining can be a coping mechanism to manage anxiety and the complicated dynamics of socialising. It can work against you, though, as you seek excessive reassurance, which can impact your relationships as you repeatedly check *Are you sure you aren't cross with me?* or take other people's moods personally. You can work on regulating your nervous system back to safety by repeating these words, *I am safe, even though I feel uncomfortable, I am safe, I am safe,* while doing box breathing: in for four seconds, hold for four, out for four, hold for four.

People-pleasing, over-sharing, and over-explaining are toxic friends. Here is a good example from the therapy room:

Susan: I did it again.

AK: What did you do?

(Note that the over-explainer always feels they are in the wrong, even when they aren't, and feel judged and unheard, ergo the need to over-explain.)

Susan: I had the conversation with Martha, and it didn't go as planned. I told her how I felt hurt when she dismissed my nervousness about going to the big dinner, and once I started, it was verbal diarrhoea. I went into how my anxiety has made me pull back from social situations, even with friends. I explained that not only did I feel exhausted by the constant dread and anxiety of what others will think of me and how I couldn't go anyway as I had nothing to wear and felt bad about how I look, but that even if I drove and didn't drink, I was now afraid of driving. She didn't get it.

AK: What was that like for you?

Susan: It was crap, she kept just saying, 'Come on, it will be fine, you know these girls your whole life, you can't let a bit of anxiety hold you back, we all feel anxious at times.'

AK: What was it like to hear that?

Susan: It was like what we talked about, I felt like I was being dramatic and to get over it and why couldn't I, as everyone else was able to?

AK: Can you see how she invalidated your experience, and even if some parts were true in terms of the need to slowly take steps to do things socially that will be uncomfortable, it seems like she didn't understand how hard you have been having it for a while? I'm sorry that happened. And can you see that it isn't up to you to convince Martha about your anxiety? I would like you to acknowledge how it is for you and to keep supporting yourself by doing what you are doing to

> take the necessary steps. How do you feel in this group of friends? Sometimes female friendships may only have length of time in common.
>
> **Susan:** Yeah, I was starting to think that myself. I mean, I'm not getting any support anymore, and when I do share tough things, I feel shot down.

Practical phrases to repeat to enable you to make yourself as important as everyone else:

- I am allowed to say no.
- I am not responsible for others' reactions to me.
- I can tolerate their disappointment.
- I do not have to over-explain myself.
- I can pause before I answer.

From now on, remember and remind yourself of that key piece of information: You are as important as they are.

Distress tolerance

As we noted with regard to perfectionism, when you start saying no and treating yourself and your time as being as important as everyone else's, you might experience some kickback from certain people. It's good to know that so you can be prepared for it. You will have to get comfortable with tolerating the discomfort of other people's disappointment when you don't fall in line. This is called distress tolerance, and it won't come easy to a people-pleaser.

But do you know what is even harder than practising distress tolerance? It is continuing the path you've been on and ending up in burnout, resentful, irritable and constantly feeling that you are not living the way you want to live.

The bit people forget is that pleasing ultimately damages relationships. There is only so much anxiety your body can put up with. And maybe the anxiety has come from the accumulation of ignoring your body's calls of distress.

Instead of pushing through, rest.

Instead of saying yes, try no.

Own your NO with the same joy and tenacity as a two-year-old. I don't know where my children heard this but when I ask them to, say, bring their plate over, they smile and cheerily say, 'No thank you'; even though it doesn't work in my favour, it is somewhat genius.

The Practical Psychology

Identify what you do to please others in all areas of your life:

Ask gently: Why do you do this?

_____

Even more gently, ask: What would it be like to not do this?

_____

Can you now see what has stopped you or blocked you from saying no or making changes that you know you'd like to make?

_____

If you answered 'yes' to that last question, what now? How do you change a habitual pattern of behaviour?

Saying no

It's not easy, it takes determination and work and self-forgiveness when you fail, but it is possible to challenge that reaction and give yourself the opportunity to behave differently. Here are some simple ways of saying no.

A social no

When you have received an invitation to a social event and you don't want to go for any reason, send a short, polite reply to decline: 'Thanks for asking/thinking of me, Unfortunately I can't make it to the event. Hope you have a lovely time/night, Julie.'

You can see what is not in that 'no' – it is not:

- over-explaining
- apologising – you did nothing wrong
- surrendering your sorry, for those who over-apologise about everything
- appeasing others
- betraying your own needs.

A relationship/family no

'I can't come over for the whole day on Sunday. I could come from 11 a.m. to 1 p.m. if that worked for you?'

Note: this is creating a clear time boundary and managing expectations.

A work no

'Julie, can you change to this other project? We need to get this over the line by the end of the week and finish the task you are working on first.'

'I can change to the other project. Can you let me know which project to focus on first? I can't prioritise both to meet the new deadline by the end of the week.'

People-pleasing scenarios
Think about different people-pleasing scenarios in your life. Are you the social organiser? The planner, the financial collector, the baker, candlestick-maker …?

What people-pleasing roles have you over-functioned within?

_____

Write out which roles you want to work on.

_____

The soft revolution: Polyvagal theory for perfectionism, performing and pleasing

As noted above, I think it is useful to consider yourself in recovery as a perfectionist, performer and people-pleaser because you will be challenged daily to rewire your default settings towards those familiar and well-worn behaviours. Valuing yourself over societal badges of exhaustion, overwhelm and toxic productivity will be challenging in all aspects and roles of your life precisely because those are the norm.

Polyvagal theory provides clear insights into how you can learn to become aware of when you are moving into, or are already in: Fight, Flight, Freeze or Fawn. This enables you to know how to move to a more secure 'ventral vagal' response, which facilitates your ability to assert boundaries and take care of yourself.

Your nervous system is adaptable. This is very important to know. It means that when you make the change to practising self-compassion, you can avail of the restorative and secure aspects that the ventral vagal state brings. In other words, your nervous system will work with you and adapt to your new patterns of thinking and behaving. This can bring a profound clarity to your life situations, often showing that the 'control' you had been trying to hold on to was the very thing that had restricted you and stolen your freedom.

Think of a time or times when you felt compelled to override your own needs to please others. Where did you notice that in your body? Was it in your in your voice, did it go up a pitch (like Ross from *Friends*: 'I'm fine, I'm totally fine!')? Or did it physically feel like the words were actually stuck in your throat, in a hard knot (called the globus sensation). Was there an internal fight as your mind shouted 'Say no!' while you nodded and smiled?

This is what I want: I want you to notice why and where you were triggered, when those physical reactions in your body started. I want you to connect with your body and see what reactivated the wound that didn't magically disappear with time. I want you to revolt against the shame, stigma or minimising narrative of *I shouldn't feel like this* and to work towards a new psychological flexibility. This flexibility will allow you to stay present, open and honest and to know that you are courageous as you change the parts of your identity that are harming and hurting you.

It is interesting that when you have rigid thoughts, they find themselves in your body. When you kick into *This is the way I've always done it* mode, how do the rigid thoughts show up physically? Do you breathe faster or more shallowly, experience a tension headache, clenched jaw, tight hips, tight neck, tense shoulders or an upset stomach? I think rigid thoughts co-locate into a tense body. Even when you say the words *going with the flow*, it feels looser mentally and physically. Living in survival mode robs you of a true and free sense of self. The way back to you is through your body. Perfection and pain are an inevitable pair, and they also share the company of procrastination paralysis, which is a push–pull dynamic, making you work harder, as everything takes longer to start, and then unable to finish because you can't hand it in until it is 'perfect'. You make yourself promises, to goad yourself into action: *If I just push through this day, this week, this month, and if I just work harder and longer, then I will relax.*

If–then thinking may be the biggest modern lie we use to delude ourselves. We need to give up placing our happiness in the future or thinking that you can only have happiness with conditions attached: *If I lose three pounds, then I'll be happy*; *If the kids get through this hard stage, then everything will be back to normal.* I am going to just come out and say it: Stop wasting your life for some mythical nirvana that doesn't exist, where you will be calm, cool and collected all the time. There will always be a mixture of good and bad. The goal is not to have a stress-free life. The goal is to learn to live life, however it comes at us, and we do that by facing life with a strong sense of self that is rooted in a balanced nervous system. The goal is to learn how to move, how to use your map to get you out of the bad times, to know how to ride the waves when they are choppy and overwhelming by using the tools in this book to make your way back to safety.

Perfection is the ultimate in faulty cognition. It delights in right or wrong, black-and-white binary thinking. I need you to know that you have choices. Part of your healing will be to compassionately check in and ask yourself: *Is there another way to do this?* and *If this was my best friend or someone I care deeply about, what would I say to them?* Part of your healing as a recovering perfectionist will be to remind yourself that you have the choice and the autonomy to change and to try it another way.

My goal is to dispel the illusion that you can control what is outside your control and to show you that you can instead, with practice, have internal state control. This starts with the acknowledgement that we can't control our external environment or relationships. I have noticed that the last line of the 'Ask Allison' questions sent in for my weekly Q&A column frequently end with the words: *How can I convince …?* or *How can I make them see?* There is no such thing as perfect parents, or the perfect couple, or perfect kids, or the perfect man or woman. Life is messy. We do our best to calm the chaos, accepting the intricacies of ourselves and others. The best approach is to accept that you have a whole lot to learn and to be generous in your compassion with your mistakes and hungry to learn what you can do to live a life that feels good for you. Good enough, not perfect.

The benefits are huge if you can work with yourself to be your own self. Equally, the costs are huge if you continue to ignore yourself. Do you know what the profile for burnout is? If you are conscientious, hard-working and a perfectionist, you are at higher risk of burnout. The next chapter looks at burnout in detail and it certainly shows how high that cost is to yourself.

The Practical Psychology

Here are two very simple but effective breathing techniques to help you become aware when the pattern of behaviour is being activated, giving you time and space to assess your options and make the best choice for you.

HALTING THE IMPULSE TO PLEASE

Box breathing: Breathe in for four seconds – hold for four seconds – release for four seconds – hold for four seconds. Repeat as needed.

As you breathe in, imagine breathing in new space for you. As you breathe out, say 'I release my need to please.'

HALTING THE IMPULSE TO BE PERFECT OR TO PERFORM

Take a deep breath in, then breathe out and say to yourself or aloud: 'I release my need to be perfect. It is good enough for today. I am good enough. I release my need to be perfect.'

CHAPTER 5

How does physiological anxiety feel from the inside?

Anxiety is not divided into three separate entities; it doesn't just show up in your body (physical) or your mind (psychological) or your emotions (emotional). It is a complex, nuanced, personal experience on a busy interchanging motorway in your mind that has many external factors outside your control. Your thoughts influence your emotions, your emotions influence how your body responds. They are talking with each other all the time. Our goal is to get you to clearly see which parts are present – often all three are there – and to look down through the messages to decipher what they are telling you. It can feel like an endless WhatsApp thread, with messages that keep piling in one after the other. If you don't have the knowledge about how your nervous system works, which most people don't, then the resultant anxiety feels overwhelming, and it is very easy to feel stuck with the feeling, *It's all too much*. I want to change this.

You've heard the dismissive comment, 'It's all in your head'? Actually it's all in your body. Anxiety is physiological, it is somatic, of the body, therefore the answer cannot lie just in your mind or thoughts. That's why talk therapy is only part of the answer. The root of the answer is in your body. How you get there needs questions asked with compassion, acknowledgement, and a somatic release (bodywork).

If you want to change your experience and relationship with anxiety, I suggest we start there. The good news is that anxiety and panic attacks respond beautifully to an integrated top-down and bottom-up approach. When you can cognitively appraise your emotions and thoughts, you can connect with the heart and soul of your anxiety. You cannot intellectualise away the problem, you need to experience, feel and process it differently rather than just think about it differently.

How it feels: Panic attacks

Jackie: I thought I was dying. I have never experienced anything like it in my life. It started with what felt like a whoosh up my legs and arms, and I started breathing faster and faster, my heart was beating too fast, like, dangerously fast, my chest felt heavy, like someone with a size 14 Doc Marten standing on me. I wanted to cry but I couldn't catch my breath, I was absolutely terrified, my head started racing, 'Oh my God, I am dying and I have lost my mind. I am going to end up in a psychiatric hospital if I live through this. Jesus, I knew this would happen since my grandmother ended up in a psychiatric hospital.' I felt so many things at once, I thought I was going to get sick, but my throat felt like it had a huge stone ball in it, I felt like someone had their hands wrapped around my throat, my stomach dropped and I felt like I needed to go empty my bowels immediately and also felt dizzy, and like I could faint, and then I started to shake and feel tingles. I had the most awful sense that something awful was just about to happen.

Linda: I was driving on the M50 and I suddenly noticed my heart beating faster, I felt flushed, and a wave of sickness came over me. Do I need to get sick or to a bathroom fast? Either way, this car is not the place to be. Christ, the cars are so close, what is wrong with me? I'm trapped, what if I pass out? Oh my God, my eyesight feels blurry, the radio is too loud, the car is too hot, how can I get off this road safely?

Sylvia: I had been dreading giving my presentation, I couldn't sleep for weeks thinking about it, they were all going to see that I am utterly incompetent, this was it. I couldn't eat that morning, barely slept and my head was exploding, it was like a band had been tightened around my head three times too tight, it was hard to see straight. I was so frustrated with myself, I knew the stuff, but it was like my brain had shut down, I couldn't think straight. I made a run to the loo again and emptied my bowels. Oh my God, what if someone comes in here now and knows it was me? What if I just leave, say I feel sick, or my fish died, anything? I have to get out of here. The ground felt shaky under me, nearly like watching your body in the mirrors in a fun-house, except this was horrific. These thoughts weren't helping, suddenly the thoughts took over, 'What if, what if', and then I couldn't catch my breath. Oh my God, they are going to find me passed out in the bathroom stall.

Suzanne: I'm nearly embarrassed to say this but I had no idea that what I had been feeling for months was anxiety, and now after doing this work, realising that it has always been there in some form or other, but I would just block it out, I didn't have time to think about it, I'd tell myself, and it would go away and then it would come back three times as bad. It wasn't until that

> first panic attack, when I genuinely thought I was dying and had fully lost it, only to get a dismissive 'it's a panic attack' said back at me in A&E, that I finally realised the level of stress I had put myself under for years.

When it comes to a panic attack, especially a sudden onset like those described above, the fear is like nothing you have ever experienced. But I want to say this very clearly: You can recover from panic attacks, they respond so well to treatment. I know it is nearly impossible to believe this, and one of the biggest hurdles is helping you regain confidence in yourself and your body. When you learn how to get around your nervous system, along with getting to the source of the pain in your body, you will feel like you again and in control, because I know that is what you want. You can learn how to manage panic attacks, how to regulate your nervous system and ride those waves that are threatening to wash over you.

Panic attacks are often sudden and frightening because they are your body's way of saying, *You haven't listened to me, so I am now, in the most terrifying way, going to make you think you are dying and/or going crazy to get you to pay attention.* I see anxiety and panic attacks as a breaking point after enduring discomfort for years. It's like hitting rock bottom with substance abuse. Anxiety feels like having your hand near a hot cooker – uncomfortable and overwhelming with worry, fear and dread. After it passes, you forget how bad it was until it resurfaces during times of high stress. I see this all the time, it's like anxiety amnesia, but the pernicious damage is building all the time and eroding your self-confidence.

This may be hard to hear for those who have experienced a panic attack, but it can be a good thing. Panic attacks can be the driver of change. I say this with utter compassion and respect: I feel panic attacks administer the shock that is needed. They tell you that you must stop and you must listen and you must pay heed to yourself. And you do, because the experience is so harrowing. The silver lining is a panic attack can be the change point, leading you to seek help and make changes. Your anxiety has reached a critical point and there is no denying it.

Please note that I have worked with thousands of people with acute panic attacks and fainting is very uncommon because your system is in Fight or Flight; physiologically, the increase in heart rate and energy mobilisation makes fainting difficult, even though it may feel like you could. It can be helpful to remember this.

So what does a panic attack feel like? In health-related terms, there are only two things that have 'attack' after them. This is important to note straight off: there is a huge difference between a heart attack and a panic attack. It is a common reaction during a panic attack to think that it is a heart attack, which exacerbates everything. If you experience a heart attack, the pain won't decrease, and you must seek medical attention immediately. It's always a good idea to seek medical care with any rapid change in health, that's just good common sense. A key red flag word for me is 'weird'. If something feels weird – meaning anything unfamiliar to you – seek medical assistance.

If you experience a panic attack, it is temporary, the symptoms will peak in intensity, then begin to lessen, it will pass and you will recover. Most of my clients who have had panic attacks went to A&E genuinely thinking they were having a heart attack the first time they had a panic attack. That tells you how severe a panic attack feels. It is also good that they have been medically checked and have ruled out other concerns; it is useful for the person to be able to know what a panic attack is and isn't. The *Diagnostic and Statistical Manual of Mental Health Disorders: Fifth Edition* (DSM-5) describes a panic attack as 'an abrupt surge of intense fear or discomfort' that reaches a peak within minutes. A panic attack lasts on average 3–5 minutes, but can last up to 25–30 minutes. It is characterised by four or more of these physical symptoms:

- palpitations
- pounding heart
- accelerated heart rate
- sweating
- trembling or shaking
- sensations of shortness of breath or smothering
- feelings of choking
- chest pain or discomfort
- nausea or abdominal distress
- feeling dizzy, unsteady, light-headed or faint
- chills or heat sensations
- paraesthesia (numbness or tingling sensations)
- derealisation (feelings of unreality)
- depersonalisation (being detached from oneself)
- fear of losing control or 'going crazy'
- fear of dying.

As you can imagine, those symptoms are like a stacked-up line of dominos that are kicked off by the quickening of your heartbeat in what feels like an unstoppable chain of events. The peak of the symptoms happens first, this is the most intense part, and as these symptoms begin to subside the length of the panic attack will be influenced by what came before, in terms of stress, and if you have learned techniques that will help you bring your nervous system back to feeling safe again. The frequency of panic attacks varies, and it can be a once-off experience, but then the anticipatory fear can lead to further panic attacks, which can become panic disorder. Don't let this frighten you, as you can learn how to change it.

How it feels: Panic disorder

Anxiety disorders are the most common mental health disorder in the world, with 301 million people experiencing them in 2019 according to the World Health Organization – that's 4 per cent of the global population. Women experience these disorders more than men. Panic disorders are highly treatable, yet only one in four people seek treatment. It is thought that this may be due to lack of awareness about the fact that it can be treated and 'lack of investment in mental health services, lack of trained healthcare providers, and social stigma'.[11]

Use the figures above to give you a sense of grounded hope that even though anxiety disorders are so prevalent, they are highly treatable. Even if therapy is financially prohibitive, start by becoming informed – this is why I have written this book. I am not suggesting at all that you don't seek therapy, but I'm aware that cost and availability can be an issue for many people. However, reading and engaging with this book can be a starting point.

The DSM defines panic disorder as a mental health condition characterised by recurrent, unexpected panic attacks. These attacks are followed by persistent concerns about future attacks and changes in behaviour related to the attacks, such as anticipatory anxiety and safety behaviours, for example avoiding people, places or things associated with the panic attack. The symptoms are the same as those listed opposite, along with a sense of impending doom or terror impacting your thoughts, emotions and subsequent behaviours.

One of the unexpected things about panic attacks is that they often occur in quiet moments. My clients often speak of their worry of having a panic attack while driving, or of collapsing and 'losing it' on a train or aeroplane. The reality is usually not like this. What I have heard from thousands of people is that it happens on their couch, 'out of nowhere'. They are sitting, relaxed, with no triggers that they are aware of, and suddenly those sensations rush through them. I often wonder if panic attacks occurring at home is down to home feeling like a safe space to release years of unresolved issues, experiences, emotions and built-up physical frustrations.

When you have experienced a panic attack, it is common to feel betrayed by your body and to lose a lot of confidence from feeling out of control. Normal bodily sensations feel scary and threatening. This sort of physical anxiety is super nasty and there is nothing subtle about it. And yet the damage people endure is often hidden. It becomes an internal fear that nobody has any idea is there. But it's always there – as you wait in line at the supermarket and your heart starts to pound and you want to run, or when you jump almost out of your skin when someone startles you. Others can't see the invisible chaos under the calm public surface, but you are extremely aware of it.

How and when you realise that you don't feel like 'you' anymore is a unique and unpleasant discovery. For some it builds, like a scratchy niggle that feels uncomfortable, and you just feel 'off'. For others it is the shocking smack in the face of a panic attack that throws their entire sense of themselves and their world into complete question. As you stand there, trying to work out WTF just happened, not only do you feel lost, you also feel you don't know who you are anymore. Fear likes to jump in at this stage and start a fight, like an aggressive sibling, making you question if you will ever feel like yourself again. It is easy to see why despair sits with anxiety at this point.

The 'usual suspects' of anxiety

If I put anxiety in a line-up, I know the usual suspects that will skulk into the room.

First in line, we'd find 'overwhelm', with 'overstretched' close beside, giving them no space to breathe or think. Next is 'perfectionism', standing straight and looking completely together, masking that they are currently in a terrified cold sweat as their ultimate and deeply private fear of being caught out as anything other than perfect has become a nightmarish reality. This presents as the well-groomed 'good girl' with 'boundaries' nowhere to be seen. Next in line, 'productivity', loudly proclaiming that they don't have time for this. This line-up contains some of the ways anxiety shows up for you and paralyses you. When you tell me how it feels, I imagine the muscles wrapping tightly around your lungs, constricting you in the scariest way, like having a five-kilo weight sitting on your chest.

Clients often tell me they want to feel confident again, and I get it, as they feel so lost and have been made to doubt everything and wonder who they are. But as we delve into the complexities and look below what presents as anxiety, panic attack, overwhelm or burnout, we find the hidden layers. This is the important work – identifying and understanding the reasons behind our nervous system's survival responses. When people don't understand why their mind and body react the way they do, that truly is a terrifying place to be. I am humbled every day to see the most courageous people walk towards what they fear most. Learning how to feel safe when you feel the complete opposite is the ultimate in courage. I can see how physically uncomfortable it is to even bear witness to the words around anxiety and panic. It's like the fear in a horror movie, as if naming it out loud will make it appear. But it is the act of naming it that begins the unfurling of the grip of panic attacks on your mind, emotions and body.

WHAT MAKES ANXIETY AND PANIC ATTACKS WORSE?

There are a number of different things that can increase your anxiety and having awareness of them is invaluable. Everyone's triggers are as unique as their fingerprints, so you need to understand what yours are. Here are some of the key elements that can make your anxiety worse and trigger a flare-up:

- alcohol
- substance misuse
- fatigue/poor-quality sleep/exhaustion

- hunger
- exposure to heat
- uncertainty and change
- hormonal fluctuations
- family history
- the usual suspects – perfectionism, hyper-productivity, overwhelm, lack of boundaries
- trauma
- health conditions
- modern life
- chronic stress
- complicated and/or unprocessed grief
- dysregulated nervous system
- prolonged state in survival mode and Fight/Flight/Freeze/Fawn mode
- ADHD and neurodiversity
- unhealthy coping strategies (see Chapter 8)
- places, situations, large crowds, or events where panic attacks occurred before (these must be challenged to break any cycle of anxiety)
- faulty cognition patterns – catastrophising, excessive reassurance-seeking, all-or-nothing thinking, over-generalising.

If you have never heard of excessive reassurance-seeking I bet you're likely to have experienced it – and it's a red flag for anxiety. It occurs when you look for repeated reassurances from your relationships, continuously asking questions like, 'Are you annoyed with me?' When they reassure you they are not, you don't believe them, and check again and again. You do this to relieve anxious thoughts and feelings if you are feeling uncertain and worried. It can be tied in with high rejection sensitivity, whereby previous experiences of social or peer rejection have led you to scan for any potential threats or risks that could lead to more rejection. This can lead to reliance on unhealthy coping mechanisms, but with the help of therapy you can learn how to create healthier coping strategies (we'll talk about this in Chapter 9).

LEARNING TO TRUST YOURSELF AGAIN AFTER A PANIC ATTACK

Many of us have lost the ability to trust ourselves and our bodies. It's something I am quick to tell clients: *You know yourself best*. My words aren't met with relief, but with a combination of a crestfallen sigh, heavy tears and choked words that I know hurt their throat: *I don't know who I am anymore. I'm scared I'll never feel normal or like myself again.*

What if the environment and how we are living is toxic? And what if this has led you to disconnect from yourself, with harsh self-discipline masked as being 'productive' to 'achieve' this ill-advised life concept of 'thriving'? I'm here to clear up some major misconceptions, for example if you only did more and were more organised you'd somehow magically find that unicorn of peace. But how has that been working out for you? Our society is set up to block hugely important internal messages, to numb and silence our inner thoughts with mindless external noise. The noise is exhausting, avoidance is exhausting, and anxiety is exhausting. So you must learn to listen to the information cues your body is sending you and to answer them, even if that is as basic as taking a break when you are tired or relinquishing some control and perfectionist tendencies. It is the small changes that can transform your everyday life.

When I ask clients, 'When did the anxiety begin?' and 'Have you experienced this feeling in another situation before?', I am always met with the same answer: 'No, this has never happened before.' I gently ask again, 'Have you experienced this feeling in another situation before?' and quite often something shifts in their mind, they see the bigger picture, start to look at all that has led to this moment, and then the realisation dawns – *I do know this*. That's the beginning of the process, the path back to you.

You can manage the fear by gently turning towards it and facing it. It is good to have support when doing this, whether from your GP or a therapist, or through bodywork like yoga or energy healing. The important thing is to connect with yourself and others again. I think people sometimes look for complicated solutions because the problem feels so complicated. But it can often be the simple changes that make the biggest difference. Nature is a big one – getting outside, moving, breathing deeply, enjoying the sights and sounds of the outdoor world. That is always hugely helpful. Another simple thing is to realise you have so much more power than you think. I often say to clients, 'You don't doubt for a second that you can have a panic attack, and yet you doubt that you can stop a panic attack.' The power of being able to identify mid-panic attack, *I am having a panic attack and I've had one before and I survived*, may not take away from how awful it feels in that moment, but it is the lifeline to grab on to when everything feels out of control. How you come back from panic attacks is by taking one step at a time up the ladder, slow and steady.

The Practical Psychology

HOW TO STOP A PANIC ATTACK AT HOME

Having ice in your freezer is an instant way to help stop an active panic attack:

- If it is someone else having the panic attack, reassure them that you are getting something that will help and you will be straight back. A person experiencing their first panic attack will be very scared and needs that reassurance.
- Get two ice cubes.
- Place an ice cube in each hand.
- This instantly jolts your system out of Fight or Flight and back into your body.

- The pain-like response sends a neurotransmitter that refocuses you out of your body and back into your surroundings.
- A cold compress on your neck can also help.

No ice? No problem. Put your hands under the cold tap past your wrists and do box breathing (see page 118).

HOW TO STOP A PANIC ATTACK IF YOU ARE OUT

This is your panic attack survival kit:

- Sour sweets, like sour fizzy cola bottles, fizzy snakes – they taste delicious and give a quick sensory distraction, grounding you back into your body.
- Always wear layers so you can remove clothes to feel more comfortable.
- Crackers – when you've had a panic attack before, a drop in blood sugars can trigger anticipatory anxiety.
- Calming statements, on repeat: *This is a panic attack, I am safe, even though I don't feel like it. This is a panic attack, I survived before, and I will be okay in a few minutes, when this passes. I am safe, even though I don't feel like it. This will pass, I am safe, this is a panic attack.*
- Box breathing – As you breathe, say to yourself: *I can slow down my breathing, one breath at a time. I am safe, even though I feel scared.*

HOW TO PAUSE A PANIC ATTACK ANYWHERE

What you'll need: a pen, if you have one. If you don't have one, use your thumb. This is a super handy vagal manoeuvre to help calm your nervous system in the moment.

- Hold a pen straight in front of you, arm outstretched.
- Focus your gaze on the pen.

- Now move your gaze beyond the pen.
- Now move your focus back to the pen.

Doing this – switching your gaze from close up to far away – activates your OCR (oculocardiac reflex), which reduces heart rate, calms your nervous system and alleviates a panic attack.

HOW TO RECOVER AFTER A PANIC ATTACK

A panic attack is a physically, mentally, and emotionally exhausting experience. Recovering afterwards, you may feel vulnerable, scared and physically depleted.

- If you can, take a rest, lie down.
- Drink a glass of water, have a cup of tea and a biscuit, banana, or crackers.
- If it makes you feel safe, use a weighted blanket for comfort.
- Keep to the basics – eat, sleep, rest well, and when you feel able bring in some gentle activity, like a walk or stretching.
- When it feels right, make some decisions about your next best steps.

How it feels: High-functioning anxiety – burnout and exhaustion

Burnout is the common name for the exhaustion that results from high-functioning anxiety. It is not recognised as one of the 11 types of anxiety under the DSM-5, but it is what I see on the therapy couch and, well, everywhere, every day.

High-functioning anxiety would be categorised under generalised anxiety disorder (GAD), with excessive worry, over-thinking, and constantly pushing beyond your physical, emotional and psychological needs. If you are living with this anxiety type, you are your own harshest critic, highly conscientious, subjecting yourself to relentless, high-level expectations in every area of your life. At the same time, you are minding everyone else's needs while juggling a thousand tasks at once; and all this is taking place behind a façade of being cool, calm and in control. Around you, people applaud you and only see a hard-working, kick-ass, confident, competent, busy person. They don't see the cracks. You never let them see the cracks. You mightn't even see them yourself.

The classic traits of high-functioning anxiety are perfectionism and a high level of caring – a person who cares too much. There can be a cost to caring. I did my master's thesis on burnout, and found it was the physical, emotional and mental exhaustion that showed up first. That was preceded by a bone tiredness that feels disgusting. Conscientiousness plays a huge part in this, so if you care deeply, but you don't put in healthy boundaries, you can set yourself up for burnout and exhaustion.

Behind high-functioning anxiety is fear. You question yourself at every turn, lying awake at 3 a.m. wondering, *Did I do this?* and *Why did I say that?* The fear ignores and overrides how you feel (hungry, sad, tired, overwhelmed). It drives you mercilessly. And beneath lies the biggest fear of all: what if others find out that you don't have it all together? Or simply that you are also human and can't do it all 'perfectly' all the time. When this is how everyone knows you; they say you're always so calm, organised and in control. The terror of the 'truth' being revealed drives you to stretch beyond your absolute capacity. And all the while, no one knows. High-functioning anxiety is anxiety hidden behind a smile. On the outside you are a powerhouse, calm, reliant, super-organised, friendly, helpful, and successful (according to what our culture deems successful). As I look around, I see a society that promotes this hustle culture and values and encourages high-functioning anxiety. Well, there's another soft revolution incoming. Get ready to disrupt with me because we are done with it all being too hard. I tell you who I see with high-functioning anxiety: people who are the warm lights, the bright sparks that light up a room, kind, helpful and articulate. They are considerate of other people in word and deed. But on the inside, it's a much pricklier experience for them as they feel they are living on the edge of a precipice that they could plunge off at any moment.

High-functioning anxiety	
What it looks like on the **outside**	What it feels like on the **inside**
Successful	Can't switch off
High achiever	Perfectionist
Never misses a deadline	Exhaustion
Detail-oriented	Fear/stress/anxiety
Organised	Over-thinking and over-preparing
Calm	
Confident	Inner chaos
Friendly/sociable	Low self-esteem and doubt
Consistently reliable	Irritable and self-isolating
Always says 'yes'	Unable to let anyone down
People-pleasing	Feel you can't say no
Always on time or early	Fear of boundaries
Always on the go/busy	Fear of being late
	Fear of being with own thoughts

While others describe you as 'competent, confident, calm', on the inside you battle with being unable to switch off. This is anxiety hidden in plain sight, in a society that values the superhero human, that values productivity over rest and material things over human connection. You are locked inside the anxiety of being known as the doer, the multitasker, the unflagging one, and yet you feel empty, depleted, utterly exhausted, and disconnected from yourself.

High-functioning anxiety in the workplace

It is in the workplace that high-performing anxiety can really take you over. One thing that ensures a cynical eye-roll from me is the work performance phrase 'consistently exceeds expectations'. It's trumpeted as a wonderful thing, a big achievement, but is it really? Honestly, not only is it not possible and not healthy to always exceed every expectation, but you know, and I know, that come your performance appraisal, there will only ever be yet more expectations heaped on for you to 'exceed', this time, the next time, and the time after that. How high can this performance bar go? When does stellar performance find its natural plateau that delivers a work–life balance? It might work for the organisation, but when I'm brought into organisations to work with employees, I see broken spirits. Can I call time on this, as an organisational psychologist and as a human being? It riles me up in the therapy room when I hear highly conscientious, competent, exhausted people tell me about the absolutely ridiculous expectations placed upon them. When you can't keep up with utterly unrealistic demands that are not only excessive but also ever-changing, how can you exceed them?

When you are living with high-functioning anxiety, this sort of workplace attitude exacerbates your own drive to over-perform and please. And, of course, it is exactly these sorts of workplace that attract this type of anxiety because they are challenging, tough and exciting, and high-functioning anxiety is rewarded financially, in status and within society. From what my clients tell me, the demands keep increasing, the timelines decreasing, the meetings multiplying and the time to do the proposed work decreasing. To me, the expected output and timelines cannot be met and are too much.

Ask yourself honestly: What is the culture like at your workplace? Is it toxic or sustainable? Or, worst of all, do they give the impression they care about your mental health, but it is merely a tick-the-box exercise? I have been sorely unimpressed by certain organisations in this regard.

I was once asked to give a stress management workshop, but it was specified that I not mention the word *stress* as they didn't want to give the staff any ideas that they were causing them any stress. Talk about doublethink! (I declined the invitation.)

The cost of opportunity

Opportunity cost is real.

I believe in hard work; I believe in tenacity and perseverance. Not only do I believe in it, I know there is no other way than to work and go through it. All the good stuff in life demands consistency and grit. But you have limits, and it's in your interest to be aware of that. Before you say 'yes' to any work-related offer or invitation, please consider and ask the following questions to weigh up the cost of the opportunity:

1. Do I have time to do this?
2. Is it aligned with my values and in line with the life I want to live?
3. What will this cost me in terms of the support I will need to do it?
4. What will it cost me in terms of my own energy resources?

Nothing is reward enough if you pay the price with your health.

If we think about what how we use the phrase 'high-functioning', such as a high-functioning alcoholic or high-functioning depression, it means that along with the presenting issue, in this case the struggle with anxiety and perfectionism, you are also achieving huge feats in your daily life. You are the one hitting the 'consistently exceeds expectations' performance metric. The public masking of the anxiety symptoms doesn't disappear just because you are at work. The enormity of the effort it takes to hide how you feel on the inside is often released with the speed of a deflated balloon at home on the couch in the evening.

> Kate came in and looked the business. She looked strong, healthy, together, she was warm, articulate and basically a lovely person.
> **AK:** What brings you here today?
> **Kate** (bursts into tears, her head dropping into her hands): I'm so sorry, this is mortifying.
> **AK:** Honestly, this is how everyone starts. Please allow yourself to have the cry that has been stuck in there for far too long.
> **Kate:** I really feel so stupid being here, I am sure you have people with real problems. I just feel like I am in a never-ending sprint. I have done very well, it feels uncomfortable saying that, but I know I am good at my job, I'm a really good mum and wife, friend and daughter, but I am so exhausted. I push hard with my exercise, I push hard with every bit of food my kids eat, I do everything to the best I can do, and I still worry that it is not enough and that I am not enough. I worry about what people think about me, they think I am so chill, and nothing could be further from the truth. I can't sleep, I can't relax, my body feels completely tight all the time. I try to control every situation from cleaning to how the kids are dressed and still I worry.
> **AK:** About what?
> **Kate:** I worry about absolutely everything and everyone all the time and I try to fix it by doing and being what they need me to be. I feel like a character in my own show, playing all these different roles, and I've no idea who I am anymore if I wasn't all these things. The idea of that terrifies me. Who am I if I am not 'Kate, everyone's go-to person'?

When you are operating within high-functioning anxiety, you can chase and pursue external values or the values of your company and forget what makes you happy. You can be so depleted by work that you don't have the energy to do what nurtures you when you collapse on the couch at home. It is easy to become lost and lose yourself so that you don't (or don't have the energy to) factor *yourself* into things anymore. Reflecting back on your childhood, this may be an ongoing trigger of you engaging in 'others first' at the expense of yourself. Part of finding your way again is to create healthier boundaries. Otherwise, you're just a ball of energy directed at ever-shifting goalposts, and your attention gets stolen away from where it needs to be. There is an excellent speech – from a high achiever – that calmly points out how to tackle this:

> *Imagine life as a game in which you are juggling five balls in the air. You name them work, family, health, friends, and spirit and you're keeping all of these in the air.*
>
> *You will soon understand that 'work' is a rubber ball. If you drop it, it will bounce back. But the other four balls – family, health, friends, and spirit – are made of glass. If you drop one of these, they will be irrevocably scuffed, marked, nicked, damaged, or even shattered. They will never be the same. You must understand that and strive for balance in your life.*
>
> *How?*
>
> *Don't undermine your worth by comparing yourself with others. It is because we are different that each of us is special.*
>
> *Don't set your goals by what other people deem important. Only you know what is best for you.*
>
> *Don't take for granted the things closest to your heart. Cling to them as you would your life, for without them, life is meaningless.*
>
> *Don't let your life slip through your fingers by living in the past or for the future. By living your life one day at a time, you live ALL the days of your life.*
>
> *Don't give up when you still have something to give. Nothing is over until the moment you stop trying.*

Don't be afraid to admit that you are less than perfect. It is this fragile thread that binds us to each other.

Don't be afraid to encounter risks. It is by taking chances that we learn how to be brave.

Don't shut love out of your life by saying it's impossible to find. The quickest way to receive love is to give it; the fastest way to lose love is to hold it too tightly: and the best way to keep love is to give it wings.

Don't run through life so fast that you forget not only where you've been, but also where you are going.

Don't forget, a person's greatest emotional need is to feel appreciated.

Don't be afraid to learn. Knowledge is weightless, a treasure you can always carry easily.

Don't use time or words carelessly. Neither can be retrieved.

Life is not a race, but a journey to be savoured each step of the way. Yesterday is history. Tomorrow is a mystery and today is a gift: that's why we call it 'the present'.[12]

The Practical Psychology

These questions are prompts for you to explore how high-functioning anxiety is showing up for you and how it impacts your life.

How do you find the performance appraisal at your workplace?

―――――――――――――――――――――――――――――

How does it impact you at work?

―――――――――――――――――――――――――――――

How does it impact you at home?
_____

Is there a discrepancy between the two?
_____

What are your fears if you didn't perform to the expected level?
_____

Are there any flexible time arrangements you need that you fear would be removed if you didn't perform as you do?
_____

If you could create or change any work circumstances, what would it be?
_____

Could you talk with a team lead or manager about this?
_____

MAKING SPACE FOR YOU

What do you need?
_____

What performance are you tired of in all roles of your life?
_____

Relationship with self:
_____

Relationship with others:

_____

Relationship with family:

_____

Relationship with work:

_____

Relationship with friends:

_____

HOW TO BRING THIS TO THE NEXT STEP – YOUR NEEDS ASSESSMENT

What needs to go?

What would you like to change or stop doing, but can't (ever or yet)?

_____

Think about ways to reduce the amount of time you spend doing this. Or are there any other possibilities?

_____

What do you want to do less of?

_____

What do you want to do more of?

_____

What parts of your day, week, month aren't working for you right now? What would help?

Day: _____

Morning: _____

Afternoon: _____

Evening: _____

Week (what can go?): _____

What are your crunch days?
_____

Month: _____

What activities do you do that you don't like (yours or theirs)?
_____

Can you share this load?
_____

What do you need to do to meet your own needs?
_____

What physical needs do you want to meet?
_____

What mental needs do you want to meet?
_____

What emotional needs do you want to meet?
_____

How are you going to meet the needs above? Be very specific.
_____

What needs to change to reduce the anxiety?
_____

Which parts of this make you uncomfortable?
_____

The hardest question: What are the consequences of continuing to ignore your basic needs?
_____

CATCHING WHAT YOU ARE SAYING ABOUT YOURSELF

Do you remember *Catchphrase* on TV? I loved that show. I often hear people's personal catchphrases or narratives, as in the stories they believe and tell about themselves and what they can and can't do. The ones I often hear are:

- 'I can't do that that, it would be selfish.'
- 'But if I don't do it, it won't get done.'
- 'I wish I could get more help, but they won't do it right or the way I like.'

Pay attention to the phrases you use about things you think you can and can't do, and note them down:
_____

Are these thoughts blocking you and how you are living your life?
_____

CHAPTER 6

Why women experience twice as much anxiety as men

It is literally impossible to be a woman. You are so beautiful, and so smart, and it kills me that you don't think you're good enough. Like, we have to always be extraordinary, but somehow we're always doing it wrong. (From Barbie, *spoken by Gloria (America Ferrera))*

According to the Anxiety and Depression Association of America (ADAA), women are twice as likely as men to experience panic disorder, generalised anxiety disorder with or without agoraphobia, three times as likely to experience obsessive compulsive disorder and five times as likely to experience post-traumatic stress disorder. These are stark statistics that need to be addressed and changed within society, work, our relationships and homes. To understand these gender differences, we need to look at a biopsychosocial model of health, in other words the biological, psychological and social factors.

Biological factors: Hormonal fluctuations, in particular oestrogen and progesterone, can impact mood regulation and increase susceptibility to anxiety disorders, along with lifelong hormone changes that we will explore below. There are also relevant brain chemistry and neurotransmitter gender differences and fluctuations, for example with serotonin, which impact mood regulation.

Psychological factors: Such as being more prone to certain cognitive styles, like rumination and worry and emotional sensitivity, which feeds directly into the social factors, such as gender socialisation and gender role expectations, status, power and pay differences.

Social factors: Women experience more forms of sexual assault and domestic violence, which naturally can lead to anxiety and PTSD. Women are often the stress absorbers in society and in the home, juggling multiple roles at once, and yet we are still living with the gender pay gap.

Women tend to experience more internalising disorders, such as depression and eating disorders, while men may experience more externalising disorders, such as substance abuse, aggression, risk-taking. The patterns can stem from social expectations around men and masculinity.[13] Accordingly, women may lash at themselves internally whereas men may lash out.[14] But while women attempt suicide more often than men, more men die by suicide.[15] There's a whole other book in how men are also being failed. You can see the patterns emerging, and why women experience anxiety at a rate twice that of men.

One of the most striking findings is that 80 per cent of people diagnosed with autoimmune diseases are women. Autoimmune diseases occur when the immune system mistakenly attacks healthy cells and tissues in the body. It may be caused by a combination of genetic and/or environmental factors. Such diseases are also linked to anxiety, for many complex reasons, such as chronic illness and/or inflammation, which may affect the brain's chemistry. That 80 per cent is a huge statistic: women live longer, and yet their immune systems are attacking themselves. This comes back to the impact of being chronically drip-fed stress hormones, such as epinephrine (adrenaline), cortisol and norepinephrine, from a toxic culture, dressed up and normalised as an idealised concept of 'success'. I shudder to think of the impact on our nervous systems and immune systems.

Emotional labour

The term 'emotional labour' was originally coined by Arlie Hochschild, a University of California, Berkeley professor, sociologist and author of *The Managed Heart: Commercialisation of Human Feeling*[16] (a book I am deeply familiar with as I did my master's thesis on the subject). It described the emotional labour required to do your job, which entails how you manage your own emotions to meet the emotional requirements of a job. Hochschild described the transition from a manufacturing-based economy to a service-based economy, and the attendant demand for service with a smile and the commodification of emotions. Rather than selling a product, what is now being sold is 'good service', requiring changing or suppressing your own emotions in line with the company brand.[17]

Hochschild described the emotional labour involved in the work of flight attendants, for example, who must be courteous and manage their own authentic emotions because they are the face of the company. At the time of the study, flight attendants' smiles were measured with a ruler. They were trained to deal with drunken passengers who were fond of patting them on the bum by imagining them as being like a baby. They were shown how to 'manage', aka suppress, their emotions in 'recurrent training'. The study found that the work required the attendants to present a particular façade, and that façade had to display the 'correct' emotions at all times. From the first greeting – (big smile) 'Hi, welcome on board!' – the attendants were actively working to manage every interaction, right up to the point of 'deep acting' – where you lose your identity in your role.

Surface acting and deep acting are two separate adaptive responses to hiding or suppressing your emotions at work. So the high-pitched, enthusiastic 'Hi, welcome on board!' over multiple flights per day is the outward expression of a job requirement that doesn't correspond to how stressed the flight attendants feel. Smiling on the outside, stressed on in the inside. You know, and the customer knows, that this is surface acting – expected but fake. It was described by Hochschild as the commercialisation of your feelings in exchange for a wage.

The process of deep acting is where you change how you feel on the inside to match how you look on the outside, which means you are identifying too much with the job. It can leave you open to losing yourself in the process and to exhaustion and burnout. If you imagine a nurse empathising with their patients, fully engrossed in their role, that is mentally and physically deep emotion work, and you can see how burnout can occur in such taxing roles.

Finding the balance between faking it and feeling it can be challenging.[18] If your personality and job fit well, your emotions will be more naturally aligned.[19] Like everything in life, I think it's not about finding balance, it's about not losing you, and this is easier to do than you'd think. So keep checking back in with your body, ask it how it is, and really listen; and do something for it. If you are tired, even a 15-minute disco nap will help (not at work!).

Many women have been in ongoing training like this their entire lives, and this is reflected in the high prevalence of GAD and panic disorders among women. The paid and unpaid emotional labour that deviates you from your authentic self can be summed up in the five most whispered words in the therapy room: 'I feel lost and overwhelmed.'

The term 'emotional labour' started out in the workplace, thanks to Hochschild's study, but it then broadened out and became synonymous with the hidden and invisible work of unpaid labour, such as running a home and the relationships within it. The lines blurred. Most women now occupy a range of unpaid and paid roles as employee/boss/wife/mother and somehow manage them all simultaneously. It's a huge responsibility that is generally not noticed, valued or acknowledged. Nowadays, emotional labour means being the person who remembers, reminds, minds and manages the physical, mental, and emotional loads of everyday life to keep everything going. Notice I didn't say progressing, just 'going'. It's also known as the mental load, which is a good description because it is a heavy burden to be tasked with shouldering the stuff of an entire household. 'The Mental Load' a feminist comic by an artist called Emma[20] explains the exasperation you feel when someone says, 'but you should've asked for help'. Even simple reminders or questions add to your mental load. Therein lies the problem. Why are you the manager of the household? Who gave you this role, why did you take it, how did this happen? We need to rethink the distribution of the demands of household and motherhood. It's time to challenge the 'Mom Manager' role. It's somewhat ironic that you are going to have to do it, but this one would be worth it. It's time to revolt against the Mom Manager role you didn't sign up for. Who is with me?

> Julie was feeling particularly irritated. She had just Revolted two separate sums for the teachers' presents, said yes to one match and needed to organise a lift to same, signed the kids up to another term in another activity and responded to two emails. She did this with a mountain of laundry engulfing her space and eyeballs. The table had grated Parmesan scattered beside the abandoned plate with an empty smoothie glass and cutlery from the night before. The sink and countertops were covered, and she hadn't even looked at the To Do list yet. It was 6.40 a.m. and Julie already felt exasperated and quite frankly pissed off.

> 'Mom, where are my soccer gloves?'
> 'Mom, where is my gumshield?'
> 'Mom, where are my football boots?'
> 'Mom, why didn't you sign me up for …?' (fill in the many blanks).
> 'MoooooooMMMMMMMMM …'
> Julie thinks, 'Where is my mind and patience?' Gone, like all the ancillary equipment and clothing scattered from pillar to post, but somehow she is responsible for it. There are demands coming from every direction, and all of them must be met. It's unending, day in, day out, and Julie can't falter for a moment or the whole house of cards will come crashing down around her. Deep breath, keep going, keep going, don't stop.

We need to acknowledge how society has normalised the emotional load as a woman's responsibility, passed down from generation to generation. Women are expected to embody traits like niceness, smiling externally as they betray their inner needs, desperately trying to 'just become more organised' so they can keep the wheels turning, reinforcing societal expectations at every turn. The statistics keep piping up with uncomfortable truths, though. Neuropsychopharmacology researchers looking at the EU population stated that mental health disorders are turning into 'the largest health challenge of the 21st century', meaning that '38.2 per cent of the EU population suffers from a mental disorder each year', which corresponds to '164.8 million' people affected.[21]

The emotional labour, whether paid or unpaid, often disconnects women from their authentic selves, leaving them feeling lost and overwhelmed. Have we learned, both implicitly and explicitly, to prioritise pleasing others and striving for perfection, at the physical, mental, and emotional cost of neglecting our own needs? Does this societal conditioning lead women to repress and suppress their true selves, potentially contributing to anxiety disorders and other illnesses? Perhaps it's time for a health warning to draw attention to these issues.

Equality and equity are essential in our workplaces and homes. I'm not interested in talking or debating this anymore. Many women struggle to assert their needs due to subtle but effective societal blockers, fearing judgement for seeking help or being labelled as being 'nagging' or bossy, meaning aggressive. Even compliments like 'You're so strong and in control' can be weaponised, reinforcing unrealistic expectations. The imagery of the board getting Barbie back in her box wasn't lost on me in the movie as she began to assert herself and question what she was made for. A question, I think of as I pick the socks, shoes and bags off the floor.

Fascinating research 32 years after Hochschild's 1983 study explored the '9/11' effect, where airline crews gained more assertiveness and emotional autonomy, prioritising safety over traditional courtesy. It became the cultural norm that they could be more assertive with passengers and have more emotional agency, thus giving them 'role shields'. Less service with a smile and more protection for them in their job. What do you need to be shielded from? What would it be like to have more emotional agency over your words and boundaries, confidently expressing when you can't accommodate certain demands? Recognising dissatisfaction and embracing the power to effect change is crucial for reclaiming personal agency and wellbeing in both professional and personal spheres. We need to ask some hard questions surrounding emotional labour. If we want change, we need to start speaking up for ourselves in our everyday lives.

The Practical Psychology

Ask yourself:

AT WORK

Do you engage in emotional labour at work?
_____

How is this for you?
_____

AT HOME

If I gave you a 'how you really feel' free pass to speak your mind, what would you say and who would you say it to? (Have some fun with this.)
_____

If you are in a relationship, both of you do this exercise:
Make a list of the domestic tasks you each do at home.
_____

Make a list of the emotional load you each take on.
_____

Make a list of the cognitive load you each take on.
_____

Have a discussion about which jobs could be renegotiated and distributed. Pause for a moment and see if any discomfort comes up for you even thinking about bringing this to your partner.
_____

How could you achieve more emotional agency to express yourself and make changes that you know need to be made?

Hormones and anxiety

Understanding the role of hormones across a woman's lifespan is fundamental in comprehending the complex interplay between psychological, physical and emotional wellbeing, and its impact on mental health. Hormones play a central role in regulating various bodily functions, influencing mood, cognition and behaviour throughout different life stages. You will be familiar with all this, but breaking down how your hormones show up over the course of your ever-changing life is helpful. Most months, I have my *Oh, that's why I have been so impatient, irritable, snappy* moment, as I laugh to myself, with those around me wondering who I am or what just happened, but at that stage I'd have tea and chocolate and all would be well in the world again.

From puberty to menopause and beyond, fluctuations in oestrogen, progesterone, testosterone and other hormones can significantly affect a woman's mental and emotional state. During adolescence, hormonal changes can contribute to mood swings, heightened emotions, and increased vulnerability to mental health issues, such as depression and anxiety. I know, who am I telling? In adulthood, hormone levels continue to fluctuate in response to menstrual cycles, pregnancy, childbirth and menopause, it just keeps coming like a hormonal juggernaut. These hormonal shifts can influence energy levels, sleep patterns, stress responsiveness and emotional resilience, to name but a few. If you are a woman, I'm going to make an assumption and say you may be familiar with pre-menstrual stress (PMS), which can bring irritability, changes in mood, aches and pains during the menstrual cycle. (I keep vowing to sign up to one of the menstrual cycle apps, but by the time I do I won't need it anymore!)

Pregnancy and postpartum periods involve dramatic hormonal fluctuations that can impact mood, anxiety levels, and adjustment to motherhood. Postpartum depression and anxiety are common mental health concerns affecting many women during this phase and can blindside you no matter what you know on the subject. As with all anxiety, you can't just intellectualise your way out of it – you feel what you feel.

As women approach menopause, declining oestrogen levels can contribute to symptoms such as anxiety, sleep disturbances and mood changes, which may increase the risk of developing mood disorders like depression (notably if pre-existing) and hot flushes. The cognitive and emotional impact can also blindside you, making you think you are 'losing it' when it's really down to fluctuating hormones.

Moreover, hormonal imbalances or dysregulation can exacerbate pre-existing mental health conditions or contribute to the onset of new ones. This is a hugely under-recognised point: so many women find their anxiety increases with their periods, pregnancy and perimenopause and everything in between. Understanding the intricate relationship between hormones and mental health is essential for providing the right care and support and for giving you a sense of autonomy with regard to your overall wellbeing throughout your life. By recognising and addressing the psychological, physical and emotional impacts of hormonal fluctuations, healthcare professionals can develop holistic approaches to mental health treatment and empower women to navigate hormonal transitions with greater self-awareness. This is the beginning of an important change in women driving their own health.

When I talk to clients about the relationship between their ever-changing hormone cycles and their mental health, I am always struck by the common experience of a deep loss of confidence around life transitions. These transitions are the ultimate identity changers, i.e. pregnancy, labour, postnatal, perimenopause and menopause, and they can be raw and vulnerable experiences. When we are discussing their anxiety or how their panic attacks are presenting, often that loss of identity is a key issue: 'Who am I now?'; 'I want to feel like myself again'; 'I don't know who I am'; 'I don't recognise who I am'; 'I don't like who I am, this isn't the real me.'

For women, these transitions are physical, moving from a girl to an adolescent with your first period, from a woman to a mother by having a child, the rollercoaster of hormones post-birth, then moving in later womanhood to perimenopause and menopause. This shape-shifting and identity-changing is powered by hormones, and yet we still see women's incredible bodies, minds and emotional states dismissed with the words, 'You are so hormonal.' The hormone narrative has to change because it is the female health narrative. We hear many complaining about the huge upsurge in women in mid-life being diagnosed with ADHD. But maybe, like our hormones, it is because the research used boys and men. For a long, long time we have failed women in their healthcare needs. Ask yourself: What comes to mind when you hear the word 'hormonal'? I'd be willing to bet that it's not positive, that it's quite possibly disparaging and dismissive.

There has long been mockery and shame around female hormones, linked with women being portrayed as irritable and unstable. You'll remember it from the time you were a teenager, how that negativity was often directed at you and your body, with 'Are you on your period?' used as a put-down.' 'Are you hormonal?' is accusatory. Many women feel they must advocate strongly for their physical, emotional and mental health, often needing to prove their symptoms and their impact. This can leave them feeling dismissed and disbelieved. Your hormones are powerful, they are creators and regulators and should be revered rather than feared.

I will not explain hormones here – there are many excellent experts in this area who are finally having their voices heard, and thankfully so. Learning the language of your hormones is key to understanding yourself with kindness, respect and with the requisite skills of how to make decisions that work for you, your body, and your health. It makes me sad when clients defend themselves by saying things like, 'Don't mind me, I'm just hormonal'. *You're right*, I'm thinking, *but what are you actually communicating when you say that? What are you telling yourself?*

There is another way to look at our hormones and their impact on us. I found this when I read a fascinating book by Joan Borysenko, a Harvard-trained cell biologist, licensed psychologist, spiritual educator and psychoneuroimmunologist, called *A Woman's Book of Life*.[22] It had a profound impact on how I thought about hormones. Borysenko speaks of the importance of the irritation women can feel before their period starts and how every month the things that have been off kilter in your life and your relationships are brought to the surface, usually via anger. This fascinated me as it echoes how I view panic attacks – that they are part of your body's self-protection mode, even though on the surface it doesn't look like that.

As Gabor Maté says in *When the Body Says No*,[23] hormones can act as our boundary protectors. Perhaps you wanted to say 'no' numerous times over the course of the month, but you didn't. The month of mounted frustrations reaches a peak in your cycle and that's when clearing conversations can occur, or it's when you have that big cry that provides a pent-up release. We can see those reactions as positive and helpful if we choose to and educate ourselves on the different seasons within our cycles to change our experience. This perspective of listening to what your body is telling you or shouting at you, which is shot down by those who seek to shame women as 'over-reactors', has alienated women from the wisdom and cues coming from their own bodies. Your body might be saying to you: *I am tired and need to rest, This is too much, It is unfair that I do the same things every day and nothing changes* – and you might really need to hear that, for your own good health. This is a radical idea, but it is extremely useful to recast your hormones as allies – they are part of you, and you're all playing on the one team. When you don't treat them like that, that's where anxiety can creep in as you try to downplay, ignore or suppress your authentic thoughts and feelings. If you try to annex off a part of you, that can only lead to division and a sense of being disconnected from yourself. And we now know that is a core part of anxiety – that fracturing of the self that destabilises your sense of self and identity. Instead, try to see your hormones as potent messengers and protectors, looking out for you, and perhaps speaking clearly to the very things you try to hide and erase.

As we explore the social and relational impacts of how being a woman influences how we can betray our physical, emotional and energy needs, perhaps your hormones are unapologetically expressing how you really feel. In terms of anxiety and tackling anxiety, this way of looking at your body and your hormones is extremely helpful. Our bodies aren't meant to go, go, go all the time, and maybe it is our hormones that force us to listen, to rest, to recover. That is a good intervention because when we consistently ignore anxiety, it can lead to the body employing the shock tactics of a panic attack to get our attention.

Postnatal anxiety

After giving birth women experience a rapid decline in progesterone levels, with a decrease of up to 70 per cent occurring within the first few days. The drop is one of the most significant hormonal changes that women undergo in their lifetime. This predisposes you to be more sensitive to stress, which can heighten worry, fear, anxious thoughts, along with all the other contributing factors after having a baby. While there is now good awareness of postnatal depression (PND), what I see more frequently but is less talked about is postnatal anxiety (PNA). Symptoms can overlap, but they are quite different. They can also co-occur.

PND is defined as depression experienced by a mother following childbirth, in the first year after having a baby, due to a combination of hormonal changes, psychological adjustments to motherhood and fatigue. It affects 10–15 women in every 100.[24] Symptoms include low mood, anxiousness, negative thoughts, inability to enjoy anything. It is classed as PND when at least five depressive symptoms are present out of the nine for more than two weeks as per criteria listed in the DSM-5.[25]

PNA is when a woman experiences severe anxiety after having a baby, adopting, or becoming a parent (the postpartum period), occurring in the first year of having a child.[26] Becoming a parent and already being a parent is a huge change and responsibility, but when the worry is excessive and all-consuming and feels as if it is out of your control and taking over your thoughts, it might be postpartum anxiety. One study found the incidence of postnatal anxiety was 17.1 per cent, surpassing the incidence of postpartum depression at 4.8 per cent.[27] But it is hard to seek help when you aren't even aware of what it is yourself. The anxiety that can follow the first year after giving birth grips you with a constant fear that you are utterly failing, and your inner critic ramps up to borderline abusive at this vulnerable stage of change. Many experience anxiety during the pregnancy and, again, fluctuating hormones are playing a key role. This is exacerbated by lack of support and intervention along with utterly unrealistic expectations of first-time mums, and each successive birth bringing its own unique challenges. Common phrases I hear are 'I think I'm losing it' and 'I think I'm going crazy.' Do you notice a pattern here? When women's mental health feels overwhelming, or you are in distress, turning on yourself with a shame or stigma lens of 'crazy' is where a lot of women go. Historically, this is because women who were deemed 'hysterical' could be placed in a psychiatric hospital against their will. How we speak about ourselves and how others speak to us is vital in changing the female mental health narrative. It's one I am here to challenge.

The symptoms of PNA can be a combination of physical, emotional and cognitive:

Physical symptoms may include (but are not confined to):

- poor sleep
- fatigue/exhaustion
- feelings of angst
- loss of appetite
- nausea or upset stomach
- tense body/muscles
- heart palpitations or increased heart rate
- trembling/shaking
- feeling short of breath or as if you can't get enough air into your lungs
- hyperventilation.

Emotional and cognitive symptoms may include:

- irritability
- difficulty relaxing
- a sense of dread or doom
- being worried, especially about the baby or yourself
- difficulty focusing
- feeling distracted
- being forgetful
- anxious thoughts
- panic attacks
- obsessive thoughts.

Common risk factors are:[28]

- pre-existing history of anxiety
- previous mood disturbances during hormonal changes, such as puberty, PMS, or birth control
- pre-existing family or personal experience of a perinatal mental health conditions
- crisis related to housing, finances, or work

- pregnancy during teen years
- previous infant or pregnancy loss
- lower socio-economic status
- limited or no social support from friends or family
- history of endocrine dysfunction, such as diabetes or thyroid imbalance.

Postpartum anxiety and OCD (obsessive compulsive disorder) can be present if you find yourself compulsively worrying about the baby, checking their safety, cleaning, and repeating certain rituals to ensure the baby's safety.[29] Mothers can experience intrusive thoughts and feel terrified by their own fears for their baby's safety and the worry they might do something to harm the baby. Even having these thoughts is deeply upsetting to mothers and many keep it to themselves for fear of what others would think about them or what they might do. Having worked with many women in this position, that last sentence is the one that needs to set your mind at ease. If you are deeply upset by your own thoughts, this is a good indicator that they are intrusive thoughts and not that you would do anything. Even thinking of these thoughts as intruders helps identify them and separate them from you. Speaking with your GP and a psychologist can alleviate this fear and support you during a tough time. Get as much support as you can.

Here are some examples of how postnatal anxiety might show up for you: Repeatedly checking on the baby during the night to make sure they are still breathing. Not being able to sleep yourself and worrying about the baby or ruminating about what you are not doing. Excessively worrying if they are sleeping enough or too little, worrying about their feeding, if they are hitting their normal milestones. Being terrified to leave your baby with anyone, even people you trust. Feeling like everyone else is doing a much better job than you and worrying deeply about how your anxiety will impact the baby and your relationship with them, especially around bonding.

Chronic heavy-duty lack of sleep, along with labour, which may have been traumatic, immense hormonal fluctuations, the change in your identity and role as a mother/parent and your relationship, along with the mental, physical and emotional responsibility of a baby, leaves many thinking their relationship is doomed. Comments on your body, what you are doing and everything in between at such a vulnerable time are a few of the contributing factors, along with pre-existing anxiety. Please bring in compassion if you feel like or ever felt like this because there are so many potential reasons for it. I wish women were checked for postpartum anxiety, postnatal depression, and PTSD six months postpartum not with a tick-the-box exercise in the post-birth haze.

In today's world, mothering and parenting nearly feel like a competitive sport. As a society it is essential to lend support to parents, especially in that fragile post-birth period and beyond. Parenting is not the same as it was for the previous generation. This is why I keep talking about the rates of anxiety and guilt and 'never enough-ing'. That so often stems from a toxic social environment that we need to call into question. I do love knowledge, but all the information that's available can leave parents feeling like they need to know everything to do a good job. You do not need to be an expert to be a parent; we need to stop professionalising parents. Never mind the present for the newborn, sit and listen to the mother's birth story, or how she is feeling, or what is keeping her awake at night, not including the baby. Let her take a shower while you hold the baby. What parents need is community, connection and care, and this is so badly needed across the family's lifespan. Please stop telling new parents how easy they have it compared to the parent with two or three children; please stop telling the parent of the toddler or the teenager that it gets harder – yes, lie to them. Every part has its own challenges, joys, exasperation, heartbreak and laughter and tears. Parenting is a full-body contact sport and the rules change every few weeks, so let's all be on the same team, and agree to disagree; what is needed is open ears and hearts.

I feel if the truth of parenting were shared in a more honest, warts-and-all way, anxiety would be lessened. The usual suspects of anxiety love gate-crashing on parenting, so we need to keep working on becoming reformed perfectionists, encourage and support boundaries, and be more patient with ourselves and others. We need to dial the pressure down and lock judgement out.

The Practical Psychology

If you related to the above, please ask and answer the following questions:

If applicable, how did anxiety show up for you during your pregnancy, postpartum, perimenopause and menopause?

_____

What did you need then?

_____

What would you like your partner, parents and siblings to know?

_____

What would practically help? (I call these practical things my B&B. My B&B is all about doing the Boring and Basic things that are good for you and really help when they are there consistently – sleep, rest, food, and movement. They are also deeply felt when absent and have a direct impact on maintaining good physical and mental health. Because they are basic and boring, we often underestimate their importance. Think of them each as legs on a four-legged chair; remove even one, and you will definitely notice the difference.)

_____

_____

What outside help do you need, from your inner circle (family and friends)?

_____

What outside help do you need, from your outer circle (GP, psychologist, nutritionist, work, etc.)?

_____

If you had to write a script to explain to others what has been going on for you, what would it say?

_____

_____

STOP THE SHOULD-ING

Seeking help is important. Make a list of who you could contact, pick up the phone, and make an appointment. It can be hard to make choices when there is so much going on, especially while minding a new baby. Even though it feels impossible or even scary to leave the baby, trust me when I say Do it. This is your not-so-gentle nudge back to feeling like yourself again. There's never a good time; don't wait until the next stage happens for your baby/child (that's 'if–then thinking' again), and don't worry if you haven't managed to do it yet. Now is the right time. If you have been arguing with your partner or feel completely misunderstood, write out how it has affected you and pull out the core emotions. I think everyone needs to write out their birth story, and if you need to speak with someone, please do. This should, a word I generally never say, be standard in afterbirth care. External societal pressure with all the 'shoulds' adds to the anxiety of how mothers think they 'should' be doing it. Fear of judgement, fear of doing it wrong and impacting your developing baby freezes many mothers and or puts them in Fight or Flight mode as they become hypervigilant to every noise their baby makes. We need to normalise the level of difficulty of the transition to motherhood and exponentially increase the support to parents.

There is no preparation for the emotional change, for the identity shift that is all-encompassing of your body and mind. Teaching parents how to regulate their own nervous system, to understand where a lot of their triggers originate from, and doing work on processing past wounds is what I would consider passing on intergenerational wealth; teaching this generation how to regulate their nervous system, move out of chronic survival mode and know how to bring themselves back to feeling safe and connected. This way you have regulated parents, who are co-regulating their children through compassion and connection. This is the soft, but empowering, revolution that our world needs now more than ever. The rates of loneliness among mothers in our capitalist and individualist society shows it's not working. The rates of loneliness across the board attest to too many feeling disconnected and isolated. The time for change is now. Use your anxiety to move you towards living a life that feels more aligned with you, your values and how you want to live.

Remember this: parenting is hugely important to the health of society. With zero training given and many different points of view, that connection to how you want to be within your own tribe can be lost. Connect with you, with your body and thoughts, do the work from your past, connect with nature, ask for help. Drop any stigma that you *should* know how to do this. We all need to help each other.

Perimenopause: The next journey

Finally, at the age when you begin to feel you've got a handle on a few things – *Okay, I've got this* – you slowly but surely notice change starting to creep in. At the start it's so subtle you don't pay much attention. It might be that your joints feel achy; you couldn't fall asleep – your mind is wide awake; you wake up thinking *Oh, I have a fever, that's weird*; or you walk into a room with great purpose only to stop dead and wonder why you're there; or your periods get heavier, or lighter, or vanish, or hit you worse than you've ever experienced in your life.

For me, it was the periods that was the first herald of change. I've been lucky with my periods all my life, and I'm grateful for that, but when my thighs began inexplicably radiating in searing pain just before my period, like the gasping pains you get in labour, I was like, *What the heck is this?* The pain would be so bad that it would wake me up from sleep, and I'd be forced to go downstairs and take paracetamol. I don't think I ever before got out of bed to take a painkiller. It seemed I had entered a new season of 'firsts' – most of them unwelcome! My initial thought was, *Okay, it's just lockdown* – we were in the height of it then, with one child in junior infants, one in Communion year and the other in sixth class, all suddenly being home-schooled and living behind masks in the 'new normal'. I knew I could feel the unfamiliar creep of anxiety, accompanied by heavy brain fog and a general feeling of overwhelm, but I racked all that up to circumstances and dismissed it as a perfectly normal reaction to the world being flipped on its head. From my work, I was well aware that Covid and the impact of lockdown were crushing people, and that it was bringing a lot of existing trauma to the surface. The knock-on effect of that was that my workload increased tenfold. I was also well aware that the 3 I's were very much present in me – I was definitely more irritable, intolerant and impatient. And the tears seemed to have decided they would show up unexpectedly, often without any forewarning, sense, or control to keep them in my eyeballs. My fuse seemed to have got a whole lot shorter and rage decided it wanted to be another uninvited guest at this not-fun party.

Given all this and the fact that all the boundaries blurred in a very uncomfortable way as we lived, worked, parented, and tried to be substitute teachers all day, every day, the overwhelm was huge. And still I wrote it off as *It's normal, it will pass, I'm just being silly.* Like so many women – and, unfortunately, doctors – I thought it was anything but perimenopause. This is a very common reaction – and it is no doubt because, as we've already noted, we are largely not listening to the messages our bodies send us.

> *Years before, Lucy had experienced postnatal anxiety that floored her, and now she couldn't believe she was back at this place where daily panic attacks and constant worry kept her from falling asleep, from staying asleep, to her first anxious thought as she opened her eyes in the morning.*
>
> **Lucy:** What the hell is wrong with me? I feel like I'm going crazy. I certainly feel like I'm losing control and my mind. I can't sleep even though I'm bone-tired all day, but as soon as I get into bed it's like I've had a triple espresso and my mind won't shut up. I'm not comfortable in bed, I'm too hot and have to change my pyjamas, I feel so irritated and then he is breathing so loudly. I'm worrying about everything, the world, my children, I'm fighting with my husband all the time and I am experiencing these rages that come with no warning. I know anxiety, I had panic attacks and general anxiety and I know my hormones impacted it.
>
> I'm thinking about giving up my job. I used to be able to manage, but all of a sudden, I seem to be losing it with everything, I can't remember why I came upstairs, I start one job and get distracted with another. I'm really concerned about my relationship with my husband, I feel so angry with him. Something has fundamentally changed, and I can't put up with being the one to do it all and to get nothing but back talk from the kids, who are in the throes of being teenagers. I know it wasn't like this when I grew up and that pisses me off and triggers me immensely, as I would never have spoken to my

> mother like that. I feel really down, like, I'm wondering if I'm a bit depressed? I'm certainly overwhelmed and have lost so much confidence in myself.
> **AK:** Have you considered if your hormones might be a factor alongside these lifestyle factors?
> *Lucy looked back at me with disgust, as if I had just insulted her.*
> **Lucy:** It can't just be hormones. This is so real. And it's making my life hell. It can't be just perimenopause or something.

Note how often we say 'just' when it comes to our hormones.

The thing is, hormones are very real and play a huge role in your overall health. They are physiological processes that have specific functions that work hard and have a physical impact. If you cut your finger, that's real. If your oestrogen is dropping, it's very real – it has measurable impacts and consequences, and they affect your whole self, body, mind and emotions. It may make you question who that self is anymore. What do you like, what do you need and what can you not put up with anymore? Bear in mind, too, that perimenopause can range from eight to ten years in duration before you finally stop menstruating and are out the other side, which is menopause. Hormones play a major role in perimenopause and menopause, affecting not only physical processes but also mental health. It's important to recognise that these changes are not merely transient or emotional – they have measurable physiological effects that can impact the body and mind significantly. The decline in oestrogen levels during perimenopause can lead to fluctuations in neurotransmitters like serotonin and norepinephrine, which are closely linked to mood regulation. These hormonal shifts can contribute to symptoms of anxiety and mood swings experienced by many women during this transitional phase. It's worth noting any pre-existing anxiety or depression that may have occurred during previous hormonal shifts and transitions, as this awareness can help you to prepare, be forearmed, and proactively manage your health from a place of thinking about and taking the next best steps for you.

I will empower my daughters to track their cycles, to understand and to speak about their hormones differently, challenging the stereotypes around hormonal changes. For us all to challenge the trite comments about being 'hormonal' and move towards a deep understanding and prioritisation of the importance of nourishing, resting and getting to know, honour and mind our incredible bodies in each cycle and change throughout our lives.

There is a problem, though, in that while this is a natural part of life and presents a whole new chapter for a woman as a new life stage, the portrayals of menopausal women do women a major disservice. Menopause is too often presented as something to mock, or as another part of the female life experience that is to be ashamed of and to hide. This is reinforced by the Western attitude to ageing women, which often portrays older women as 'Karens', menopaused into irrelevance. This, in turn, can make women resistant to accepting this new life stage and recognising that they have entered perimenopause – and that it might account for some of what they are feeling and thinking. As a result, many women see anxiety and depression in the hormonal shift of the perimenopausal journey. That said, it is all too easy to miss the symptoms of perimenopause, or attribute them to something else, because there are so many and they are often a bit vague, they come and go, you end up not sure what you're feeling and doubting your own interpretation of it. I can't give you chapter and verse on perimenopause, but these are the common symptoms I see in women who present with anxiety, panic, low mood, or depression, when I have to question if they are in fact experiencing perimenopausal symptoms – as they often are:

- change in periods (heavier, lighter, longer, shorter)
- headaches
- migraines

- itchy eyes
- itchy skin
- needing to urinate more and with a feeling of more urgency
- overwhelm and anxiety
- irritability
- loss of confidence
- feeling down
- more tearful
- insomnia
- difficulty getting to sleep
- difficulty concentrating
- memory challenges
- lack of focus
- lack of confidence driving
- low sex drive
- heart palpitations.

Those are the physical symptoms, but there are also the even-harder-to-pin-down psychological effects of this life change. It is a time of questioning – you find yourself questioning everything: your life, relationships, who you are, what you've been doing, whether you can keep working. This is often accompanied by a diffuse rage that you find very difficult to suppress – even though you've been suppressing anger all your life. Now you find it hard to tamp it down, and often, you don't want to anymore. This feels like a new anger – and it means business.

I remember being asked one Valentine's Day to do an interview on *Prime Time* about the increase in divorce rates for women over 50 in Ireland. It felt somewhat unromantic and unfair on my husband as I went off to talk divorce on Valentine's Day – but there were striking figures to talk about. It was clear that there was a shift under way and many women over 50 were initiating divorce and choosing a different second half of life. To my mind, and based on my own observations in the therapy room, it seemed that the statistics correlated with women hitting perimenopause and questioning their lives to that point and thinking, *Hang on a second, this relationship is no longer working for me.* This has been facilitated by the social change women have experienced over the past 50 years, which has left many in a financial position where they can make this choice.

As a psychologist, I find the rage very interesting. Women are conditioned to be the 'good girl', as I've already spoken about, to not be difficult, to not offend others and, quite frankly, to ignore their instinctive emotional needs. However, the process of age can bring a fresh clarity – and that is something I think we need to harness and encourage. I'm not saying just because you get older you gain more clarity, I don't think that chronological age equals wisdom, but do I think that after 50 years of garnering experiences and picking up some emotional injuries along the way, your boundary lines become much clearer for you in terms of what you will and will not agree with, what you will and will not accept. It's not that there were blurred lines, it is that you accept that you have rights and are not willing to betray yourself or your needs anymore. This comes as something of an awakening – it's something I hear women say again and again, both in therapy and among my friends. There's a sort of astonishment at what they accepted before, and a new sense of self that allows them to simply say 'no more' as they acknowledge that what they have been doing has been putting too much specifically upon them.

This is why anger is an emotion that I encourage women to understand and to relate to differently, by embracing it and listening to what it is trying to convey. In psychological terms, anger is a secondary emotion – it always stems from another thought or feeling that is buried under it, protected by it. Beneath the outburst you will find the primary emotions, which may be disappointment, sadness, fear or worry. The female narrative around the 'good girl', who is not difficult, comes into direct conflict with the anger you are feeling, and that can be a battle for the ages. But this is where your hormones are so helpful – they push those under-feelings to the surface, inviting you to get angry about the right things, not redirecting it back at yourself. They give you the end-of-tether feeling to say: *Hang on a second, this is rubbish. Enough!* I always invite anger to the couch. I ask the client to imagine their anger as the Disney character from the superb movie *Inside Out*, which explains the functions of your emotions in the most relatable way. This helpful visual of anger, all red with its head on fire, can start the ball rolling on seeing why 'Anger' is angry. Anger is there to motivate you or give you the fire to express when you feel something unfair or wrong has occurred.

From my perspective, the perimenopause, rather than an unravelling, can become a very clear line in the sand of what you will and won't put up with anymore. With age, experience, and a body that has been overworked for years, we experience rage that feels so alien and unallowed. Many women tell me they can't stop crying and it is these two emotions that turn up in sessions, from pregnancy to postnatal anxiety to perimenopause. When sadness meets the rage and they are finally acknowledged and listened to, it may initially provoke trepidation and fear about self-identity and aspirations, highlighting the perceived gap between who you are now and who you aspire to be. Maybe this time is about pausing to question and to find the bridge back to your authentic self. The anxiety, panic attacks, doubt, sadness and overwhelm may be the red flags saying *This is not who or how I want to be; something has to change.* Questioning the speed of life and trying to do and have it all, but at the cost of what and to whom? Bringing it full circle back to wanting to be a relaxed woman, a rested woman, living a life aligned with your own values and with clear boundaries that protect your time and energy and joy.

The Practical Psychology

How do your hormones impact you?
Name the physical, emotional, mental and cognitive impact your hormones have upon you:

Physical: _____

Emotional: _____

Mental and cognitive: _____

Which phases or transitions in your life did you find challenging?
_____

If relevant:

Becoming pregnant: _____

Pregnancy: _____

Giving birth: _____

Post-labour: _____

If you feel you may be perimenopausal, what symptoms have you experienced and/or have surprised you? Remember nuance and list the good and bad.

_____

Let's invite in some emotions that may be present.
Have you noticed any sadness and if so, have you questioned what it is about?

_____

Have you experienced irritability, anger, shortened fuse and/or rage?

_____

Looking at it through the lens of compassion, what would you say to these emotions from a place of tender care?

_____

What are they communicating with you?

_____

What do they need?

_____

What support do you need?

_____

If you are post-menopausal, what did you find difficult and what has surprised you?

_____

PART 2
Revival mode

CHAPTER 7

How to leave survival mode

You did what was necessary to survive, physically, mentally, emotionally or all three. I saw an animation of a person holding a huge stone boulder over their head filled with words such as *worry, dread, anxiety, panic attack, trauma, frustration, loss of confidence*. The caption asked, 'Why are you holding that?' They looked confused, they could feel the weight of it now that they were made aware, but it had become their norm, and they were so disconnected from themselves they had no idea what to do next. I recognise this in what many clients say to me: 'I know it's there, but what do I do next, and how do I do it?' I'll let you in on a great psychological secret that I really want you to know, practise and embody. If you question why you, or anyone else, is behaving in a certain way, especially when it seems to be working against you, compassionately ask Why. *Why have I stayed in survival mode?* Move away from the frustration with yourself and stop being cruel by asking yourself, *Why can't I just stop or relax or forget?* Your body remembers, that's why. Have you ever noticed that your body brings emotions to the fore seemingly out of nowhere? And then you realise it is around a particular date, place, person or even smell that brings you back to a difficult experience?

Survival mode is the physiological and psychological adaptive state where your body and mind are fully focused on your survival needs in that moment. The goal is to protect you from perceived threats and danger. Your body physically responds in preparation with a release of the stress hormones cortisol and adrenaline, which heightens arousal. This is the state of hyperarousal that facilitates you to Fight, Flight, Freeze or Fawn, depending on the circumstances.

Why you go into survival mode makes sense, but why do you stay there? From my perspective, there are lots of reasons and they are systemic in nature. We have to look to the chronic experience of stress, financial worry, housing, childcare, physical and mental health crises. Your own and others' trauma, past and present, Big T and small t. Huge geopolitical uncertainty, wars and genocide in the world. Westernised consumerism, hyper-productivity, the environment, and the push towards individualistic culture. Everything is connected, we are all connected. We are numbing out emotional pain or processing emotions through use of substances or social media because the deeper conversations are veiled. Add to this the addictive quality of the stress hormones that lead to chronic overwhelm and stress becoming the 'normal' state, and relaxing, resting and having time to think feeling intolerable and painful. The irony of the loss of connection with ourselves and others is that it still adds pain and, rather than it going away, it demands we sit up and listen, often doing so dressed up as a panic attack or anxiety. But I am here to say this is an opportunity to explore what it means to live a life that feels safe and authentic for you. I hope that reading this book will make you understand the complexity of the toxic norm that isn't working for any of us and needs to change. That you will truly see how we are living in chronic survival mode.

The last year has changed me. I have always been a huge advocate for mental health, fairness, equity and equality in our world and our environment. Covid really highlighted our interconnectedness. I had always seen it, but it became crystal clear how our behaviours impact everyone in our world. Like our environmental problems, I see the level of chronic stress and mental distress rising like a hot thermometer. It isn't sustainable. Having worked for over 20 years with anxiety, panic attacks, trauma and how they show up in all our relationships, I have learned that learning how to leave survival mode is crucial because our nervous systems aren't built to be permanently 'on'. Understanding the many contributing factors and seeing clearly what you can do to learn how to regulate your nervous system takes the blame and shame away. You have the ability and autonomy to change, but there is some privilege in that, it may not be the same for everyone; some may continue to be in traumatising situations. Your goal is to access radical acceptance of where you are now and to take it one step at a time towards more neutral ground, so that you can engage and connect with others as if your very survival depended upon it.

This section is about your revival. You now know how to spot the patterns and usual suspects of anxiety, you know how it shows up in your thoughts and moods, and I am excited to share with you how to put all the practical psychology you are learning into your everyday life to make a real and lasting difference.

It's not your fault

If you watched the film *Good Will Hunting*, you will be familiar with the scene where Robin Williams, in the role of a therapist, repeatedly and with great compassion, says to Will (Matt Damon), 'It's not your fault, it's not your fault …'

Blame, shame, *Why can't I keep up like everyone else?* and inner frustration will only serve to keep you stuck and feeling rotten about yourself, your relationships and your life. You can't 'keep up' because relentless capitalism and consumerism is a machine that is wreaking havoc on our nervous systems. We've been fed the drug of chaos alongside a daily diet of addictive stress and, guess what? When it's all calm, that's when it feels most unnerving. And then we wonder why no one can sit still for more than a few seconds without picking up their phone.

Anxiety is not your fault. It's a reaction to triggers, past and present, and there's a genetic predisposition, too. But anxiety is telling you, loudly, that you want things to be different, that it's not working as it is, that you don't want to accept things as they are, that you have other needs and desires you would like to pursue and fulfil. Instead of fighting against anxiety, you might be surprised to discover that it is the one that has been holding its hand out, beckoning you to seek help, get support to rest, to recover and to process. It had to then proceed to waving bigger and redder flags to get your attention. The good news is you have seen the messages now and understand that anxiety may be your ally.

You have read all about survival mode – and you might have recognised a lot of yourself in there. You also know how insidious it is, how it can take up residence inside your body, and how it can be interwoven with early experiences in your life, and that means its roots go deep. While that is all true, you can heal and you can recover. If the idea of managing your anxiety and tackling its root causes makes you feel despairing or paralysed, ask for help. You don't have to do it alone.

As a psychologist, and as a human being, I love psychology because it makes sense. We are sense-makers. An odd word I hear from people when they talk about psychologists is that they 'poke' to get information. Nothing could be further from the truth. The evidence-based approach of compassionate inquiry is trauma-informed and takes into account the role of your neuropsychology and the mind–heart–body connection.

Laddering is a psychological way of uncovering people's core values and beliefs. Most kids do this exceptionally well by continually asking 'Why?' until you get to the absolute root of your beliefs – and the end of your patience if you are a parent. As explored earlier, our implicit beliefs can be inherited, learned, and very often they go unquestioned as we simply accept them as they are in our unconscious. Part of therapy is to perform compassionate laddering to understand why you believe X or why Y is important to you. It is like a guided walk around your own self, with the therapist there to make sure you don't step into mental and emotional quicksand. Through talk techniques like laddering, you can climb out of the pit of shame and self-doubt that has been feeding your anxiety and come to see that not only is it not your fault, there were lots of reasons why you responded as you did, often trauma or emotional injuries you may not have even been aware of, and that there is something you can do about it.

Hope can then bloom again.

Leaving survival mode

Is this the happy ending? No, it doesn't quite work like that, but it does get better. We met the SOS switch in Chapter 2, where you learned that you have the ability to move from survival to safety. This is our aim now, to enable you to use that switch as and when you need it to move towards safety.

But what must be made abundantly clear is that you won't ever be completely free of anxiety. That's not really a possible state as a human and, most important, anxiety will still exist because it is there to protect you. What you will learn is how to keep resetting, figuring out where you are now and where you want to get to by naming how you are – *I'm noticing that I've been feeling overwhelmed and my body feels tense. I need to do some things to move me out of survival mode back to feeling more grounded and settled in safety.* Like everything in life, it is a process, not a destination. Having no anxiety is not the goal. To never have a panic attack is not the end goal. 'Yes, it is,' you say to me. No, I promise you, it isn't. But each time you interrupt the anxiety and panic attack dominos, you are changing it and, much more important, you are building back trust where self-betrayal had set up permanent residence. Not only were all those negative and unhelpful thoughts living rent-free in your head, they had embedded and squatted down to live painfully in your body, giving you digestive issues, no energy and tension – and that was just for starters. The answer you are looking for is not what you think. Step away from the quick dopamine, the quick-fix 'control', the no-more-anxiety-ever-again fallacy, because it is making it worse.

Instead, we are going to focus on something much more sustainable. It is beautifully encapsulated by a single sentence by Gabor Maté: 'Safety is not the absence of threat. It is the presence of connection.' This line, to me, feels like what happens in a therapy session: I throw out the 'buoy' and the client grabs it. We connect in a moment of threat and upset. Life and all its uncertainty happens outside the therapy room. You need practical tools that you can rely upon that will support you when it all feels rotten, terrifying, frustrating and tough. In fact, it is especially in those challenging moments of anxiety that you step towards the very things that make you uncomfortable and learn that you can tolerate the distress more than the absolute desire to run and hide. Connection buffers and builds your ability to take those hard steps. It is exceptionally challenging, but championed with connection and compassion you can move towards what you need.

You do not have control over what will happen in your life. Bad things happen to good people; our lives can change in a moment, sometimes, unfortunately, irrevocably. If you can reach out in your vulnerability and seek help and share how you feel in the hardest, darkest moments, that connection can save you. The connection is first to yourself, your emotions, your experience. It is not reliant on anyone else, but having your experience validated and understood by others fosters connection that brings that essential human connectedness that we do actually need in our deepest desire to be accepted as we are and to belong. It takes immense courage to share how you feel, it takes courage to share the parts of yourself that you keep hidden. When vulnerability meets empathy, we connect.

I know this is a challenging idea. I know you might be thinking: *What do you mean? What's the point if 'it' or the panic, overwhelm or excessive worrying doesn't completely disappear?* Anxiety is like grief – it doesn't disappear, but you grow around it. Why? Because you have no choice. But with anxiety, dread, anticipatory anxiety and overwhelm you do have some choices, and you can change how you interact with them. There is a way, it might just take a different route than you expected. Let's say you feel back in control in situations that previously made you want to flee; you will heal that one thing and then find yourself activated by other people or situations. This is not a message to dishearten; it is honest and helpful. The goal is to notice, name what is present, and adapt in a way that is healthy. In a way, you are going into observant scientist mode; you don't become upset or frustrated that you have anxiety again and say mean things to yourself, but you do say, *I'm noticing that I am anxious, what do I need to do next that will help?* And sometimes less is more.

Coming home to you

What if anxiety is the vehicle to your homecoming, your return to your self? What if anxiety is part of the solution? This is a completely different way of looking at it – and it might feel counterintuitive to you – but I do believe that anxiety serves a purpose: it forces you to stop and listen, it urges you to make changes, it tells you to prioritise your healing and growth and mental health. It is not fighting with you, an age-old enemy; no, it is trying to alert you to perceived and real threats on the horizon. What if it wants to help you get to a place of safety?

It is in safety where you can flourish, grow, and heal. Learning how to connect, feel, process and practise self-awareness and compassion creates a profoundly new relationship with yourself that embodies a different way to live in your mind and body. Where you can once again tune into the instinctive knowledge provided by the messages of interoception that tell you when and what upset you. Interoception, also known as the eighth sense, is part of your inner senses. It refers to the inner cues that tell you how you feel on the inside, so you can tell when you are hungry, tired, or how you feel. Part of the work will also be to befriend these inner signals as they can be too keenly noted when you are in a state of anxiety and are hyper-aware of your inner body, from your heartbeat to knowing you feel too hot or are sweating, having palpitations, breathing fast or feeling dizzy.

Neuroception refers to the subconscious process that your nervous system uses to detect cues for safety and threat in your environment. You are not even aware of it, and yet it influences your thoughts and behaviours. A face that seems friendly leaves you feeling safe and you connect and socially engage easily with them. Whereas if you pick up a tone or facial gesture that seems threatening, your body may feel in a heightened physiological state and stress. Dysregulation of neuroception due to trauma and being in chronic survival mode can make it difficult to perceive safety. Cultivating regulation and healthier interoception and neuroception can be part of your path back to safety. This is what leaving survival mode looks like: it's noticing and differentiating when you find yourself habitually going into defence mode or feeling on edge or thinking everyone dislikes you. *What did she mean by that? Why did he look at me like that?* Being able to read and interpret whether you are safe or in danger is a huge part of moving towards a revival where your body isn't always switched on and looking for the next bad thing to happen, from a panic attack to losing your cool. When we are connected to those inner cues, it makes emotional regulation much easier because it is interoception that communicates to you your body's state. Unfortunately, losing that inner compass – often drowned out by the voices of others (family, society, social media, and all the *you shoulds, you shouldn'ts*) – is exceptionally easy. Coming back to understanding your body and interoceptive cues is like bringing a nervous system translator to help you distinguish between what is a threat and what is a real danger.

This homecoming brings your heart, mind and body into a place of safety. I didn't say *back* to a place of safety because many have never known what it feels like to be safe in their body. You may not initially recognise yourself in that last line, but can I ask you how you find relaxing or resting or, even bigger still, being by yourself with your own thoughts? If the idea of those things brings on a sense of dread, it may be that you have been living in survival mode, never knowing a true sense of safety. Rather than a nervous system, imagine how different life would be if you had a calm system. Ask yourself: What would that look like for you?

Author and teacher Cory Muscara put it beautifully: 'We want to meet our emotional pain in bits (titration) and develop skills to re-ground when we feel overwhelmed (pendulation).' The concepts of titration and pendulation are two words to become familiar with as they take the 'all or nothing' sting out of our perception of progress as linear. Clients are often deeply frustrated when they think they are going backwards when they meet inevitable difficulties. If you invite yourself to change how you approach emotional pain or trauma, you can consciously adopt a gradual and gentle approach, in smaller, more manageable doses (titration), in terms of how you experience it in your body (somatic experiencing), to avoid it being triggering, re-traumatising, or flooding your nervous system. Intentionally integrating interventions bit by bit allows the somatic processing of difficult emotions and experiences.

If you've ever played music, you may know what a pendulum or a metronome looks like and that it helps the musician practise a rhythmic beat as it swings back and forth, cultivating control and consistency. In therapy, pendulation, a term coined by Dr Peter Levine in 2010,[30] speaks of the rhythmic movement that occurs as you fluctuate between different states when activated and anxious or overwhelmed, self-regulating back to calm and feeling grounded. This is what I mean by becoming aware when you are in that anxious state and learning how to move, using your inner GPS, towards regulation and safety bit by bit. It's worth repeating: the goal of your nervous system isn't to be calm all the time, it is about learning, practising, and noticing when it feels too high (Fight, Flight) or too low (Freeze, Fawn) and to move back to feeling regulated with compassion and flexibility.

While you are reading this book, pay attention to the experience of the impact of the words in your body. When you read something that 'hits home', where does it hit? Do you feel it in your back, neck, shoulders, throat, head, chest, or stomach? Somatic experiencing is a therapeutic approach developed by Peter Levine that teaches clients how to track and regulate how anxiety and trauma show up in the body using body-centred awareness.[31] We know it shows up in the mind, and as clients start to explore painful experiences, I gently ask them where they feel it in the body, and what it feels like, facilitating the gradual resolution of stored physical and emotional tension and unresolved trauma through titration and pendulation. I help them to choose their own psychological toolbox (see page 328), that they can use when they feel dysregulated to create an internal safe space or support outside themselves, most often a combination of both.

The concept of pendulation helps you learn how to identify when you are overwhelmed and what to do to feel safe and grounded in your own body again. Cory describes creating this safety as a 'homebase'. I love this, and the word that came to mind for me as well is showing you how to cultivate your own 'homesense' through using your inner sense of what 'home' feels like to you in your own body. When the emotions are swinging too hard and it feels overwhelming, you need to know how to catch that with compassion and ground yourself back into your senses in a way that feels safe for you. My job is to show you how, and to reassure you that you will have your own inner guiding voice as you take the action necessary for what you want and need. The following chapters have plenty of practical techniques for you to regain your own 'homesense' when you need to do that.

The heart of the matter

That, in a nutshell, is my reason and aim in writing this book: I do not want you to walk away from this book feeling tickled intellectually – *Oh, that's very interesting* – I want you to walk away with the practical knowledge of how to integrate your mind and body. I want you to know how to feel safer and more connected more of the time. This will take time and a lot of practice and self-compassion, but you can heal, you can recover, and you can find yourself again, and again. You have to feel to heal, it isn't 'all in your head' (another clanger), it is also in your body. You have heard this line, but this is so important for you to realise because this is where you need to go to make the changes you have wanted to make for years. Blocking doesn't just happen online; it can be a protective inside job when thinking about it is too much. This can come as a surprise to clients, when they genuinely say at the start of the process, 'I had a very happy childhood'. I think it is impossible to give such a black-and-white answer, life is much more nuanced, much more specific to how it was for you. The 'good' or 'bad' narrative gives a flat answer, whereas people's lives have depth from years of experience. Think about what they ask you at a job interview: 'How many years' experience do you have?'

It also cuts your experiences into whether you see yourself as a success or failure, or as good or bad. This dichotomous idea is limited and flawed. When I paint, it is the contrast that defines the space in a painting. Examples of this necessary duality are present in our daily lives, too, as the dark of night opens to the dawn of a new day; there is time for growth, letting go, death and the rebirth of spring. It can't be summer all the time. So why do we expect to live in this neverland of happiness or to stay the same? Widening this rigid and unhelpful narrative brings compassion to how experiences are for you.

Comparison is the thief of joy in far more ways than you might think. Empathy, compassion, being present and listening to someone's experience is a hard thing to do. Naturally, you want to add in your thoughts or experiences and you can, I suggest, if you want to help someone, hold that space for them. This is hugely missing in our society. We are in a perpetual hyper-fixing mode – *Have you tried …? Did you see …?* – rather than sitting with how something is for yourself or for others. That is a practice we have become unaccustomed to and uncomfortable with. Listening is a challenge I compassionately set for you. Start to notice how much you want to interrupt or add to what someone is sharing with you. Then consciously choose silence and see how that feels and how it impacts the interaction. This action of being still and tuning in is part of the antidote to being stuck in striving.

I see too many people who are stuck in 'survive' while the concept of 'thriving' is shoved down our throats every moment of the day, wrapped in that toxic message of 'Do more, be more'. Can you see how you've been robbed of the joy and peace of taking time to just be? Productivity and competitive comparison have become the ultimate peace-destroyers. Social media is now the epicentre of damaging comparison, a constant stream of other lives to watch and measure yours against. But if you are comparing yourself to people who have teams behind them, the poison of *never enough* starts before your feet have hit the ground in the morning. It's unrelenting.

This is why we are not aiming for 'thriving' here – that is an abstract concept that is certainly not 'one size fits all'. The idea of reviving is to give back to yourself. It might be to accept yourself as you are, and that's not as easy as you'd think. To rebel against the grind, and to live a life that feels more aligned with how you want to live. The revival is to breathe life back into who you are in a gentle, non-striving way. To ask yourself daily, *What do I like? What would I like to do today?*, to stop striving for eternal happiness and instead look for more moments of joy that glimmer throughout the day. Noticing the small moments that warm you, that nourish you, that connect you to yourself and others. This is the revival I hope for you. With work and patience and compassion you can move out of constant surviving, feel more in control of your body states, and exercise more choice in how you respond to what you feel. You can revive that sense of connection and control that has been eroded over time. When you notice and are aware, that is when you can use the practical tools described in this section to regulate your emotions and feel a greater sense of confidence in yourself. It's not a script for 'happiness' or some sort of perma-calm state, it's simply the means by which you can reset that inner compass so that it can guide you effectively.

What will it be like to exit survival mode?

After a fright, a shock, or an intense emotional experience, have you noticed that you experience an energy crash? We've colloquialised this experience with phrases like 'Then I crashed and burned' or 'I burned the candle at both ends.' I warn clients after the first session that they will feel exhausted, and prescribe them sleep, if possible. I've personally experienced this due to ongoing demands, not by choice. Something similar happens when you undertake the work described here and it's very important for you to know that as you exit survival mode, you will not be met with abundant energy and the best feelings of 'I did it', even though you did. When you have been living inside a chronic state of Fight or Flight, it's only natural that changing from that takes a toll on you. You learn how to accept the feelings and sensations present and tolerate them being there, but before that you have a whole host of catching up and emotions that need to be processed, wept over, allowed, grieved and released as you peel back each layer of who you thought you were, which may have been who you had to become to survive.

Take a moment to let that sentence settle.

I think tolerate is a great word – we met it before in the theory of distress tolerance (see page 112). In a dopamine-fuelled society of quick fixes, eternal positivity, 'just be happy' and FOMO, the truth is that we are missing out, and on so much. We are missing out on quiet and silence; space to repair, process and heal; space to hear and attune to what our body and mind are telling us. We are missing out by feeling the relentless drive and pull for more and the fallacy of future happiness (in the form of if–then thinking: *if I get this new role, then I will be happy*). We are missing out on calmness, ease, and the joy of being. We are missing out on rest and recovery. What we are lacking is showing up in bodies that ache and hurt and are tense, and our minds are the same.

Hyper-productivity is a disease that capitalism profits from. Companies use baited expressions such as we need to be 'delighting the shareholders' in order to pressure their employees to work even longer hours for them to increase corporate profits. Our priorities are in the wrong place. We need to not only question but to push against what we have been sold as 'normal'. I ask you one question: What are you willing to sacrifice? If you have been sacrificing your own self, your own wants, and needs, if you are weary of sacrifice and can see no end to it, it is time to recognise that you are living in survival mode – and that you want to change that. If you have been living with anxiety, trying to push it away, damp it down, control it, hate it, reason with it, then you are exhausted. If you want things to change, for your own sake and the sake of those you love, it is time to take a long, hard look at who you are and how you are – and how you would like to be. That is exactly what revival mode is – it is your chance to switch the priorities, switch the lens and the perspective, and to learn to switch from survival to safety.

All of this is acknowledged with the awareness that there is no happy state that we can live inside happily-ever-after. We all know the life truth: bad things happen. There is no way around that fact, no matter how much we try to numb it out; life will serve us all painful and difficult times. What we can do, though, is not live in fear of that fact. Because the other truth is that pain and discomfort give us a lot of information. If you are numb to physical pain and you have an injury, the likelihood of doing more damage is higher if the pain is masked. It is important to not pathologise all pain. Our emotions serve functions with important messages. If we never sit with the harder or more uncomfortable feelings, we won't have developed those skills to be able to tolerate it with others. Forewarned is forearmed, as they say, so it is best to know and accept that you can't eradicate anxiety or unexpected and unhappy events from your life. But you can meet them from a better place, where you are internally aligned with your true self, and swing back and forth to a safer pace and place, where you know how to accept the bad along with the good, where you are not constantly in hyperarousal or hypoarousal, where you have the tools to calm and regulate yourself. It's simply a case of being better able to live within the truth of life, with all its beauties and difficulties. So that is my bittersweet twist on what it is like to leave survival mode.

The Practical Psychology

Try this quick and effective technique when you need to interrupt anxiety:

- Breathe in – *I am safe* …
- Breathe out – … *even if I don't feel it yet.*
- Breathe in – *I am safe.*
- Breathe out anxiety, panic, fear.
- Breathe in – *I am safe, I am safe.* (Place your hand on our heart as you say this.)

CHAPTER 8

The great disconnect: Unhealthy defence mechanisms

Compassion starts at home, in your body, mind and soul. It isn't about seeing yourself as an ongoing 'self-improvement' project and getting stuck in weaponised wellness. Life is nuanced. Tolerating and embracing imperfection and the mess of holding many truths and emotions simultaneously is the ultimate in human honesty. You can love being a mother and still need space. You may feel overwhelmed yet capable, happy yet frustrated. Rather than trying to mould yourself into something new, you can radically accept, understand and manage all parts of yourself.

Please don't swap survival mode with striving. True compassion starts with accepting who you are, and why. That's the first step. You can't simply scrub out the bits you don't like – instead, you need to accept, talk, figure out all the parts and then learn how to manage them in a way that makes sense and is meaningful for you. No one likes this bit; the shinier version of the 'quick fix' is so much more appealing. 'Do this for a few weeks and you will look and feel completely different!' is a damaging and dishonest sell. Remember my B&B (see page 162)? It is doing the boring and basic most days that garners the results that align with how you want to be. Naturally, you must also factor in being human and the fact that life usually delivers unforeseen events, sickness, relationship issues and so on. If you don't factor these in, you will feel you are failing, but you are not.

This chapter is about having a revealing, compassionate and constructive private check-in: identifying, naming, and separating out the parts of you that were there to protect you, but have now become unhelpful and unhealthy defence mechanisms. The starting point of those mechanisms was survival and to protect you. The problem arises when you are stuck in hypervigilance as you keep looking out for perceived threats, leading to behaviours to avoid embarrassment, failure or a panic attack. You knit a comfort blanket of habits and wrap it tightly around you, to keep yourself safe, to keep the feared thing at bay. Not only did it serve a function, can you see that it makes a whole lot of sense?

These 'habits' were defence mechanisms and trauma responses. They served a purpose. So can you take the blame, pain and shame given to by yourself, and to you by family or society, and put it down? Please acknowledge what it was like to go through what you went through. Even if something happened in your family, you each had a different experience of it, because every experience is unique. Where you want to get to now is to move out of simply intellectually knowing that it put your nervous system under stress, accepting that you are living it, and make integrated, somatic, body-based changes that fully embody who you are and how you want to live. Don't get stuck in feeling bad for doing things you wish you wouldn't keep doing. Think about what you have learned so far and reflect upon the neurophysiology of inbuilt survival and how your body instinctively and unconsciously responds. The job at hand is to explore what needs to go, but without any self-blame or flagellation. Learning how to override (when safe) your inbuilt system for avoiding threat and danger is an active practice. This is an inside job, and you are stepping into the driver's seat. Buckle up and let's go.

Stop deadheading your emotions

My mum loves gardening, and she tells me how satisfying it is to pull out a weed by the roots. If we imagine our daily lives as a garden, we can picture anxiety as the weeds that are constantly trying to grow up around the flowers and choke them. The weeds want to take over. If we deadhead the flowering weed – hey presto! – the garden looks neat and tidy and blooming again. The problem is that the root is still in the ground and it will immediately begin growing again. 'Deadheading' can come in the form of the positive spin, like advice that starts with the words 'just', 'relax', 'don't be anxious', 'don't worry' or 'be positive'. It can also come in the form of minimising your thoughts, feelings, and experiences: *It's not that bad*; *Others have it worse* and – the worst offender – *What doesn't kill you makes you stronger*. In my considered, trauma-informed opinion, not only is this incorrect, it is utter rubbish. This type of thinking, which skirts around the actuality of your inner life, causes damage to you. As you actively stuff your emotions even further down, trying to beat them into submission, you end up feeling bad for feeling them in the first place. This puts you at war with yourself. Burying how you feel will not work. I know you know this intellectually; I am talking to your emotions here.

How do you deadhead and minimise your thoughts and feelings? I know it's not only other people saying it to you. Most people I see are excruciatingly fed up with themselves as they take in the public façade of everyone else who seems to be able to cope with everything. Trust me, one thing I know as a psychologist is that the public and private pictures can be quite different. Why? Because there is so much pressure to look as if you are coping. Society is more interested in how things look in the short term than how a person feels. Wanting the quick fix makes sense but it doesn't ever work. It's always down to trying what works for you and your nervous system and understanding that this is an ongoing, adaptive, dynamic work-in-progress. Life and you are always changing. It is a myth, and a dangerous one, to believe that you can make a one-off change to your health and that's it, done. As I have mentioned, I often say to clients who are upset that they are 'back at therapy' that they don't feel the same way when they go back to the GP if they get sick again. The difference I feel is that there is less blame and shame when it comes to physical health – there is still some, but it seems to feel more personal when it comes to our mental health, which is affected by such a multitude of contributing factors. The work is to actively do something about them. You don't feel like it's a personal failure when the weeds grow, you just notice them and go about getting to the root of that particular weed, knowing full well more weeds will grow again and there is no personal fault within that either, it's a normal process of growth and life. Placing this idea beside our mental health, I ask you to not deadhead the emotional cues. Instead, use the trigger, understand and bring compassion to the anger and seek to do something that restores, regulates and heals. Then do it on repeat with care and kindness.

Numbing out

There is a sweet seduction to numbing out all the noise and pretending it's not even there. We all do it, to one degree or another. There are so many ways to do it as well – with alcohol, drugs, or retail therapy, or screens, or sex. The modern world offers us so many enticing opportunities to get outside our heads and stop thinking. It's very hard to resist. When I hit the Instagram refresh button and see the circular timer move as it prepares to bring me something new and shiny, I feel like Pavlov's dogs, hungrily anticipating my 'reward'. When it comes to any kind of activity that we compulsively engage in that gives a quick reward and also has negative consequences, it comes under the 'numbing out' umbrella. We are looking for that dopamine hit it delivers and we are looking to distract, ignore and numb out the overwhelming thoughts and uncomfortable feelings. As you look at your To Do list, it's easy to swap it for a mindless scroll. Let's be honest and not vilify numbing out because we all do it; shame is not allowed here and it's not going to help. I'm much more interested in why we feel the need to numb in the first place.

We'll look at screen addiction mainly here because it's the one very many can relate to and often confess to with embarrassment in the therapy room, but this discussion applies to whatever you might be using.

Let's be perfectly blunt – your phone can be a drug to which you are addicted. Is that the case for you? Is it stealing your peace of mind, your time and your focus? What we have at our fingertips is one heck of an addictive behaviour loop: not only does your brain like it, your body craves it too. The reward is chemical, it's a pleasure hit, and with FOMO hanging over you as well, you don't want to miss a moment, a clarion call of breaking news – you want it all. And yet the reality is, we are missing out. How many times has someone – maybe even your child – been talking to you, but your attention is fractured and you're only half-listening to them? You are there and not-there because your phone is taking your focus and attention.

DO YOU HAVE A SCREEN ADDICTION?

I will not be burning my phone at the stake, but the time is well overdue to be real about the impact on our brains being permanently 'on':

- How many times does your phone distract you every day?
- What do you struggle with most?
- Do you get annoyed at how much you reach for your phone?
- Do you find it difficult to initiate a task you need to do and notice you reach for the phone instead?
- How difficult do you find it to stay on task?
- Think and write down how the phone impacts you and your day.

It is also worth noting the psychologically charged words used by social media: *Status, Like, Friend Request.* These are the words of 'connection' and 'belonging' and they activate our primal need to be liked and accepted by the tribe. The entire set-up of social media platforms is specifically designed to appeal to us deeply, to call us in sweetly, and then to unleash a wide arsenal of weapons to keep us there, craving our hits and rewards. It's a pretty fearsome opponent. When the weekly time notification pops up on your phone, it can be a bit angst-inducing. It can feel a little like the warning on a cigarette box or on the bottle of alcohol. It's your weekly slap on the wrist: 'We told you it is addictive, and you are doing this to yourself.'

I think dual responsibility is needed. Getting back your focus, attention and concentration isn't as easy as you think. These apps also have a responsibility. Are you controlling your devices and what they take from you, or are they controlling you? Peek behind the curtain at the tech giants, and it's very likely you will find that they are playing the tunes as we follow the tech Pied Piper. This entertainment-based way of getting and keeping our attention is insidious and deeply effective. I was watching the series *Painkiller* one night, and the Richard Sackler character played by Matthew Broderick said something that was so chilling and it made me think of our widespread addiction to numbing out: 'All of human behaviour is essentially comprised of two things, running away from pain and towards pleasure. Pain, pleasure, pain, pleasure, it is the very essence of what it means to be human ... if we place ourselves right there between pain and pleasure, then we have changed the world.' Those words leapt out at me and made me think about how we numb, why we numb and why we fear feeling.

Here's the thing, and it's unfortunate: it's very hard to make good choices and changes and a lot easier to make bad ones. I wish this wasn't the case, but it is. If you want to tackle this, it's important to stay aware of where your attention goes. You've heard of intellectual capital and emotional capital, added to these is attention capital. You need to think about how to protect and invest your attentional capital in what is a fiercely competitive market, where so many different things are vying for your attention.

WE'RE ALL SCREENING INSIDE

I have noticed this in my own home, and I hear it a lot from clients as well – there is a 'witching hour' that hits most homes every evening. I have noticed my own tolerance level dip around those evening hours of dinner prep, activities, taxi ferrying and homework. For me, it's all the noise, from the TV and from the devices. As I am speed-peeling potatoes, answering homework questions and fielding moods and post-school meltdowns, against a background of high-pitched voices from the TV that sound like they are talking at 1.5 speed, I can feel my stress levels rising as the over-stimulation begins to fill my body. But it's not just the noise. Whenever I listen to the noise targeted at children and teens via whatever digital device they use, the psychologist in me is appalled by what they are being fed on a constant drip. It is high-octane, high-pitched, and highly emotive 'content' assailing their senses and emotions. The content from TV to screens is dysregulating and makes them anything but content. Every character is either incensed or having a panic attack; it's like having a bystander panic attack.

That's what I notice most of all – the call upon their emotions. It's an emotive tactic, drawing them in with shouting, tears, sadness, hysteria, anger, frustration and exasperation, and it's a tactic that works. I'd love to see an fMRI scan to see the impact it is having on their developing brain. (A functional MRI (fMRI) is a special kind of brain scan that shows which parts of your brain are active when you're doing different things, like thinking, moving or feeling.) It's like an emotional net that catches kids and keeps them stuck in this highly reactive state. It is anything but calm and the impact of it creates inner chaos and sensory overload. It is a bombardment of their senses, but it is also the speed at which their brains have to manage the constant switching that leaves them twitching. We all know they are feeding kids 'shorts' all the time and using highly emotive voices and speed or urgency in their content to fight for their attention. Yes, the cute videos are nice, but I have noticed how they use emotionally evocative content to anchor the viewer and keep them watching. Then the algorithms keep serving up more and more of it. It has the effect of a sort of paralysis – a digital loop feeding frenzy that's going on around your child as they sit immobilised at the centre of it.

The children seem to tune out completely, not hearing you if you call, not even feeling hunger until the screen is turned off. It holds them captive as their hearts and brains race to keep up with the constantly changing flow of information and images. It's important to start to notice this, to pay attention to the effect it has on you and on your family members. I have trained myself to notice the impact of the onslaught of virtual (and yet very real) noise on my body. I recognise when my window of tolerance is closing in. I can see the wavy pattern as my thoughts speed up and my patience goes down and irritability takes hold. If we imagine it like an emotional weather forecast, I can now see the change in the incoming conditions and realise quickly that I need to act now. That's the point we all need to reach – realising what is happening and deciding how we want to handle it, and that applies to every one of us, of every age.

Regulating the witching hours

Sometimes, at these stressful moments, I simply walk into the garden and take a few deep breaths. Removing yourself from the environment is a powerful antidote to what's happening in that environment. It's simple and effective. From personal experience I can also recommend Loop earplugs. These are great for parents; you can hear exactly what your children are saying, but it just turns the background volume down. Think about the pinch points across your day, when those 'witching hours' occur that you find it difficult to navigate, and think about what would support you to cope with those moments in your day.

Pinch points in your day	Practical ways to prepare/support/protect
Dinnertime	Prepare meals in advance or have quick and easy nutritious dinners, batch cook or use leftovers, meal plan/prep for your busy days/evenings. If you have the time, some weeks you will be a batch queen – the next week, not so much.
Transitions (school, activities, etc.)	Have one set place for all the paraphernalia for the different activities to live (helmets, hurls, gum shields, etc.) where it can be found by everyone.
Noise	Encourage quiet time, e.g. no phones/devices while eating, two hours before bed. Create connection time with no phones, like a movie night, so it's a connecting experience. Bring mindfulness to when their mood changes and why: is it from what is being consumed digitally or on the TV? Encourage boredom, expect resistance.
Overwhelm	Can you add in consistent rest time before the busy times in your day? Even 3–5 minutes will help.
Deep work time	Turn notifications off and turn 'Do not disturb' on to maximise your working time.

Create your own phone plan that puts you in control
Morning routine
Instead of peeling open your eyes and thinking *What have I missed?*, which sets up the brain to scan all day, try this:

- Take a deep breath and release
- Come into your body
- Feet on the floor
- Go outside and get some sunlight into you
- Heel drops (see page 330)
- Challenge – eat your breakfast without your phone.
- Compassion – acknowledge it's a hard habit to change and spend some quality time attending to you.
- Start by choosing three mornings you would like to do this. Remember, everything needs to be sustainable.
- Breathe in, connect with yourself, breathe out.

Night-time routine
Instead of bleary-eyed scrolling:

- Check in with you.
- Write out anything you need to get out of your head. Leave it on the page and out of your brain.
- Do a body scan. Lie on your bed and go through your body from your head down or toes up, noticing any areas of tension. Notice any sensations of wanting to check out and catch up with friends or scroll out. With compassion, notice how challenging it can be to start winding down, especially if this is the first time you have done it today. Bring compassion to this, recognise that it is good that you are challenging and changing in new ways, and that it is not easy. Give space to the fact that it is hard.

- Turn the lights down, light a candle (if safe – don't fall asleep!), read, wash your face, teeth, etc. I know you do this already, but doing it mindfully is a different experience.
- Keep your room clear and uncluttered. (Chuck stuff in a basket if necessary and put it outside the door.)
- Give yourself permission to be finished for the day. This means that while not everything may be finished, you are choosing to rest and sleep.

Pausing anxiety

Don't forget that you have the power to hit the Pause button. Say to yourself: *Okay, I am feeling overwhelmed, hot, hungry, I've reached my noise threshold limit, there are too many things being asked of me at once. I have reached the end of my tolerance.*

When you name the problem, you can activate your self-regulating tools, which brings a greater sense of control. In therapy, we 'name what is in the room.' For me, I check in: *Okay, feeling a bit frazzled now, what can I do next?* I take a deep breath, acknowledge how I feel, meet the moment with some compassion: if I'm feeling tired and frustrated, I get a glass of water and a snack as I know I get 'hangry'. Water in, blood sugar stabilised, the next thing I can tackle is the noise. I ask for the TV and other devices to be turned down or stick in my ear plugs. It's very simple: you put your needs first and ask for them to be met. You breathe. You pause the environment and reset it. It's straightforward but powerfully effective. Look within and look around your environment and see what you can control from the inside out.

Flooding and information overload

Sune Lehmann, a physicist and professor at the Department of Applied Mathematics and Computer Science of the Technical University of Denmark, became acutely aware that he was losing his ability to focus. He wondered, as I did, if it was simply to do with ageing – was it a case of grumpy oldster shouting 'Turn down that TV!'? As he delved deeper into it, however, he moved away from the micro-picture of his own reactions and posed a new, macro question: what if it is our collective attention span that is shrinking? 'Flooding' is a term that describes what happens when your brain feels emotionally hijacked and overwhelmed. This can often happen mid-argument, when you are wound up and emotional and your racing mind is trying to think of how to express your emotions. Those emotions are getting in the way of their own expression, though. When your heart rate goes over 100 bpm, the prefrontal cortex gets flooded and this cuts off the ability to connect to the logical, thinking part of your brain. That's the emotional overload we so often read about. But Lehmann suggested there is a flooding that occurs from too much information swamping our brains all at once. He described the effect of this type of flooding as having a deeply negative impact on our ability to focus.

It's easy to see how this dynamic works in our modern lives. The smartphone in our pocket serves as a gateway to a vast universe of information, continuously buzzing with updates, videos, comments, and stories. It's incessant, never granting a moment's rest. Many of my clients express a simultaneous attraction to and repulsion from the news sometimes because it can trigger their own trauma and is sometimes too much. The constant stream can be highly triggering, igniting intense emotional reactions that often find no outlet, as the news leaves us feeling powerless to enact change.

However, since we have become the first generation to witness a live-streamed genocide in Gaza, the landscape of information consumption has transformed drastically, and so has my opinion in relation to it needing to affect you and to activate change within you. Having a lot of experience and hearing the personal stories from traumatised and displaced asylum-seekers in Ireland who were victims and prisoners of war and genocide, it has been a very different experience to bear witness from afar. I spent the first while in disbelieving horror – *How was this happening, why wasn't it being stopped?* – but then felt activated to know that we can enact change. Whenever natural disasters had occurred in the past, I'd always encouraged others to see the 'upstanders' – the medical staff, the police, all there working as one to correct and protect and for us to do what we could and donate. In the wake of this social and human injustice, a fervent call for justice has emerged, sparking a wave of worldwide peaceful heart-led activism that transcends individualistic concerns. This collective movement reflects a shift towards communal empathy and action, where individuals unite in their commitment to social change. The digital sphere, once a platform for incessant updates and distractions, now serves as a catalyst for meaningful dialogue and mobilisation. As societal issues rightly demand our attention, individuals are compelled to channel their emotions and energy into constructive engagement, standing up and actively fostering a culture of collective caring, activism and action.

The world is always changing, there have always been power struggles and many egregious wrongs throughout history that we don't seem to learn from. I would have said to clients to be mindful of their digital information consumption, and I still think this, but in the context of my hope for this book in changing how we are living, a big part of it is challenging the systems that are oppressive. An unveiling has occurred as people's hearts have been activated and this soft revolution I speak of is unfurling where everyday people are standing up and saying No.

Being mindful of what I have just said above, as you answer the following questions, categorise your digital consumption into parts that you can let go of and see which parts call to you to move towards collective care, community and action.

The Practical Psychology

DIGITAL INFORMATION

What are you consuming and why?

_____

What do you get out of it?

_____

Does it make you feel more or less in control or both?

_____

What is consuming you and your thoughts?

_____

Your mind and your body are not separate. What you think affects how you feel, not just emotionally but physically.

Think of the last shocking thing you read, saw, or heard on the news.

Where in your body did it hit you?

_____

Did you gasp?

_____

Did your heartbeat increase?

_____

What emotion did it elicit? Disgust, fear, worry, helplessness, horror, despair?
_____

Did it affect your feelings towards people, or your sense of hope for the world?
_____

Did it instil fear for the future?
_____

Did it bring worry or anxious thoughts?
_____

Was it triggering for you?
_____

Or did it worry you that you didn't feel anything or were desensitised by what you read or saw?
_____

Or did it motivate you to think beyond yourself and to move from the perspective of 'I can't look at this, it is so upsetting' – to 'We need to do something to help?'
_____

Was there something you could do?
_____

How did you feel when you made a change?
_____

We discussed personal activation within our own nervous system. Social activation, particularly in response to social and human injustice, can be collectively healing. Rather than negatively impacting mental health, this activation may stem from our innate drive to survive, belong, and engage socially. The horror of genocide highlights the importance of human connection and our sense of meaning and purpose in mental health. Moving people away from mindless pursuit of numbing out with consumerism for things that we don't need to connecting back to our deepest realisation that people matter. As Gabor Maté has told us, 'Safety is not the absence of threat but the presence of connection' – a line worth repeating to ourselves as we absorb and read distressing news and to funnel that energy into collective action, protecting humanity and worldwide healing.

What can you do to down-regulate your nervous system after hearing difficult, upsetting, and tragic news?

Recognise the impact it has on you, your mood, your emotions, and physical state.

———————————————————————————

Notice what thoughts you are having about life, people, tragedy, the world, loss of control.

———————————————————————————

What does it mean to you specifically?

———————————————————————————

Is there anything you can do to help?

———————————————————————————

What support can you get?

_____

If you are doing something to help, are you surprised at the positive impact it is having upon you?

_____

Have you found a new group of like-minded people or a sense of community that may have been lacking?

_____

Remember – you are allowed to reduce the amount of news you consume. That remains your choice. Like everything in life, taking breaks, getting enough rest and using the resources available to you is important.

If you feel too full of information, do this:

- Choose to disconnect from all your digital devices. Breathe in through your nose. As you breathe in, imagine breathing clear space into your brain. Place your hands on either side of your head if that helps you to connect to the experience.
- Breathe out anything you need to let go of.
- Stretch your arms up and out.
- Breathe space into your throat, and release.
- Place your hand on each place as you go if it feels comfortable.
- Breathe space into your chest and lungs, and release.
- Breathe space into your heart, and release.
- If you need to cry, let it go.
- Breathe space into your stomach, and release.
- If you feel angry, tend to that feeling.
- Breathe space into your pelvis.

- Breathe space into your legs and into your feet that support you and keep you grounded.
- If you can, stand barefoot on the ground or grass.
- End by taking in what you need …
- … and releasing what you don't.

What can you do to facilitate reducing your daily content?

_____

Could you set a daily time limit on how much digital information you consume, nearly like a daily digital content intake allowance?

_____

What practical things can you do to help with distressing news?

_____

Which apps or digital platforms do you struggle with most?

_____

What small change might be helpful?

_____

DIGITAL REDUCTION OPTIONS:
- Subscribe to a newspaper.
- Disable news notifications.
- Allocate an hour for focused work on a single task.
- Set aside 30 minutes for task switching.

This is a daily practice, challenging but ultimately the path forward.

Take a dual approach by asking 'What can I do?' and taking action on that while being mindful of the things you still have to do in your everyday life, even if you don't want to. This can help pull in more focused space. This change from individualistic focus to caring for others collectively is a change that is badly needed.

When being online leaves you feeling that you aren't doing enough as you compare yourself to others, pause when you notice a change in your mood or cues from your body:

- Are you comparing yourself?
- Is it making you feel you are not doing enough?
- Is it making you feel better or worse?
- How is it impacting your energy?
- Is it making you feel angsty or anxious?
- Look out for body cues – are you hunching your shoulders?
- Are you holding your breath?
- Do you have any tension in your body? If so, where?
- Is your jaw clenched?

Why it is hard to stay focused?

In today's world, it can be exceptionally hard to maintain focus, even when you desperately want and need to. Sometimes staying focused on task with concentration feels like trying to hold water in my hands: impossible and frustrating. With every beeping interruption, every brain-rousing notification, the struggle to not reach for the phone is very real. Sometimes, for the craic, I count how many seconds pass before I am interrupted. It doesn't take long to lose count. I know I am not alone in this; it is especially difficult if you work from home. If your phone and other digital devices keep interrupting your gargantuan effort at doing whatever it is you are trying to do, it's kind of torturous.

In *Stolen Focus*, Johann Hari brilliantly describes this state of living, pointing out that we are flooded because we are 'soaked in information' as if we were 'drinking from a firehose'.[32] Hari outlines three research findings that help explain why it is hard to stay focused:

- Three minutes is how long an average adult office worker stays on task.
- It takes 23 minutes to get back on track and focus after being interrupted.
- A US study showed that in an average day at work, you never get one uninterrupted hour of straight work.

No wonder you feel frustrated: you are on the go all the time and yet somehow you are behind!

Now add to this the fact that it is happening to everyone – your family members, your friends, your colleagues – it's across the board, a shared stressor. This means it isn't just an individual problem, it's a systemic one and it infects all the systems you are a part of – the family system, the work system, the relationship system all suffer from this attention gap. The system is broken, and the results are all around us: physically, mentally, emotionally and environmentally. How can you be integrated when your focus, energy and senses are being overloaded? No wonder our nervous systems are constantly nervous. Ask yourself:

- How many books do you have that you haven't finished (or started) yet?
- When was the last time you read a book and didn't feel the pull to look at your phone?
- How long does it take you to get back on track after you've been interrupted at work?
- Can you switch off?
- Do you worry about your focus and concentration?
- Do you feel in control of your digital consumption?
- Do you feel stuck in procrastination paralysis?
- Do you find it hard to stay on task?
- Do you feel overwhelmed by the information load and yet empty at the same time?

- Does your brain hurt at the end of the day?
- Do you feel tense in your neck and shoulders?
- Do your eyes hurt?

How does numbing out tie in with anxiety?

Why do we do anything? We are driven by the pursuit of pleasure and the avoidance of pain. This pleasure–pain balance forgot to mention a crucial piece of information in our world of overwhelming accessibility to pleasure that it paradoxically leads to an inability to enjoy pleasure, which is known as anhedonia.

Why do we numb? To avoid pain, to avoid discomfort from our minds and bodies. To avoid what we need to do, to avoid thinking and feeling overwhelmed as there is so much to do. Picking up your phone doesn't feel the same as picking up a cigarette and yet instead of asking, 'How many do you smoke a day?', we might need to start asking, 'How many times a day do you pick up your phone?' to bring conscious and compassionate awareness to the habit of picking up your phone.

If it worked, if it made you feel grounded and regulated, I'd say go for it, but what we are left with is a roundabout of an avoidance of pain, combined with the hope of a quick hit of dopamine. That may happen at first, with a funny reel to hook you in, but then you see a peer or a celebrity who is posting how well they are doing in real life and you groan as your To Do list is looming, but you don't know where to start, so you freeze into procrastination paralysis, doom scrolling and being annoyed at yourself. You may notice your mood has changed, you are making self-derogatory comments about your body and then start generalising about how everyone else is rocking at life, in the job, as a parent, and you are just stuck pressing the button to get more dopamine. Check in with yourself and ask, *What do I need right now?*

I'm sure you have heard of dopamine, it's a popular topic these days, and you may have a good understanding of this important neurotransmitter. Something you might not know, and this is where the nuance makes all the difference, is that scientists are suggesting it may play a larger role in the motivation to obtain a reward than the pleasure of the reward itself.[33] So it is the anticipation that is the sweet spot, which might explain the frustration you feel when you know you have been on your phone too long, when you only went on for a second for a quick break from the difficult task you were working on. I find it so interesting that anticipation and uncertainty, two hallmarks of anxiety, also share a reverse pleasure–pain balance. A study exploring what happy people do differently showed that they embrace uncertainty and discomfort, actively engaging in risky endeavours like going on a date or trying something new.[34] This insight offers one of the most intriguing paradoxes: that satisfaction often stems from engaging in activities that feel risky, uncomfortable, and sometimes even negative, which to my mind makes perfect sense. When we numb out or stay in our comfort zone, the avoidance of the pain increases the pain, if we take anxiety as the case in point. It's always good to be straight with yourself and say both are hard, but choose the 'better' hard.

Rather than asking why we numb to cope, part of the answer is above, and it makes absolute sense. The other part is understanding the adaptive strategies of survival we have explored. There seems to be a better acceptance of our activated fight or flight response. It may even be valued – *That's good you fought back, well done* or *I can see why you left the meeting, I hate presentations as well*. There is misplaced shame when people go into the immobilisation and shutdown of Freeze and Fawn. *Why didn't you say anything? Why didn't you stop it? What are you doing? Put that phone down and do something productive.* It can be hard to see that the passive, somewhat immobilised process of being on your phone is Freeze. Overwhelmed by past trauma, scared of the future, sacrificing your health to be able to manage the cost of living and then not being able to work if you get sick, while swatting off the unending pull to your phone, if even to manage the constantly changing updates and activity schedules that are time-specific.

The word *cope* carries a weight of failure, but it's crucial to understand the physiological and psychological reasons behind our actions. By becoming more aware of our nervous system, we can recognise when we need a break and ask ourselves: *What do I truly need?* Whether it's scrolling through our phones or freezing in a moment of danger, our responses are often rooted in survival mechanisms. Shaming someone for their actions overlooks the deeper reasons behind their behaviour. So many feel stuck, and whether it is coming from trauma or the everyday experience of living in a toxic culture, shaming in the form of *Come on, get up, what are you doing?* misses why the person has collapsed or escaped into their phone. The phone isn't looking for anything from them. I am not advocating being on your phone incessantly, but rather to widen your understanding of why you do what you do. Technology offers a lifeline to your complex emotional and neurological drives towards connection, without the threat of being scolded or let down: *You didn't say you were having a hard time!* Shutdown, a common response to trauma, can inhibit our ability to express how we feel in words because the Broca's area in your prefrontal cortex, which is your language centre, is effectively shut in that moment.[35] You know when you want to say something in a difficult moment and can't find the words, and then hours later, when you are alone, you suddenly think of the best response ever? Well, that's the reason why.

Understanding these complexities through compassion and the polyvagal lens not only provides accuracy but also releases misplaced shame, directing us towards the changes we seek.

Focus facts

Guy Claxton, Professor of Learning Sciences at the University of Winchester, appears in conversation with Johann Hari in *Stolen Focus*. He recommends that 'we have to shrink the world to fit our cognitive bandwidth'. In other words, you don't have to keep taking on board more and more, expanding the amount you take in, making the big picture bigger and bigger – rather, you need to make the world fit around you and what you are capable of processing. If you try to be 'better' by going faster and consuming more information, all you achieve is to overload your abilities, which ultimately degrades them. Claxton explains that when we live at a human speed, not tech warp speed, it makes us smarter because it trains our focus and attention. 'Slowness nurtures attention, and speed shatters it,' Claxton says, and that sounds like wisdom. You cannot keep overloading yourself to the point where you feel as if you are going to explode. That is an incredibly anxious state to live in.

If you take on the external pressure to keep going, to push, to strive to ignore your needs, if you accept this as 'normal life', which is how they sell it to us, then you downplay your inner feelings and that leads to overwhelm, exhaustion and burnout. The anxiety attached to this brings us back to the autonomic system and the vagal states, which we set out in Chapter 2. It is important to stop during the day and ask yourself: *Am I in survival mode now?* Knowing where you are on the polyvagal ladder is a good visual to keep you aware of what state you are in and if you wish to focus on switching to a different one. This is the action and practice of resilience. When you work on the vagal system in this way, you increase your capacity to tolerate and to become more psychologically flexible, which allows you to adapt and switch states as required.

The polyvagal ladder:

- Calm, connected zone = ventral vagal – safe, secure
- Stressed, anxious zone = sympathetic state, mobilised – Fight or Flight
- Low energy, disconnected zone = dorsal vagal – immobilised, collapsed

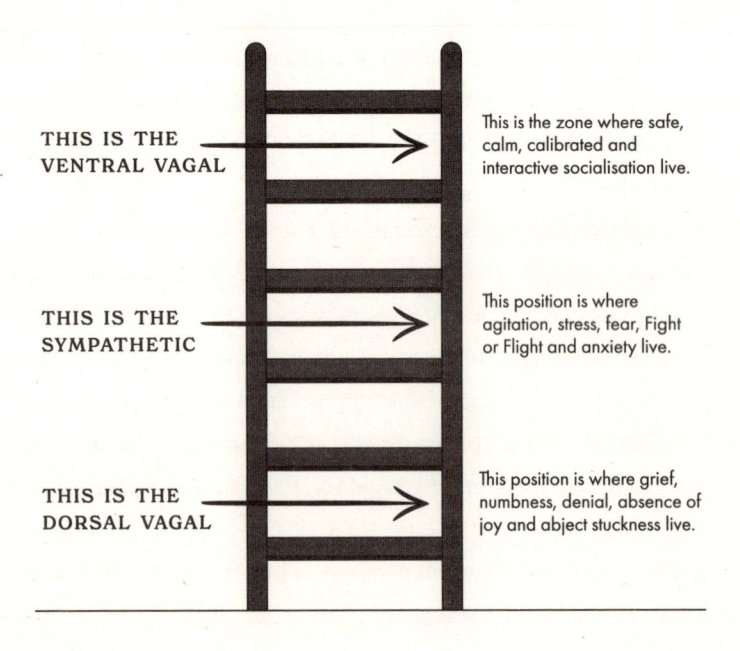

```
THIS IS THE          →    This is the zone where safe,
VENTRAL VAGAL              calm, calibrated and
                           interactive socialisation live.


THIS IS THE          →    This position is where
SYMPATHETIC                agitation, stress, fear, Fight
                           or Flight and anxiety live.


THIS IS THE          →    This position is where grief,
DORSAL VAGAL               numbness, denial, absence of
                           joy and abject stuckness live.
```

One of the key things you can do to address this anxiety is to swap some screen time for some green time. Anxiety and your nervous system respond well to time spent in nature, to fresh air, sunlight and being outdoors. Nature soothes, invigorates and refreshes weary bodies and minds. It calms and connects us with ourselves, others and the present. Orienting yourself to your environment is the perfect antidote to disconnection – and it's free. Go outside and find a space that even by simply being there provokes a sigh of relief. I have noticed that as soon as I set foot on a local walkway among the trees, I heave a physiological sigh (see page 329). I don't intentionally do it – my body does.

Reconnecting: Why you need to practise orienting

To practise orienting, find somewhere you can safely sit, take a few deep breaths and come into your body. Turn your phone to silent and allow yourself to be present for a few moments.

Turn your head to the left and notice what you can see, hear, smell, touch and feel. Bring your head back slowly and look in front using your five senses, and then turn to the right. Breathe in and release any tension and the pull towards the future. What are you noticing? Can you hear the birds singing, the wind in the trees, or the sound of waves rolling in and out? What can you feel? Are you sitting on grass or sand, or a bench, can you feel it support you? Close your eyes. Do you feel warmth or wind on your face? Are you aware of any smells? Do they bring up any fond memories for you? Open your eyes. What do you see? Is it green or blue, is there grass, a blue sky, fluffy clouds? Now allow your attention to go where it wants, practise being present. As thoughts come up, allow them to be there and then focus back on your surroundings, a beautiful tree, or its branches, the green of the grass, whatever your mind is drawn towards. Notice what this experience is like as a sensory experience and what impact it is having upon your body and mind. No judgement, no yogi pressure, just keep gently reorienting yourself back to you.

By regularly practising orienting in nature, you will deepen your connection with yourself, enhance your sensory awareness and connect back into a regulated body. It cultivates micro-moments of presence and wellbeing when you are feeling anything but calm.

To find the root of anxiety, you must go back to your home, meaning your body, and process what is there and, like any normal garden, it's imperative that you know the truth that there won't be just one weed, there will be lots, some of which are obviously weeds, and quite possibly a lot of weeds you haven't been aware of but have also caused a lot of psychological injury.

Living this accelerated life, with no time to process, think or feel in any depth, leads us to feel distracted and disconnected. Avoidance as a defence mechanism against the potential distress of dealing with psychological injury is the reason we distract and numb. However, being disconnected from yourself, and others, is not your true nature. You run deep, you have many layers, and your brain feels fragmented when it is taxed with mentally switching every few seconds. It's not a healthy human pace of life.

Finding out why you are choosing numbness

It might sound counterintuitive, but it is not a good idea to avoid pain. We are being encouraged to numb away our pain and move towards pleasure. The bit the dopamine-seekers forget is that it is the anticipation they seek. Do you ever find that you enjoy the anticipation of an event more than the event itself? Similarly, when you eat something you haven't had in a long time and it tastes delicious, the pleasure would diminish if you'd had it every day, no matter how delicious it is. In ways, I feel by having so much we are robbing ourselves of pleasure. Too much of anything isn't a good thing as we always adapt, adjust, and need more. Your tolerance needs more to get whatever relief or pleasure you got from it before, but it impacts your body, mind and soul.

Look at what we are consuming. We feel empty, frustrated, upset, and so we fill ourselves up. But the feelings and difficulties keep coming and the cycle continues. Without going full Freud on you, the mouth is the ultimate pain soother. Has the food, alcohol, drugs, sex, products/retail or digital information given you what you need? Has it solved the problem? What emptiness are we stuffing with digital noise, busyness, work, and whatever cocktail of numbing agent is at our fingertips? With all the other crises, this digital one actively impacts every minute of our waking day and now night.

How do you feel now that you understand why your body chose to numb to avoid the pain or discomfort? Rather than a coping mechanism, was it a defence mechanism? A coping mechanism is healthier in that you try to adapt to challenging or stressful experiences by engaging in mind and body techniques such as relaxation, seeking support, exercise and practising the polyvagal exercises we are about to explore in Chapter 9. In contrast, a defence mechanism protected you at the time, often as an adaptive survival response, but over time became maladaptive. We need to pragmatically acknowledge *Okay, this does not work for me anymore* with zero judgement. In fact, I'm going to ask you to bring acceptance of who you are, how hard it has been, all the work you have done and the inner challenges that I bet a lot of people don't know about.

It's important to hear this, as what may be externally construed and commented upon as *You're not trying hard enough, not doing enough, not making enough of an effort* or *You're lazy; Why can't you just …?*, adds to the layers of shame that you need to let go of. No one except you knows how hard it has been for you or the possible reasons behind the behaviour, such as trauma, anxiety, mental and physical health issues and neurodiversity.

When staying present with thoughts and emotions that are overwhelming and triggering, picking up something like your phone to distract from that niggly, tricky emotion is understandable. I repeat, no shame here. Even being aware of the social comparison, especially within the weaponised wellness sphere, which, ironically, is making people feel even worse about themselves. When people tell me they want peace and yet fear silence, I understand. Because they may never have known 'peace' or safety, as they have always stayed alert and waiting, which was exhausting.

I am asking you to take your cue from what you see that triggers the escapist numbing behaviours and to pay gentle attention to the wounds beneath that require your attention.

The Practical Psychology

We all want to feel connected; it's an innate human need, and yet it has never been easier to disconnect. Most often we disconnect because it is too much. Even the idea of working through issues or emotions that are painful isn't something you will be drawn to. I am gently encouraging you to do so, to see that technology can divide us from others and mostly from ourselves. We can't always entertain the pain away, that is why therapy is called 'work'. I am never asking you to do this alone; remember the important intervention of titration as you build up the doses of processing to work through intense or distressing emotions. Seeking therapeutic support and/or speaking with your GP is the first line of defence.

Here, I present you with 'opposite action'. This is a therapeutic technique used in dialectical behaviour therapy (DBT) to manage intense emotions. Say you feel the urge to pick up your phone or eat food or drink alcohol to numb yourself from uncomfortable or distressing emotions. Pause and ask what the opposite action of that would be. Say you felt alone and isolated, what would be it be like to call a friend – yes, I said 'call'. Too much? Okay, do a voice-note. Or if you feel frustrated that you've spent too long scrolling, swap the scroll for a stroll: stand up, shoes on, out the door. In a world that can feel too much, less is more. If you feel exhausted, rest, even if it is a disco nap – a short nap before you go out or even if you stay in! Or if your brain feels overstimulated, intentionally bring silence into your day. Have a look below and see which options you want to engage with.

PRACTISE SILENCE
Spend time each day in silence
The antidote to the noise is silence. First, hold silence for 30 seconds. Start with 30 seconds and notice what occurs. You are not practising to be a monk, so expect a lot of mental monkeys jumping around from

one thought branch to another. That's okay, just acknowledge them. Then return to your breath, and the ultimate luxury of momentary silence. Intentionally spend time in silence by building it into your daily timetable.

Morning silence

Please don't hate me, but I'd like to suggest that you get up before everyone else. Then get up a little earlier again, to get you ready for the day. This is time for you, before you go into planning and list mode.

- Take a breath.
- If you can, have your warm drink outside.
- Sun factor on, hat and coat on, and dress for the weather – but get outside into the air.
- Leave your phone in the house. Sunlight before screens.
- Notice your surroundings.
- Ask what you need. Some reassurance? A hug? (Yes, even from yourself.)

Afternoon silence

When could this happen? Think of the pattern of your day. How are your transitions from work, to pick-up, to 'otherings' (minding others). Can you find 1, 3, 5, 10 minutes? You choose, according to your schedule.

Where is there space for you?

_____

If there isn't, can you create some?

_____

One minute of being still, silent, and coming back into your body is more effective than nothing and is more rejuvenating and powerful than you might think. I'm going to call these the 'in-betweeners' – finding space when there is none: waiting in the car; on the sidelines; in the queue.

Bring yourself back home to your body with grace and ease. When you are in constant go-go-go mode (check which F you are in – Fight, Flight, Freeze, Fawn), starting and stopping, know that you can also ... PAUSE ... if only for one minute. This is how you practise using your vagal brake.

Even in these tiny in-between moments, you can find some space. It may be to switch off the noise, the news, the chatter. Or blare it up and sing along. Let's normalise how to self-regulate. It is in the very moments of life when you need it that you meet yourself as you are. You could start with a physiological sigh (see page 329).

Evening silence

There is something about night that brings you back inside yourself, like the warm curling-up of a bird tucking under their wing for the night. Your circadian rhythm (24-hour clock) needs this time. The darkness ushers in the sleep hormones that set you up to rest and digest, that allow you to unwind. That all sounds lovely in theory, but I'm well aware that the reality can be so very different. There will be no lecturing or 'shoulding' here, but the cold, hard truth is that you need to sleep and rest. I am specifically mentioning rest as well because just lying there is rest, too; don't fight it, it's the truth.

Here is my suggestion: pick a time to get off the phone or PC and commit to making that a weekly, then daily, practice. I would suggest starting by cutting back 10–15 minutes first, for a week. I bet you are thinking, *That's too easy, make it an hour!* Trust me, start there and then build to 20, 25, 30 minutes, etc., until you get up to 60 minutes. Do it slowly and steadily, then it will also be less noticeable to your brain, so it doesn't crave the night-time meme fest.

There is something you'll need to do in order to be able to create and enjoy your silence – and you might not like it. I'm going to ask you to do a surface clear of your bedroom. The clutter is anxiety-inducing and makes it hard for your brain to say, *Okay, the day is done*. My friend Sinéad Brady, a psychologist, author and busy mum, shared a brilliant idea she uses to tidy up at the end of the day – it's known as the 'Chuck it Bucket' in front of the kids, but really it's her 'F**k it Bucket'. I love the concept. I suggest you adopt your own 'F**k it Bucket' for the family to quickly declutter at the day's end. No need for Marie Kondo-level tidying, just toss it all in the box/bucket and out of sight.

Next step is going to bed earlier. I'd recommend 30 minutes earlier than usual, but we can agree on 15 minutes if that's all you can manage. Get that habit going and keep increasing by 5 minutes until you're giving yourself 45 minutes extra every night. Turn off the main light. If you have bedside lamps, turn them on. Fresh sheets for the win, and light your candle. Now get ready for bed: wash your face slowly, take your time, put on some night cream if you like to do that. Once you are comfortably in bed, surrender the day and let it go:

- Lie on your back, legs and arms like a starfish, breathe in, and feel your body, surrender to the bed, let the bed hold you. As thoughts come in, acknowledge them. If they feel pressing and persistent, address them by writing them on a notepad by the bed (always helpful to have a notepad!).
- Breathe in what you need: *I need … quiet, space, peace …*
- Breathe out the day: *I am letting go of the day, letting go of tension, this is my time.*
- Notice areas of tension and intentionally release them – they might be in your jaw, neck, head, shoulders, pelvis.
- Place your hands on area of tension, bring appreciation for what you did that day and connect back with yourself.

- Allow any tough feelings to go, and know that tomorrow is another day.
- It can help to say *Soften, soften and release* in your mind.
- Listen to the quiet.
- If it isn't quiet, put in your ear plugs.
- Acknowledge any noise you can't control and bring it into your rest – *I can hear the cars, the dog, the TV and this is my time to myself* – bringing your mind back to your body.
- Be in the silence.

CHAPTER 9

Healthy coping mechanisms for emotional anxiety

I hope you have left the last chapter with a deep understanding and appreciation of why you have been doing things you don't want to do. I hope you have put down the huge boulder of guilt, shame and frustration you've been carrying and feel a whole-body release. I am sorry for all the experiences that led to needing to create those defence mechanisms. I hope you understand that your nervous system's function is to protect you and to survive and that this realisation brings compassion and clarity.

I am excited to go into the next three chapters. You have been doing some deep work and I thank you for your time, perseverance, patience and openness to facing painful experiences and memories. In the next three chapters we are going to look at what helps alleviate and manage anxiety, dividing it into emotional, psychological, and physiological, as we did in the in-depth chapters, to increase your ability to notice and be aware of how anxiety is showing up for you. Often all three can be present at the same time, but when you tune in you can notice the details of triggers and responses: *It started in my body, my stomach felt off, and then I had the thought, I don't think I can do this today, there isn't enough time and there's too much to do, which led to anxious thoughts about why it is so hard for me, everyone else can do this, I feel so upset, frustrated and sad.* Whatever way it shows up, this separation is to help you signpost and flag which aspect needs your attention first. At the beginning of therapy, it can feel like a set of jumbled-up Christmas tree lights – as soon as you unravel one part, you find the tangled knot has embedded into another part. Being able to see how one leads into the other is so hard when in the grip of anxiety. Remember, untangling these complexities can feel overwhelming, but we'll navigate them together.

We explored the fundamentals of emotional anxiety in Chapter 3; now let's get to the good part – how to cope and how to change.

How do I make the change?

Here's something I hear time and time again in the therapy room: 'Why do I stay the same when I know what I need to do? I am so stuck and frustrated with myself.' Change is a powerful ability, but it can also be a terrifying prospect. And even when you are certain you want to change and feel filled to the brim with energy and determination to make the change, you can find that you do not know what to do next, you end up feeling lost, not sure in which direction to turn. It is deeply frustrating. Everyone says they want to be happier, more relaxed and calmer, but how do you put that into practice?

The basic building-blocks of change are straightforward when you read them, as you will see in the list opposite, but they can be challenging to put into practice. Putting them into practice can mean going against your own ingrained habits, thoughts, feelings and experiences. This is where change forces us to dig deep – it's never a once-off effort, it's an ongoing practice to maintain those new ways we have adopted. It's a challenge to change something you are used to doing and that, crucially, everyone else is used to you doing. That can be the real kicker. But a theory I really like in psychology, and that makes a lot of sense to me, is the practical power of opposites. This states that it is often the opposite of what you think will help that will actually help. For example:

- To be more productive, you need to rest.
- To process painful emotions, sit with the pain.
- To fall asleep, you need to let go of trying to sleep.
- To overcome fear of socialising, take social risks.
- To alleviate loneliness, go places alone.
- To feel well, do hard things.
- To fall in love, surrender and share your vulnerability.
- To help yourself, actively help others.
- To break the cycle of anxiety, confront avoidance.

I didn't say it was easy, but nothing good or worthwhile in life is easy. That fairytale philosophy has set us up for a fall. So, what can you do? There are nine key practices you can do that will directly help you to manage anxiety.

1. Cultivate sleep hygiene that works for you.
2. Nourish your body.
3. Move your body.
4. Connect with yourself and others.
5. Engage in daily active rest.
6. Remember that nature nurtures.
7. Set boundaries.
8. Re-parent yourself.
9. Learn and practise how to regulate your nervous system.

We have explored the importance of cultivating silence in your day, and how to nourish your mind and body in terms of seeking support and exercising. I hope you have many takeaways from this book that will work in your busy schedule. If you could add a daily walk, even around the block for 10 minutes, and go to bed 15 minutes earlier every night, while prioritising nutritious and joyful food, you will feel so different – and I will be delighted for you.

Can you see how each aspect complements all the aspects of your health? From actively minding yourself to taking a break, fuelling your body, moving your body, it all helps to connect you to yourself and others. This is habit stacking, where each habit supports and builds upon what is there. And when one habit falls away for a time, as it naturally will, you just start again. That's it. No guilt. This is the practice of start, stop, pause; what we can think of as the psychological cycle of life.

ENGAGE IN DAILY ACTIVE REST

What do I mean by active rest? Is that not an oxymoron? If we take exercise often, the 'no pain, no gain' mantra is held as the gold standard, but that may not align with what your body and, more specifically, what your nervous system needs when it is already anxious. High-intensity cardio can tax an already stressed system; when your stress hormone cortisol is already high it can put the body further into Fight and Flight. Understanding your body's exercise needs is important. That is not a green card to never exert yourself, but it is to question harsh exercise regimes and look at a different mindset of active rest. You might dislike the idea of meditating, but that doesn't mean you can't go for a walk. There are many meditative experiences that don't involve being cross-legged. A mindful walk in nature is not only meditative but also deeply restorative.

Active rest may bring in modalities such as Pilates, yoga, walking, hiking. If you have done any of these, your shaking legs will be testament to how tough they are. From my perspective, I am challenging the hard, punitive hustle culture and inviting some inner support along with more everyday joy that provides physical, emotional and mental fitness. I am inviting you to think about joyful, purposeful discipline. Life is genuinely hard enough.

BOUNDARIES

We will look at these in detail; see page 239.

RE-PARENT YOURSELF

You might view re-parenting as a new concept, but if you are a parent, trust me, you have experienced it. If you find your anxiety is triggered when your child or adolescent speaks back to you, or doesn't listen to you, maybe you weren't listened to as a child, and your child ignoring you may bring up fast anger: the quicker the reaction, the older the trigger.

Always stay curious in the face of these emotional reactions: *Wow, I am really annoyed right now. This is a strong reaction. I need a moment to connect to what is really coming up for me here.* Notice where it is in your body and, if you can, place your hand there, close your eyes and see what you feel. As always, bring the 3 Cs to these emotionally tough situations: Challenge with Curiosity and Compassion.

Emotional regulation

When you feel more controlled by your emotions than in control of them, it's a horrible feeling. You say things you regret. You go from zero to 100 in a second. You get tripped and triggered in ways you or others don't appreciate. You feel really dreadful about yourself and then the doubt, guilt and shame climb aboard and make everything worse.

Emotional regulation is the control you have been looking for. Imagine learning specific skills and knowing how to turn some emotions down (down-regulate) and knowing how to turn some emotions up (up-regulate). This ability gives you the psychological flexibility necessary to adapt, pivot and respond appropriately to emotions as they arise. The goal of emotional regulation isn't to 'not think about your emotions' or to suppress them, which might be how you were envisaging control. Instead, it is knowing how to reappraise your thoughts and process them somatically in your body to be in control in a healthier way for you. So it is the control you want, but not as you currently know it.

Think of it as making a new friend. As you befriend your nervous system you don't shout at it or demand that it changes immediately. You get to know yourself, which means you challenge yourself with compassion and with curiosity, which is so immensely different from staying stuck, giving out to yourself and feeling that you cannot change. It will feel different and uncomfortable at first because it isn't familiar. The chaos is familiar. But you want to live differently, and you want to feel different, and this is the way forward.

You can self-regulate your emotions through:

- nature
- movement
- breathing
- somatic body work
- connection with self and co-regulation.

Various methods offer pathways for emotional regulation, each playing a crucial role in navigating emotional landscapes. Connecting with nature provides a grounding experience, offering solace and perspective. It triggers the ventral vagal complex, promoting feelings of safety and connection amidst emotional turbulence. Movement, whether exercise or gentle activities like walking, fosters emotional balance, stimulating the ventral vagus nerve, releasing endorphins and dissipating tension. Conscious breathing techniques serve as anchors during moments of stress, facilitating shifts from sympathetic to parasympathetic dominance, enabling a return to calmness and clarity. Somatic body work through practices like somatic experiencing, massage or yoga, attunes you to the sensations in your body, allowing you to identify areas of tension and consciously release them. This process not only promotes physical relaxation but also enables the processing and release of emotional tension stored in the body.

Hyperarousal and hypoarousal are physiological states related to the arousal level of the nervous system. Hyperarousal refers to a state of heightened physiological and psychological arousal, often associated with intense emotions such as anxiety, fear or anger. In this state, you may experience increased heart rate, rapid breathing, heightened senses, and a feeling of being on edge. Learning how to down-regulate away from that state and towards feeling more neutral is the objective.

If you are feeling low in energy, and stuck, that is hypoarousal, often associated with emotional shutdown or disengagement, where you may feel emotionally numb or disconnected from your surroundings. Learning how to up-regulate out of that state is another key skill.

A huge caveat: following these useful activities will not create a permanent change, but it will show you how to move between the different states and enjoy and benefit from the flexibility that can bring to your everyday life.

HOW TO DOWN-REGULATE WHEN IN HYPERAROUSAL

- Deep breathing: place your hand on your chest and stomach and see it move.
- Use a weighted blanket, which provides proprioceptive feedback. This pressure mimics the feeling of being held or hugged, triggering the release of neurotransmitters like serotonin and dopamine that are associated with relaxation and feelings of wellbeing.
- Shake it out – see page 305.
- If you are sitting at a desk, a foot roller or a tennis ball will provide proprioception, the body's sense of its own position in space. This plays a key role in regulating the nervous system. This input helps to ground and distract you, in a good way, and provides a sense of stability and connection to the environment. The pressure also releases tension.

- Calming music: I really like binaural beats, which have an immediate impact on your brain (you will need headphones). Research suggests that binaural beats can influence brainwave patterns, promoting a shift from higher-frequency beta waves associated with alertness and stress to lower-frequency alpha or theta waves associated with relaxation and calmness. This shift in brainwave activity may contribute to the reduction of anxiety symptoms.
- Furiously write out how you feel. (It can be scrawly.) When you've finished, rip it up or throw it away.[36]
- Scream into a pillow or punch it.
- Press your outstretched arms against a wall.
- If you are feeling fatigued or overwhelmed, lie on your bed and put your legs against the wall at a 90-degree angle. The familiar and supportive environment of your bed can provide a sense of safety and security, helping to alleviate feelings of stress or anxiety. Lying down allows your body to rest and recover, promoting relaxation and restoration of energy levels. This is a yoga pose known for its calming and restorative effects on the nervous system. The inversion also stimulates the parasympathetic nervous system, leading to a decrease in heart rate and blood pressure, and is particularly beneficial for reducing stress, anxiety and fatigue.
- Go for a quick walk.
- Do a pat down (see page 340).
- Grounding: go barefoot, notice the texture and temperature of the floor or ground beneath your feet.
- Get back into your body and out of your mind with yoga or Pilates.
- Connect somatically to your body where you feel an emotional irritation. Place your hands there and acknowledge what you feel. If it is anger, honour it, allow it, and then let it go, often in the form of tears or words, either spoken or written.

HOW TO UP-REGULATE WHEN IN HYPOAROUSAL

- Skipping – yes, go out and get a skipping rope. Why? Because it increases heart rate and blood flow, activates the sympathetic nervous system, boosts energy, focus and mood. It also connects to the body with proprioceptive feedback. (You know your own body; don't do this if you have injuries or physical issues.)
- Listen to dance music (upbeat, with a heartbeat tempo).
- Write out why you feel the way you do, and attend to those feelings.
- Have a shower and, for a reset, turn on the cold water at the end to what feels tolerable for you. (This is not to shock you, so don't do it if it doesn't suit you.)
- Chewing is a good jaw release and is regulating, so crunchy or chewy food is a good regulator. There are 'chewables' that you can put on a pen/pencil.
- Create strong, invigorating smells – like basil, lemon, verbena, mint, orange – in diffusers, candles, room sprays.
- Open the blinds or curtains, open the windows – let in natural light and air.
- Step outside and get some sunlight, see what other senses you can bring in: what can you hear, see, feel, taste, touch?
- Connect with how you feel: if you feel stuck, acknowledge it; if you feel exhausted, ask why. Listen to what your body is telling you and find out what it needs next.

The role of emotional agency in emotional regulation

In Chapter 6 we discussed a study on airline crew that observed a shift in emotional culture, resulting in the '9/11 effect'. This change established a new cultural norm that allowed crew members to be more assertive with passengers, creating a role shield and giving them increased emotional agency.

I love the concept of emotional agency because it puts you front and centre as an agent for change. It is healthy to recognise when things are not the way you want them to be and then to recognise that you have the power and agency to change this. As we have discussed, the noise, distraction and constant doing of modern life is dulling our ability to have clarity and focus on our next best steps. The key here is to identify the problem, because then you have something tangible that you can examine and change. Increasing your emotional agency allows you to express yourself and to make changes you know need to be made. Take Julie as an example, who came to the therapy room worn out and a verging on feeling hopeless. We worked through the ways in which she could exert emotional agency to self-regulate better, and she made a promise to herself to try and put them into practice:

> Julie knew she was in a negative spiral; she knew she was tired. She went outside and had her breakfast and a cup of coffee. She forced herself to just sit there. The urge to pick up her phone was strong, but she knew her brain was fried. She acknowledged how hard it was to just sit and do 'nothing' and yet she knew that was exactly what she needed. She needed to eat in peace, she needed to taste the food, to hold the mug, to watch the steam lift gently off the coffee. To be and to not be doing. Then the thoughts kicked in again: 'Get up! You have so much to do! What are you doing?' 'Ah, hello, inner critic,' she thought wearily. 'I am being productive, I am allowed to eat my breakfast, this will help me throughout the day.' She acknowledged the inner struggles and just let them be beside her.
>
> She remembered talking about emotional agency and decided she needed 10 minutes. She did some deep breathing, nothing fancy, just in and out as it felt good for her. She decided

to eat lunch in silence that day as well, and to limit talking with Susan as she found her persistently negative and frantic. She recognised the emotional contagion of others in her space and put some boundaries around the time she would interact with specific people that day in the office.

Part of the spiralling was because with every meeting, the time to do the work she needed to do kept reducing. She'd come home in the evening, and the mess added to her sense of it all being messy and out of control. She knew she needed to make some decisions to give her more space inside her head.

She needed to do some deep work, without interruption, so she decided to wear her noise-cancelling earphones that day to signal to everyone that she was in the zone. She had her new favourite playlist, which was the recommended binaural beats and focused music that she found soothed her mind and brought much-needed focus as she reduced the environmental noise around her.

She placed her hand on her chest and felt the warmth of the sun sink in for a moment and gave herself credit for soothing and down-regulating her nervous system. This was what she was working on, it was a practice, not something she'd do every now and then, she had to practise it daily.

She knew collecting the kids from school later would be much less frantic and recognised that by minding herself for a few minutes, she was in fact minding everyone else. Julie had long been struggling with intense 'mom guilt' because her patience was at zero, she was snapping irritably at everyone at home, and then feeling awful as they walked away from her. But this sense of hope and emotional agency gave her the room she needed to make her next best steps.

Do you feel stuck in your own life? Can you recognise that sense of overwhelm followed by zero patience and snappy irritability? If this is familiar to you, your emotions have been piling up relentlessly on top of you, leaving you feeling like you're drowning in them. Trust me, you aren't alone, but that isn't okay. It is exhausting. And if you find yourself saying 'I just need to get through this week, it will all calm down then,' you need to be honest about your if–then thinking because you and I know it won't calm down. This is the time to focus on what you are feeling, and what you need to do to feel supported in what your emotions are conveying to you. To manage them with compassion and to clarify what you would like to change to make things better and easier for you. Don't wait for the right time, it isn't coming.

When you seek out change, the first obstacle you may hit is yourself. It's okay. Be kind; you now know why that's happening. It is due to homeostasis and the homeostatic impulse. Homeostasis is reflected in the inherent human tendency to seek stability and avoid the discomfort associated with change. While this inclination can serve a protective function in certain situations, it can also hinder personal growth, adaptation and resilience in the face of new challenges or opportunities for change. The homeostatic impulse works like a powerful magnet to pull us towards staying the same. It's like an energy-saving mode because change requires a lot of energy. It's important to acknowledge that, because I know that energy might be the last thing you have right now. That's okay. You can slowly and gently work towards those changes bit by bit, so you don't deplete yourself. You also don't want to change so much at once that it's unsustainable. But it's useful to know that there is a psychological reason for the difficulty – homeostasis – and that is not your fault, it's just a human trait. But with a sense of commitment and compassion, you can increase your emotional agency and your emotional flexibility, both of which will allow you regulate your emotions and decrease your anxiety.

This next part is to guide you through.

The Practical Psychology

Identify and write down what you want to change. (e.g. 'I want to feel in control, less anxious and overwhelmed; 'I want to feel calmer'; 'I want to be able to stop worrying and over-thinking'.)

_____

Why do you want to make that change? (e.g. 'I need things to change as I know I can't keep going like this'; 'I don't know who I am anymore, and I don't like who and how I am being every day')?

_____

What needs to happen for that to happen? (e.g. 'I need non-interrupted time in my day to think'; 'I am going to get up earlier; however, for this to be sustainable, I am going to go to bed earlier.')

_____

Take a realistic look at your life and name the blockers that are getting in your way. (e.g. 'I don't have enough time to do what needs to be done'; 'I don't have the support to facilitate this change'; 'I can't afford to stop working'; 'I'm scared of change and changing'.)

_____

Now think of your life and your specific circumstances and, with compassion and integrity, try to identify exactly why you find change hard.

What one change can you make that would help?

_____

What other changes would also be helpful?

_____

When would you like this to happen?

_____

What supports do you need to facilitate this?

_____

What do you need to let go of or surrender for this change to occur? (e.g. check your beliefs and inner critic – 'I can't do this'; 'I've nothing to be anxious about, other people have it so much harder than I do'; 'Why can't I just be positive?')

_____

Just for today, imagine you have made the changes you wanted to make. What would be different? Note your energy, thoughts and emotions that surround this.

What would help you have a sense of emotional agency?

_____

What would need to change for that to happen?

_____

With the things that can't be changed, how would reframing to a place of acceptance with some minor changes work for you?

_____

What would bring you from emotional labour to emotional joy?

_____

Boundaries

When I say 'boundaries' from this point forward, I want you to imagine your front door. You are in charge and have full responsibility over who or what you let in and out. For every request made of you, be it for your time, energy or even company, ask each and every time: *Do I have enough space for this now?* Doors open and shut, so before you speak, pause and ask: *Am I going to invite or let this in or do I need to close this off at this time?* These are your boundary doors and they are dynamic and are operated by you.

Boundaries play a central role in effectively navigating and mitigating feelings of anxiety and can land an emotional punch. The ability to set and re-set your own boundaries is the practice of healthy coping and it delivers huge benefits to you in your efforts to regulate your emotions and control your own space, both mental and physical. A word of warning, though – it's not easy to shift established boundaries. What might surprise you is that you might not be your biggest obstacle when it comes to setting or redrawing boundaries – it might well be those around you, including those you hold most dear. This is where you might see opposites in action again, when you are trying to do the opposite of what you are currently doing – and other people might have a big problem with that. The truth is, everyone gets comfortable with your behaviour, not just you, so when you want to change it, you might find that you come up against other people's anger and disappointment.

WHAT ARE BOUNDARIES?

Boundaries protect your time and energy. They are your choice of what works best for you. There are four types of boundary:

1. **Physical:** Your own personal space, bodily integrity, and your right to privacy.

2. **Emotional:** Connection to self and others, being able to own your own emotions, being clear about where you end and others begin, knowing what is and is not your responsibility
3. **Mental:** Your right to your own opinion, your right to your values and core principles, your right to hold your own perspectives that might be different from the perspectives of others in your life.
4. **Time and energy:** Choosing who you spend your time with, managing how you spend your time, understanding what drains you and where to draw the line, actively protecting your energy, being mindful of not taking on too much.

There are healthy and unhealthy boundaries. Healthy boundaries align with your core values and your sense of self. Listen to your body and emotions to guide your decisions. Use emotional cues as a compass to understand triggers and make choices that respect your wellbeing. Healthy boundaries inform your choices and evolve as you do over time, allowing for temporary disappointment from others while maintaining healthy relationships.

Healthy boundaries facilitate the expression of the need for alone time or space to recharge without feeling guilty. There are three types of unhealthy boundary: limited or non-existent; loose or porous; and rigid.

Limited or non-existent boundaries

A limited or non-existent boundary refers to a lack of clear limits that define one's personal space, needs and preferences in relationships or interactions with others. When you don't know where you end or begin, neither do those around you. In such situations, individuals may struggle to assert themselves, to communicate their needs effectively, or to protect their physical, emotional and mental wellbeing. This lack of boundaries can lead to difficulties in maintaining healthy relationships, as well as increased vulnerability to manipulation, exploitation and emotional exhaustion. The temporary betrayal of your own needs exacts a huge toll on relationships as there will be resentment. We have explored one of the origins, which is to choose being 'nice' as a result of the Fawn response (people-pleasing) to avoid conflict or disapproval from others.

Loose or porous boundaries
A loose or porous boundary refers to a boundary that moves with decisions being made from an 'others first' perspective. Individuals with loose boundaries may have difficulty distinguishing between their own and others' thoughts, feelings and needs. As a result, they may be more susceptible to external influences and may struggle to assert their own identity or preferences. This can lead to challenges in maintaining autonomy, setting limits and establishing healthy relationships. This can be a learned response where you became parentified as a child, as in you thought of your parent's or parents' needs before your own. This blurred boundaries between a parent and yourself, fostering a sense of obligation and guilt to prioritise others' needs over your needs.

When you have loose or porous boundaries you could be someone who frequently allows others to impose their opinions and decisions on you, often feeling overwhelmed or controlled by external influences. This boundary may have been established due to a lack of assertiveness or a fear of conflict. For instance, if you grew up in a family where your opinions were dismissed or overridden by more dominant family members, you may have learned to suppress your own desires in order to avoid confrontation or maintain peace.

The impact of this porous boundary on anxiety and emotions can be significant. Constantly prioritising others' needs and opinions over your own can lead to feelings of resentment, frustration and powerlessness. You may experience heightened anxiety in social situations, fearing judgement or rejection if you express your true thoughts or desires, and an erosion of self-esteem.

Rigid boundaries

A rigid boundary is inflexible and tightly enforced, often without consideration for the needs or perspectives of others. Individuals with rigid boundaries may have strict rules or guidelines for themselves and others, and they may be unwilling to compromise or adapt to changing circumstances. This can lead to difficulties in forming close relationships, as well as a lack of empathy or understanding of others' needs. Rigid boundaries may also contribute to feelings of isolation or alienation, as individuals may struggle to connect with others in a meaningful way. The establishment of unhealthy boundaries often stems from various psychodynamic reasons, with protection and survival frequently being key motivations.

When a person refuses to engage in discussions about their emotions or vulnerabilities with their partner, it can destabilise the relationship. This boundary may have been established due to past experiences of emotional vulnerability being met with rejection or criticism. For instance, if you grew up in a family where expressing emotions was discouraged or belittled, you may have learned to shut down emotionally as a way of protecting yourself from further hurt. As a result, you have a rigid boundary around sharing your feelings, believing that vulnerability is a sign of weakness and fearing that opening up will lead to rejection or abandonment.

Goldilocks boundaries

What you are looking to establish are your 'Goldilocks' boundaries – not too rigid, too loose or non-existent. Creating boundaries that are 'just right' is an ongoing process. Remember that all the changes and practices you put in place will change over time, as so many factors will influence and impact your abilities. If I could stick a Post-it note to the front of your brain, it would be a constant reminder to embrace psychological flexibility, to understand and accept that you, your environment, and life are in flux.

Martha knew this was the moment she had been working towards.

'Martha, can you do it or not?' Alex's tone was impatient, as if her pausing to even consider the request was an affront.

'I can't this weekend, and I've been wanting to talk to you about how we can manage Mum's care going forward.'

'What do you mean you can't? Well, I can't either, so one of us is going to have to,' Alex said angrily.

'There are three of us, and I think it is fair to say I do 90 per cent of the caring through the week and every second weekend, you do the other two weekends, and you-know-who does nothing. I am burned out, we probably won't be able to get Jamie on board, so we now need to look at outside care as well.'

'But we can't afford to get outside help,' Alex shouted.

'My health can't afford to keep doing this and working and managing my own home. Alex, I am going to ask you to stop shouting at me. We can take a break if you need, but we need to find a solution that doesn't cost me my health.'

'I am stressed as well,' Alex said angrily.

'I know you are. Let's take a 20-minute break; this is a tough conversation that has been building for years. Meet you back here in 20, I'll bring us a cup of tea. This can't continue, and something has to change.'

'No, let's sort this out now,' Alex said quickly.

'How we have been talking with each other also has to change. I am going to go take a moment, come back, and then we are going to sort this out. When I'm back, let's pretend we're at work – you wouldn't be allowed shout at your team.'

Martha smiled gently at Alex and walked away. Her heart was pounding, but she had to stand up to Alex. In that moment she had drawn the line, and she knew what she would and

> wouldn't do anymore, and she knew she wouldn't sacrifice her health and relationships. The betrayal of her boundaries had ended. She couldn't wait to share what she had done at her next therapy session.

How do you know which areas of your life need new boundaries? Think of your daily struggle points – what's causing them? Think about your personal interactions – is there an argument you keep repeatedly having? What's causing that? Think about your levels of exhaustion – are they always high? What's causing that? Are you finding the routine and status quo of your daily life is leaving you empty, maybe resentful? What's causing that? I think what you'll find in examining those questions is that the underlying cause in all cases is an absence of a boundary or the existence of an unhealthy boundary. The first step is identifying the problem you'd like to solve, then you can look to the cause of the problem, and if that cause is a boundary issue, you can honestly assess the boundary in question and why it's not working for you. After all that, you can then choose which boundary you need to put in place to change the situation.

As noted above, you must be ready for these changes to bring resistance from those around you. When you try to put a new boundary in place, you might find it makes other people angry because they were benefiting from your previous lack of boundaries. Your unhealthy boundaries made their life easier, and they'd like to keep it that way. So you might hear things like: *What's up with you?*; *Why are you being so difficult?*; *Why are you acting like this?*; *You've changed* – said in a tone of voice that makes it clear this is not a compliment! I'll be honest, it would be easier in the short term to stay the same. Even when you want to make 'good' changes, your body will bring you back to that state of homeostasis that is familiar to you. Familiar is comfortable, change is not. Change brings uncertainty. Uncertainty loves anxiety.

But what I would ask you to do is to look down the road at the longer term – can you see yourself feeling good and content if this current pattern of behaviour stays in place? If the answer is no, it's best to be clear about that, and get stuck into making those changes. It's for your benefit, but I know it's hard.

The breaking of patterns and habits is not a once-off, it requires ongoing awareness and work. Don't let this dishearten you. But it is important to realise that putting yourself first once doesn't mean everything has changed and this is how it will now naturally happen. Remember those resistors – they will be there, ready to push you back into the old habits. So if you go into this thinking, *I am going to finally tell my mother how I feel and then everything will change* or *I will stand up for myself in meetings when my comments are ignored and then everything will change*, you are setting yourself up for disappointment. It's a slow and ongoing process, and you have to monitor it and keep communicating it. I know you want things to change and for you to not have to think about it again. I admit, that would be wonderful. But it's not how it works. It might sound odd, but the idea of never feeling anxiety again, or that you could set a boundary once and it's set permanently are fallacies that are ultimately disheartening and inhibit normal growth. It involves hard work, and there's no getting around that. But then, staying the same is hard too, and it's hard on you.

So you have to make a decision and choose your hard. If you choose change, you will have to get comfortable with uncomfortable conversations and learn to live with and tolerate the disapproval of others. Has this been one of the core reasons why you haven't stood up for yourself in the past? Has your fear of the other person's reaction inhibited and silenced your ability to say how you felt when someone crossed a boundary with you? If that sounds familiar and you recognise yourself in there, then I know all this talk of boundaries will be challenging for you. People-pleasing is a trait so many of us share, to one extent or another. I understand that you are feeling queasy at the mere idea of thinking of your own needs first. But you need to hear and adopt this truth: You are not selfish for thinking about yourself and your needs. You are not selfish for safeguarding your time and energy.

HOW TO DRAW NEW BOUNDARIES

I need to circle back around to the key myth and realities of boundaries because this is essential for you to take away from this discussion:

The myth: 'I am going to tell them no and that will be that.'

A damaging myth in mental health is the idea that change happens once and lasts for ever. This leads to self-blame and stigma when setbacks occur, and it carries a hefty stigma as if you 'should' somehow magically just know better. Do you feel personally responsible or blame yourself when you have a cold?

The reality: They might not hear you until the third, fourth or fifth time and then get cross with you for setting the boundary in the first place.

Creating boundaries is tough and maintaining them is even harder because: it is not a quick fix; you will get major resistance and kickback; your lack of boundaries may have been working well for others. Others' resistance does not mean your boundary is wrong.

You will need to expand your window of tolerance (see page 51) to tolerate other people's disappointment in you. Remember, this is not your fault, and it's not your responsibility. I like this definition by Mark Groves: 'Walls keep everybody out. Boundaries teach people where the door is.'

The big question now is: how do you draw boundaries? There are 10 key ways to draw healthy and sustainable boundaries:

1. Set your limits.
2. Your body never lies.
3. Remember to Pause.
4. Be direct.
5. Give yourself permission.
6. Practise self-awareness.
7. Be mindful of your family history.
8. Engage in real self-care.
9. Do it.
10. Baby steps.

1. Set your limits

Setting your limits is the beginning of questioning and establishing where you draw the line about how you spend your time and energy in relation to your physical and mental self and emotions. Set clear boundaries across all the important roles and relationships in your life. Starting with yourself, set emotional, physical and mental limits, then explore these across your relationships, work and how you spend your time and energy. Even though it will feel daunting and scary at first, this is the beginning of a new relationship with yourself and others that ultimately will deepen and replenish rather than drain and bring resentment.

When you set limits, it will clarify to you when a boundary has been crossed. To be able to do that, you first have to know where your line is. Is there a gap between what you want and what you think others want of you? Break this down into the different relational categories in your life, from home to work.

Work out the gap between what you want and what others want with regard to:

- yourself
- home/family

- relationships
- parenting
- workplace.

Cognitive dissonance is when there is a gap between what you think and how you behave. The bigger the gap, the harder it is on you because it doesn't feel authentic or good. Living a life that is misaligned with your own values contributes to feelings of disconnection and anxiety. Is there a gap between who you are and how you think and behave and how you believe you 'should' behave for others' approval, acceptance, or love? With compassion and curiosity, can I ask why?

As you explore the gap present in your roles and relationships, know that you will need to practise distress tolerance of other people's disapproval, so that you can live with it. Managing their temporary discomfort is pivotal to holding boundaries that are important to you and to the health of your relationships.

Notice with compassion when your window of tolerance moves towards: physiological and emotional activation – *Stop pushing me – you are always on my back* (Fight); or *I don't have to listen to this – I'm out of here* (Flight); or immobilisation – *Sure, I can do that, no problem'* (Fawn – people-pleasing), or *Hey, are you even listening to me? Answer me! Why are you saying nothing?* (Freeze – shutdown mode activated).

To establish your boundaries, you must first discover what and where your mental, physical and emotional limits are. Let's take examples of each type of limit, using the client story of Joanne to illustrate the common boundary problems that can arise.

> **MENTAL LIMIT**
> In the therapy room, Joanne said: 'I need specifics. It's like I know a boundary has been crossed in the moment and after the fact.

It's an immediate internal reaction of no, but I keep saying yes and having that delayed reaction, which is doubly annoying. I do know it doesn't suit and can't believe I've gone and said yes again. I then explode later at the wrong people, feel bad for doing that, and feel so guilty that I've done it again. I can't help but go back into the "What is wrong with me?" spiral. So I want to say no to the new project that has just landed in my email as I haven't finished the other two. My head is already switching between two projects and all the other interruptions.'

Script for Joanne to set a mental limit:
'Thanks for the update. Which project would you like me to prioritise under the time set out for projects A and B that I am currently working on? Or would you like me to focus solely on project C and redistribute the other projects?'

Boundaries do need to be specific. Creating your own unique scripts for different scenarios can be hugely helpful. This type of solution-focused thinking can bring clarity to an issue that you may have felt stuck with or overwhelmed by. Pausing old reactions, which may have been reactive and full of upset or anger, and teaching others how to treat you can feel empowering, hopeful and liberating.

PHYSICAL LIMIT

Joanne: I feel I have no physical space. I know every mother says it, but they stand outside and wait for me to come out of the toilet. I struggle with having healthy physical limits with myself and bypass my own physical limits all the time. It's like this awful feeling of guilt follows everything I do. If a friend asks me out and I'm exhausted, I go. If my manager asks for the report early, I stay up late to get it done. Even when I have the choice to say no, I don't. If my husband asks for a favour and it doesn't suit, I'll go out of my way to do it; he wouldn't say anything to me, but I have this huge sense of doing something wrong if I don't do it.

AK: That feeling of doing something wrong, how long have you felt that?

Joanne: I can't remember that feeling not being there.

AK: What would it be like to not push through your physical limits?

Joanne: I know the right answer to say, but the truth is I feel stuck in this repetitive loop, and I don't know if I can overcome it.

AK: Who would you be letting down if you met your own needs?

Joanne: Everyone.

AK: Did anyone call you selfish if you put your needs first?

Joanne: Yes, my mum. She was sick for years, it was so hard, I felt so bad for her, and it was hard to rest when I knew she was more tired than me. I'm not blaming her, she didn't want it either. In a way I think that made me want to help even more and not have her feel like a burden.

AK: That must have been so tough on you, I'm sorry, I know it wasn't anyone's fault but it's time to make some adjustments as things as they stand aren't working. Start by naming what it is like with your husband so that he can encourage you to say no. Like an accountability buddy with yourself, you will do this yourself in time, but it is okay to get support as you make small changes.

EMOTIONAL LIMIT

Joanne: I have a friend who emotionally dumps on me, it's very one-sided and I feel guilty if I try to shorten the time we spend together talking as she says she only can talk to me like this.

Emotional dumping is a common pattern that friendships and relationships can fall into. I think it's good to name it so you can identify and notice when it is happening.

I reminded Joanne that she wasn't her friend's therapist and that even a therapist would bring awareness when someone is stuck like this. I told her it was important to set a limit on these conversations.

Joanne: Sure, that's great, I know this, but what do I do when I need to make the dinner and I literally can't get her off the phone, Allison?

We got specific again, with another prepared script.

Script to stop emotional dumping:

'I have noticed that there is a lot going on for you. I understand, our lives our so hectic, aren't they? I'm certainly no therapist, but have you considered getting support with a therapist? As your friend I can help to some degree, but as your friend I am limited in being able to help you process this.'

Joanne felt the response she would get would be: 'I can't afford a therapist and I have no one to speak to about this but you', or perhaps just a passive-aggressive 'Fine'.

We discussed what she would reply to these responses: 'This friendship is important to me; as your friend, I can't be your therapist.'

There is every likelihood that you are reading this and thinking, 'I can't do that.' But the truth is, your friendship will not survive if you don't speak honestly because you will start to withdraw and perhaps ignore their calls and/or feel resentful – all of which spells the end of the friendship anyway. It's not about being brutal or unfeeling, it's about gently explaining where you end and your friend starts. I don't believe in harsh truth, but I do believe in honouring the integrity of your own needs.

It is a testament to the health of any relationship if you can express a healthy boundary and be heard with compassion and understanding. If you have a friendship or relationship in which you cannot express a healthy boundary, you need to check on the relationship, assess it and make appropriate changes. This may mean limiting the time you spend with that person, or limiting the one-on-one time, or limiting what you share with them. It is your right to choose your personal capacity in terms of how much of this friendship you can shoulder. If you don't speak out, you can end up tolerating an unsatisfactory friendship or relationship, and tolerating relationships isn't good for anyone. It needs to be a conversation, not a monologue. Therapists explore difficult things with their clients in a safe, objective space, and as a friend, you might not be able to create that kind of space, depending on the connection or level of the friendship. As a result, you mightn't be able to say what needs to be said, especially if your friend is stuck. Can you see how that helps no one and depletes everyone?

A friend who is stuck in emotional dumping behaviour is in danger of becoming stuck in rumination, and that requires therapeutic support. Rumination is linked to depression because endlessly talking about an issue without making any progress in your thinking only makes it worse. People are often encouraged to share their struggles for the sake of their mental health. I'm going to say this carefully: this message, although well-intentioned, can leave a person feeling even more alone, misunderstood, and judged if they get the wrong response back. This isn't anyone's fault. Think of it in terms of the medical field: if you had a physical complaint and shared it with your friend, they could not assess, diagnose or treat it correctly. So why do we expect emotional expertise from our friends and loved ones? They might not be equipped to help, so constantly seeking help creates anxiety for both of you.

Our lack of boundaries often stems from a fear of letting people down or disappointing them. But you are betraying yourself, and it's a self-betrayal of your time, energy and right to choose who to share your thoughts and physical space with. For all the negativity around age, especially for women, I think it's worth noting that I do think something shifts after 40, when you remember that you are a person as well. I wish women and men felt this earlier in life. That said, it's never too late to start identifying and setting your personal limits.

2. Your body never lies

Pay attention to your body's signals and sensations when interacting with others or making decisions. Your physical reactions can provide valuable insights into whether a situation aligns with your boundaries and values. There are two reliable red flags that tell you one of your boundaries has been crossed: a feeling of resentment; and a feeling of discomfort. If a request feels controlling, or manipulative, or you know you do not have the time or energy to meet it, then say no. Calmly, clearly, say no. And that is it. Remember the advice: 'No is a full sentence.'[37]

Do you notice if you have any resistance to this?

_____

Do you over-explain yourself? Do you immediately start justifying your 'no'?

_____

Over-explaining is a trauma response, stemming from past experience when you may have had to defend yourself if you weren't believed or if your caregiver didn't respect your mental boundaries because they held different values, beliefs or opinions. See your body as an instrument of the truth that lies within. If you are trying to decide yes or no, use the physical response to help you make an aligned decision. If you have the time or it is a big decision, I recommend imagining that you have said 'yes' for a day and take note of how that sits in your body and mind; do likewise with the hypothetical 'no'. You don't have to justify why you can't come, or do something; you can always be kind and mannerly. but it's time to end over-explaining.

3. Remember your Pause button

Take time to pause and reflect before responding to requests or making commitments. This allows you to consider whether the request aligns with your boundaries and whether you genuinely want to agree to it. When someone asks a question that begins with *Can you ...?* or *Will you ...?* or *Could you just ...?* or starts with *I need you to ...* – do the practical pause (see page 329) and give yourself time before answering.

You can do this physically, if it helps, by pressing your index finger and thumb together. This is your pause gesture, reminding you to pause, think, then reply. If you keep practising this physical pause gesture, it will create a neural link that will signal to your brain to be aware of the thoughts you are having about the request and to tune in to the response in your body. By tuning into those internal messages and being aware of the interoceptive cues, you are centring your needs and can then act in your own best interest.

If your mouth is about to say an automatic yes, but your thoughts are conflicted about what you want to do, and your body is feeling the familiar prickle of not wanting to let the person down, listen to the information cues coming from your thoughts and body. The practical pause will give you the few seconds you need to breathe and allow yourself the space to know and honour your internal response.

> *'The mind narrates what the nervous system knows.*
> *Story follows state.'*
>
> *– Deb Dana*

4. Be direct

People cannot read your mind, so don't expect them to. Clearly communicate your boundaries and preferences to others without ambiguity or apology. Tell the person directly and concisely if something doesn't suit you. You don't have to defend your no with a 'good enough' reason. 'Thank you for thinking of me. On this occasion I can't make it. Have a lovely time.'

When you are honest like this, you give others the ability to be honest as well. This is not to say that you get to be a hermit – remember that social connection is so important to your health. You are allowed to say no, but it might also be helpful to ask yourself why you are saying no. Bring it back to how you feel after meeting that person. Ask yourself: is that person a drain or a radiator? Drains are, well, draining. These are relationships or situations that leave you feeling drained and tired. They may not suit your social preferences, so one person's drain is another's radiator. Radiators are relationships that are engaging, warm and supportive. The difference between a drain and a radiator is that a drain takes energy, while a radiator gives energy. Could it be that this is where your no is coming from?

Friendship expert Professor Robert Dunbar of Oxford University describes maintaining friendship as 'extremely costly' because your two resources of time and energy are normally quite low, especially in our fast-paced world. Life and relationships and the psychology that underpins those experiences are nuanced. For example, you might be aware that a particular person is a drain, but you might share a relationship out of duty or obligation. Nonetheless, you can protect your boundaries by being mindful of your time, what you share and your right to privacy. You have a right to mind yourself. No one has endless energy.

Radiators	*Drains*
Who brings warmth/energy?	Who drains you?
_____	_____
_____	_____

Keep this list private, or better still, get rid of it.

5. Give yourself permission

Grant yourself permission to prioritise your own needs and wellbeing. Recognise that it's okay to say no to requests or to take time for yourself, even if it disappoints others. How do you know if you struggle with boundaries? Notice and pay attention if these three show up: fear; guilt; and self-doubt.

Instead of an immediate reaction of fear – *What will happen if I say no?* – try a new response:

Acknowledge where this thought came from.

_____

Ask: What are the consequences of staying the same?

_____

Take practical action (e.g. tolerating their disapproval and disappointment).

_____

Bring the 3 Cs – support yourself with compassion and curiosity as you challenge this process.

*What **compassion** do you need to bring to the fearful thoughts or sensations?*

_____

*In a spirit of **curiosity**, ask yourself what led to those fearful reactions, what made you feel like it wasn't okay to say no?*

_____

*Combining what you have discovered from questioning this with curiosity and compassion, how can you **challenge** this in an effective way and what needs to change for that to happen? Write out the steps.*

_____

Instead of reacting with guilt, try this new response:

Who first made you feel guilty? _____

About what? _____

How does guilt show up in your life right now? _____

How does guilt disconnect you from what you want? _____

What has guilt taught you? _____

How do you want to live going forward? _____

The function of guilt is to make you feel uncomfortable about something you've done that is wrong according to your own or others' moral compass. Separating your own sense of what is right or wrong for you from that of others is a hugely beneficial exercise with major freeing consequences. This, like most boundaries, will elicit resistance from others that 'this is not like you', but perhaps they are right. Becoming aligned to and living according to your own inner compass and values and being conscious of how others' comments and beliefs have been assimilated as your own will keep you feeling stuck and 'not feeling like yourself'.

This leads directly into when and why you stopped trusting your inner signal system. If you are to understand anxiety and your experiences in general, it is essential that you are able to understand yourself from the inside out. If you have lost your inner compass, perhaps it is because it has been drowned out by the voices of others (family, society, social media, all the *You shoulds* and *You shouldn'ts*). Like so many topics highlighted in this book, you can take what may initially look or feel bad or negative and find out what message it is giving you. If we park judgement, or fear of being judged, there is always great information to be picked up. So when we look underneath guilt we might realise, *Okay, that's interesting, this guilt isn't even mine, I was made feel guilty, I have assumed that I should feel guilty, but I can now see this internalised guilt isn't helping in any way and is keeping me stuck.* Pulling yourself out of conditioned guilt can, ironically, make you feel more guilty, but unless you are doing something wrong, explore whether it is shame that you need to name and let go of.

Compassionate inquiry allows layers of yourself to be explored with an open mind that wants better for you.

Instead of reacting with self-doubt, try this response:

Who does that critical self-doubting inner voice belong to?

_____

Part of setting boundaries is pausing and asking these questions to help with decision paralysis and procrastination when you don't know what you think.

When did the self-doubt start? _____

Think of specific times of self-doubt using the 4 Ws:

Who? _____

What? _____

When? _____

Where? _____

Look back into the origins of your boundaries, or lack thereof:

Emotional boundaries – *were you allowed to express how you felt?*

_____

Mental boundaries – *were your thoughts validated or diminished, mocked or greeted with anger?*

_____

Physical boundaries – *were you allowed your own space?*

_____

Time and energy boundaries – *how were these questioned?*

_____

Self-doubt is a learned experience, often arising from the experience of being invalidated or mocked, or through receiving negative feedback. You no longer trust yourself or your ability to assess a situation and make a good decision. You lose the sense that you have the right to say no. It leaves you floundering, unable to make a choice because you are racked with doubt that it isn't the right choice. This can lead to a gap between what you want to say or do and what you actually say or do. You can watch for this gap when answering a request by asking yourself: *Do I want to do this?* or *Do I feel I should do this?*

It is important to question what role fear, self-doubt and guilt have played in your setting of boundaries or inability to set boundaries. If you arrive at the realisation that one, two or all three of these have been affecting your decisions, you need to gently re-engage with your own sense of personal autonomy. Pull your power back and integrate the pieces to feel more like 'you'.

6. Practise self-awareness

Cultivate self-awareness by regularly reflecting on your thoughts, emotions and behaviours. Understand what triggers stress or discomfort for you and identify patterns in your boundary-setting tendencies. Listen to your initial physical response: what is your body's response? It is most likely correct. When it feels uncomfortable and/or too much, saying yes is only going to make that worse. Every time you say yes to someone else, you are saying no to something for yourself. This can be an upsetting experience. Deciding to value yourself and to interact and love others in a way that also meets your needs may be a novel experience for you. Take it one step at a time.

As you become more self-aware, you may become angry and/or grieve for older parts of you that you wished had these boundaries. Clients often become very upset as they make progress and admonish themselves, *How did I not know this?* and *Why didn't I do therapy sooner?* It is good to allow space for those thoughts and feelings, but getting stuck in them won't help you move forward. Keep practising self-compassion along with your self-awareness.

7. Be mindful of your family history

Reflect on how your family's dynamics and your upbringing may have influenced your boundary-setting tendencies. Understanding your family history can help you recognise and address any unhealthy patterns. Were you the 'good daughter' or the 'good son'? Dig into your family roles and see what role you took on. This might show you why creating and preserving healthy boundaries is so difficult. Have you been known as the one who always says yes, the one who everyone can depend upon? Or perhaps you were known as the organiser? Maybe by doing it all you are in burnout? Being a reliable person is a good quality, but not if you don't show up for yourself.

Healthy boundaries are about self-respect, about respecting your time, your energy and your mental and emotional peace of mind. Feeling overwhelmed, exhausted, angry and resentful does not make for long-term healthy relationships. This is why self-awareness is your key to creating healthy boundaries. Has your norm been that you put everyone else's needs before yours? If so, it's time to change this and to stop people-pleasing. You cannot keep on betraying your own needs.

8. Engage in real self-care

Prioritise genuine self-care practices that nourish your physical, emotional and mental wellbeing. This may include activities such as exercise, self-regulation, resting or spending time with loved ones. The core of self-care from a psychological perspective, though, is setting, creating, holding, maintaining, and resetting your boundaries. Sure, a bubble bath would be easier, but it won't garner the results you really want.

Let's blow the aspirational self-care stuff out the window. I'm interested in healthy boundary maintenance and managing anxiety. 'Maintenance' is a good word in this context – when you see something isn't working, you assess and implement the required change. Self-care may start with the question: *What do I need first?* Now ask: *Which boundary do I need most at this phase in my life?* Write down what renews you, whether it's a walk in a forest, a park, or by the sea. A coffee with a friend. An exercise class. Meditation. Dancing. Perhaps it's alone time. The point is, you know what works for you, and all I'm asking is that you start doing it in with consistency. My expectations are slow and low. Every week brings new challenges, new appointments, sickness, work demands. If you don't get some space for you this week, fine, start again tomorrow. I don't have a scarcity mentality with self-care, I have a realistic one. Whatever it is, seek out what nourishes your mind and soul. Put a boundary around the time you take out to do that. Then, and only then, can you be fully present within your relationships.

9. Do it
Take action to assert your boundaries and prioritise your health. Follow through on setting and maintaining boundaries, even when it feels uncomfortable or challenging. Don't have that angry rant in your mind. Blaming others takes away your autonomy and ability to be responsive. You have power, so decipher what you can and cannot change and align with that. Ask *What can I do next?* You can do this. Whatever is out of your control, you can still decide how you want to feel about it and intentionally regulate your nervous system, even to neutral.

I felt ____ (angry, upset, frustrated) when you said/asked/expected … I am not comfortable doing this anymore and I wanted to let you know that because our relationship and you are so important to me.

What other scripts do you need? Write them down and keep them for when you need them. The very act of writing them down will give you a greater sense of clarity and confidence in your ability to say what you need to say. The first few words are always the hardest.

10. Baby steps
I love watching babies who have just started to walk. They wobble, stumble and fall, it may be one step forward and two backwards, but they get back up and try again and again. Remember that establishing healthy boundaries is a gradual process. Take small, incremental steps towards

asserting yourself. Celebrate your progress, even if it's slow, and be patient with yourself along the way.

Boundaries are the foundations of your life. But you can't be rigid or perfectionist about them because they will change and be tested, and they will require ongoing negotiations. You can play your part and let people know what doesn't work for you. You can also accept fully that how other people behave is out of your control and is not your responsibility. The consequences of others trespassing or ignoring your boundaries does come back to you.

As I write this, I can think of two boundaries I need to express. The thought of that feels like a dull, apprehensive feeling in my gut. I know what I have to do, I know what I have to say, and yet the idea of it feels super uncomfortable.

Let's do this together, one hard conversation at a time.

Make a list of what is acceptable and unacceptable to you in all relationships:

Personal: _____

Romantic: _____

Parental: _____

Daughter/son: _____

Friend: _____

Employee/boss: _____

This is your starting point. Well done, you have set your limits. This is huge work.

The Practical Psychology

COLD THERAPY

When you immerse yourself in cold water, it quietens the noisy mind as you come to focus on your breathing and movement. It brings you to a point of crystal clarity – *This is freezing, I am taking this breath, I am moving my arms, I am kicking my legs.* It brings you right back into your body and the mind takes a backseat for a while. That can be freeing and has a huge impact on the nervous system and anxiety. It is a form of direct connection with nature that brings you back to yourself.

David Sinclair, a Harvard biologist and leading researcher of longevity, explains that we are used to experiencing 'metabolic winters' because our ancestors had to adapt to living in the cold when the seasons changed. However, we are now all snug in winter in our warm, temperature-controlled homes, so we are not answering our natural desire for cold and the outdoors.

Cold therapy is rooted in the science of the body. After 10 to 15 minutes of cold exposure, 'the sympathetic response causes blood vessels to vasodilate, a process called cold-induced vasodilation (CIVD)'. What feels like shock cold to you is your peripheral blood vessels alternating between vasoconstriction and vasodilation. In cold water, your body rapidly alternates between the two, narrowing and widening blood vessels, respectively, to regulate body temperature.

Anna Lembke, a Stanford professor and psychiatrist, prescribes different forms of hormesis. Hormesis is the idea that some amount of pain is good for us. This is something I have been thinking about for a while now. In our never-ending quest for eternal happiness and pain-free existence, the 'happily-ever-after', I fear we have taken a wrong turn along the way. According to hormesis, as Anna Lembke described it, our bodies respond to cold-water immersion by 'up-regulating' good feelings like 'dopamine, serotonin and norepinephrine' as a way of 'compensating' for the cold. So while people like to poke fun at the dryrobes and the zeal of the sea-swimming converts, there are good reasons and huge benefits from cold therapy, however you choose to practise it.

Dipping in

- Ice holds – to stop an active panic attack, hold an ice cube in each hand.
- Diver's reflex – place your face in a bowl of iced water: you will experience an immediate mind–body connection, increased focus and attention and stress reduction, which can aid regulating mood and emotions.
- When you need a moment to reset when feeling anxiety, run cold water over your wrists.
- Regular cold showers – build up your tolerance by starting with 10 seconds and gradually increase the intensity and duration to what works for you.
- Paddle in the sea – take off your shoes and socks and walk in the cold water.
- If you can swim, try the sea, or have an ice bath. Don't be pressurised by trends: if a bowl of ice will do the trick, stick with that.

A word of caution: Cold water can be a physical shock, so, like everything else, implement it in doses and know your own medical and psychological history, and your swimming capabilities. Check with your GP for medical advice before taking the plunge.

CHAPTER 10

Healthy coping mechanisms for psychological anxiety

What are you worried about?

The difference the person's tone makes in asking that question is remarkable. I ask it very gently in the therapy room, but many people hear in it a tone of exasperation and impatience when they are asked this outside the therapy room. What is said is *What are you worried about?* but what they can hear being said underneath that is *It could be worse, It might never happen, This is all in your head.* The difficulty with anxiety is there is still a lot of shame and blame on the person, that they 'should' be able to 'let go', 'relax', 'get over it' and, the worst one, to my ears: 'Just relax and stop being anxious'. *Wow, now I'm cured, thanks so much for that*, said nobody ever. From your side, inside, you feel you are dripping in fear, stuck in a loop of over-thinking and catastrophising, trying to imagine and control future outcomes. And the fear and worry isn't just your own, it's for your loved ones and even strangers you read about in the paper. The dread and doom can feel that it is who you are, and then the fear of the fear thinks, *This is it now, I will never change.*

Do you really think anyone wants to live that way? Restlessness is an awful experience, when even your thoughts feel like a threat, and you can't get them to stop. Anxiety doesn't just feel like racing thoughts, it's a daily mental marathon. That is the psychological experience of someone whose thoughts, emotions and body are enmeshed in a constant push–pull of inner frustration, of knowing what to do and yet fearing the anxiety is gaining strength, without the understanding of how their life and story impacted their nervous system.

I start this with appreciation for the courage of people who experience anxiety and panic attacks. I genuinely think they have been too strong for too long and, as I mentioned, I feel the body presents panic attacks when it is fed up as you continue to try to push through each day. This is where I see toxic resilience, which often leads a person to believe that they 'can't cope' or 'aren't strong enough' or 'feel weak', overlooking the importance of a trauma-informed understanding of themselves, which I hope you have now. The body, mind and emotions inform the body of my work. Understanding why and where trauma is stored in your body is the key to understanding yourself and the root of your anxiety. You will not out-rationalise a panic attack, you will not intellectualise your anxiety away, and yet that is exactly what I see so many people trying to do, and where I see most people become stuck and deeply frustrated. They have a lot of information, and yet it can make them feel worse when the change hasn't happened. I hope you can see the function of why we feel fear or flee and have compassion as to why many of us try to numb noisy heads.

I always thought the phrase 'a body of lies' was apt in helping people dig below the surface of who they think they are, to reveal to them the many masks they wear in order to feel accepted, valued, worthy, liked and loved. Uncovering the 'lies' we hold about ourselves – *I'm just lazy, I've always just been a worrier* – and who we think we are can be quite an unsettling process. Your own accepted ideas about what you perceive to be your 'personality' or *That's just who I am* may have missed the bit where that is who you became to survive.

We are back to the usual suspects: people-pleasing, perfectionism, the good girl/boy. These are the masks your wear to protect yourself, and they can lead to you feeling overstretched and overwhelmed. A lot of times the truth is hidden in plain sight. Look at the word 'Belief' and go to the centre of it: Be**LIE**f.

Your inner critic

The root of psychological anxiety lies with the inner critic who nests inside your brain and has an opinion on everything. You can look perfectly functioning on the outside, smiling and competent, but on the inside there can be a steady stream of angry and mocking dialogue all aimed directly at you. Your inner critic is a powerful force, and it can be the source of a constant sense of psychological stress and anxiety. It's like a battle of wills going on inside you all the time – sometimes you feel like you're gaining the upper hand, sometimes it's a knockout and you're down and out on the floor.

Ask yourself: Why do you notice and remember the bad? Your brain will notice all the mistakes and take note with the fluorescent marker of shame. I want to ignite in you the practical psychological skill of noticing the good, in yourself and in others. It won't be easy, it won't come naturally, but just noticing when the inner critic walks into the room is so insightful. And when you start noticing, that awareness will help you feel a little more in control. It is a skill because you have to actively and consciously override your brain's wiring to notice the bad, which is linked to the evolutionary need for survival, to act first and then think if you were in danger. Here, you are trying to notice the quiet good that is being overshadowed by the loud bad.

I get my clients to make their inner voice a character, to give it a name and personality – that helps to spot them as soon as they arrive, looking to make trouble. I find that picturing my inner critic helps me, too. I know my inner critic is an absolute bitch. The things she says to me could bring you to tears, and they often do. She brings her own posse with her as well, and they are a powerful bunch. She's the leader, but standing behind her are Doubt, Inferiority, Criticism, Fear, Perfectionism and 'What if?' I ask clients to name their inner critic to help identify when it shows up. I have always been fully aware of my own active and mouthy inner critic but hadn't thought to name her, until during a panel discussion on this topic, someone in the audience asked, 'What's yours called?' and without hesitation I said, 'The Bitch'.

Time to meet your personal inner critic:

- When does that voice show up and why?
- What is the fear under the initial feelings of shame, those thoughts of 'I shouldn't have done that or said that' – what are you really afraid of?
- Have you noticed a pattern?
- What needs haven't been met?
- What hurt or past emotional wound is showing up?
- Identify what happened and what changed as a result of that experience(s).
- What do you need for that to feel attended to and minded?

Now for the big question: How are you going to soften what your inner critic says to you? The answer is: Pretend it was said to your sister, mother, friend, or someone you deeply love, be aware of how it sounds when directed at someone you love, and then stand up for them, say what you want to say – but say it to yourself.

This might look like this:

Inner critic: *I'm such a complete and utter failure, everyone thinks I am doing an awful job. I am awful at everything. I can't do anything* right. *Everyone else is doing so much better than me. No one likes me. Why am I like this? What is wrong with me?*

Imagine for a moment bringing in your own counter-voice to what your inner critic has just said. To set the scene, I'm going to invite in the concept of radical acceptance,[38] which is used therapeutically to help process intense emotions and to aid emotional regulation. If we look at the words above, what we see is a rejection of the self in the most personal and definitive way. A great way to help spot red flags within critical language towards yourself is to notice when words such as *always, never, everyone else, complete and utter failure* are present. There is no nuance, no room for humanness and it would leave you thinking nothing could change. If we ran all those words through a radical acceptance sieve, it might poignantly relay back a different story, one that showed a lack of self-belief, past hurts, peer, social and family rejection that warranted masking up to be 'perfect'. Practising radical acceptance first would allow some much-needed tears and sitting with the emotions present. Perhaps there is frustration, embarrassment, shame, not feeling good enough, a history of being criticised, a fear of getting it wrong in front of other people and past experiences of this.

Countering your inner critic with compassion might sound like this:

This is hard. Max did make a snide remark, but that isn't the whole team. It did trigger that old familiar feeling of getting it wrong and being disliked. I know the rest of the team like me. I might reach out to Amy and get her take. I acknowledge even doing this makes me feel even more vulnerable, but this is what I have been working on. I'm not stuck, this bit isn't working, but that doesn't mean I am failing. In the last project I felt the same way at this stage, and then it was really well received. I am allowing myself to ask for help and know that I would always help anyone out and rather than thinking less of them, I think more of them. Okay, that was hard, I'm going to take some deep breaths, write out this experience and then go for a 10-minute walk and go and talk with Amy.

Changing the inner critic narrative will take compassion, patience, and lots of practice. Your inner critic has been holding court for a long time and will not take kindly to your new, supportive voice. It will berate you and seek to minimise the work you are putting into having a kinder relationship with yourself. Don't be afraid of that critical voice – it can shout its worst, then you can counter it with reason and compassion and good dose of reality. When the self-doubt kicks in, place your hand on your heart and repeat to yourself:

- Compassion over perfection
- Progress with compassion
- Keep going
- One breath after the other
- This is unfamiliar and uncomfortable and that's okay
- I am learning
- I am allowed make normal human mistakes.

A word on mistakes ... Make them. If you aren't making mistakes, you might be stuck, frozen or in a cycle of avoidance. It takes huge courage to do uncomfortable and hard things and I'm sorry to tell you this, but there isn't any safety net. Not exactly what you wanted to hear, but the truth will open the world back up to you. 'Staying safe' when it is a defence mechanism is the enemy of overcoming anxiety. I mentioned the study on what happy people do differently, and it is doing things that make them temporarily uncomfortable. It's back to the opposites: to connect you need to take the social risk and say 'hi'.

I struggle where I see in too many facets of life where mistakes are deeply discouraged, we are robbing people of the invaluable tool of trying, and when it doesn't work out trying again. This is resilience. No one feels good when they make a mistake; you feel exposed, as if everyone can see the parts you try to keep to yourself. You don't smile and think *Wonderful, a learning opportunity*, you probably curse yourself and feel mortified. Ironically, please think about people you have connected with, people you like, and I bet you like their normalness and their human flaws.

Ask yourself where your abhorrence for making mistakes comes from. Two places frequent the therapy room in relation to criticism: home and school. If you think about it, as a child you are in one or the other at such an important and impressionable stage of development. You looked to these figures of authority to get a sense if you were on the right track. Being shamed in front of your peers at school is a common culprit. The other is when there was a critical parent. Even when they stop that behaviour, many have already internalised the critical parent and that voice becomes their inner critic.

Conscious drinking

It is very common for people experiencing psychological anxiety to reach for something to numb out those feelings. We looked at screen addiction in Chapter 8, but the other classic mind-number is, of course, alcohol. This is something that comes up again and again in the therapy room with my clients, and we all know it's a widespread problem, even though it's so often hidden. And this doesn't necessarily mean addiction, it's very often an unhealthy relationship with alcohol that means you are relying on it to an extent, but unable to see or admit that. The problem is, alcohol is never an effective solution and can contribute to anxiety – both while you are drinking and the next day and beyond. It's important to be aware of the effect alcohol has upon your anxiety levels, and what I intend to propose here is a good plan that will genuinely make you feel better.

As I observe our cultural attitudes towards alcohol, I believe it's time to reconsider accepted norms and social practices. Even before the World Health Organization (WHO) published a startling statement in the *Lancet Public Health* in January 2023 – 'When it comes to alcohol consumption, there is no safe amount that does not affect health'[39] – a noticeable shift had been occurring in people's awareness.

It seems that alcohol may be the new smoking. Covid lockdowns may have accelerated that process, causing people to question their relationship with alcohol.

If you want to make changes to your life and feel better: what would that look like for you? This is a call to question drinking, to practise conscious drinking or, if needs be, to rethink your drinking. It's very easy to fall into mindless drinking, where you barely notice how much you are consuming. If you are going to have a drink, have it at the table with dinner, for example. That way, you're not quaffing away while the TV distracts you and you don't notice the end of the bottle arriving fast. By drinking consciously, you are more mindfully aware of every sip. Associations are powerful. If TV on + sitting on couch = alcohol for you, that's an unconscious association and it's easy to just fall into it every time you sit down. Creating new, conscious habits is about building on small changes that make a big difference and then maintaining them. This may apply to a wider audience as most will deny any attachment to alcohol, and it's easy to see why; our norm is not normal.

The best way to find out what your relationship is with alcohol and how it affects your anxiety levels is to implement a new, conscious habit and take note of how it makes you feel. You might decide, for example, to forego those glasses of wine on a Friday night. Now ask yourself: did you sleep better or longer? Did you feel sharper the next day? Did you notice any difference in terms of anxiety and inner critic? Try it out and take notes and find out what does and does not work for you.

This is, of course, a societal problem, as we all know. To me, it's plain that our accepted norms and highly pressurised social practices need a rethink. So many people – those I meet both professionally and personally – are questioning their relationship with alcohol, making changes and reducing their intake. They are more intentional now, slowing down, consuming a small amount, choosing not to numb and feel out of sorts the next morning. Changing this relationship with alcohol carries huge benefits.

For anyone who feels that living without alcohol would be a good thing to try, there is a movement called sober-curious that encourages you to try it and see how it feels. As I said earlier, for anyone who experiences anxiety or panic attacks, this is a fantastic idea. Cut it out, and see what that feels like for you.

Anxiety and alcohol are not a good mixer. The number of people who hadn't been drinking the night before their first panic attack is tiny. This is a pattern that I have seen repeated over the last 25 years. From my experience, alcohol and panic attacks have a toxic friendship.

Ask yourself: do you think that last sentence will change how you feel about drinking?

Have you become more sober-curious or just curious about your drinking in general?

If you were to make any changes, what adjustments come to mind?

If you were to practise conscious drinking, how would that look for you?

Did you know about the connection between alcohol and anxiety/panic attacks?

Have you experienced hang-xiety?

If you were to give up alcohol, how would that look for you?

Conscious socialising

I noticed years ago, while training to do an exercise challenge for a morning TV programme, that there was a whole other way of socialising that I had never known existed – and that this way and the way I was used to doing it were as opposite as night and day. To add some real-life honesty here, I met the group of lads I was doing the challenge with at the bottom of Howth Hill at around 9.30 a.m. on our first day of training. Suffice to say, I had never cycled up the hill before and I had only gotten *into* bed at around 4 a.m., so as you can imagine, I was not exactly in incredible shape to get on a bike and heave myself up a hill – having not been on a bike since I was a kid and having been in bed for only the blink of an eye!

But I did it, and I committed to keep on doing it. We continued to train at weekends, always early. Our first daughter was just six months old at the time, so this waking up early thing was part of the deal anyway. But I was so pleasantly surprised to see so many other people around my age and older out swimming, walking, cycling, hiking. I had no idea there was this whole early morning fun going on. Saturday nights may have been rocking late into the night, but Sunday mornings had their own crew, too. I ended up loving it and wanting to be one of the Sunday morning crew. Pre-kids, I would have balked at this grim idea: weekends were for fun, going out and sleeping in and why in God's name would you do early starts and exercise? But as I kept going, I found that I had an appetite to socialise, connect, move, and feel good in a different way. Connection, being in nature and outside and doing something with others that was challenging was a real eye-opener for me. It took me a while to realise that sleeping in wasn't my authentic self. As a kid, I had loved getting up at 6 a.m. to watch cartoons. I liked the quietness. Funnily, my eldest likes to get up at that time now and I feel like saying, 'No, this is *my* quiet time!' When I asked her why she was up, that was her exact answer: 'This is my favourite time of the day and the only time to myself.' The apple doesn't fall far from the tree.

This is what conscious choices are all about, not just rolling along in the same habits because they're habitual, but actually asking yourself what works for you. The practice of realigning with your authentic self is an essential part of tackling and managing anxiety. Are you a natural night owl or a natural early bird? By getting up earlier, you start your sleep process from that exact point because you will naturally go to bed a little earlier. If you get up earlier, you need a fresh head, so going out late changes that. I am not suggesting you no longer go out late, but I am asking you to consider your circadian body clock and to be aware that how you spend your day influences the quality of the sleep you have at night.

Making conscious choices is an underrated adult skill. 'Boring' is often thrown at those who want to live and feel better. You'll find friends saying: 'What, why are you going home? Oh come on, have one more drink, I'll promise we'll go home after this one.' Know that they are speaking from their own agenda, and you do not have to share that agenda. It's your choice to make conscious decisions that make you feel better in yourself.

Cognitive behavioural therapy

Cognitive behavioural therapy (CBT) is an evidence-based talk therapy. It is helpful in teaching people how to notice, identify and change unhelpful and negative thought patterns and behaviours that lead to distress and mental health issues. It is based on the idea that thoughts, feelings and behaviours are interconnected, and as you impact one, it positively influences the others. The therapist and client work collaboratively on specific goals. Cognitively challenging certain thought patterns, such as all-or-nothing thinking or catastrophising, and working upon behaviours, such as challenging reactions to stressful situations.

This cognitive approach effectively sprays the weed with thought weed-killer, but I am always interested in what is hidden below the surface that can't be seen. We all have blind spots; and it is incredible in therapy when lightbulb moments reveal aspects of the person's life to them. They often feel it is impossible: *How did I not see that before? How did I not know this?'* Please know it was because thinking about it was too painful. Keep reminding yourself about all the different times, experiences, situations, and overwhelming emotions your brain has protected you from. This is why only you can get to the point as to when you are ready, to look at and process what you experienced.

Pause to process the protective nature of why you couldn't or didn't feel or see what happened:

The Practical Psychology

As we explore the psychological impact of anxiety, which can feel like an isolating experience, especially for people wearing the masks of perfection and high-functioning anxiety, there are many effective practices to help soothe restless minds. Remember the Gaviscon ad where the fireman hoses down the red, inflamed stomach? This is my version for your brain, and these exercises are the cooling blue fire hose.

HOW TO QUIETEN YOUR MIND

I have been asked a thousand times by exasperated clients: 'How can I get my mind to stop?' To be perfectly honest, there is no mythical peaceful nirvana state that you can achieve to give you a still mind. If you have no thoughts, you are flatlining. If you are alive, you have an active mind, that's part of being human. However, when you feel your mind is overwhelming you, there are things you can do to help:

What is going on for you on the inside? Identify any thoughts – be specific, write them down:

_____

Identify any worries:

_____

What is coming up for you?

_____

Are these helpful thoughts?

_____

Can you have these thoughts and emotions and allow yourself a few moments for them to be there and for you to also take a moment to reset?

_____

Now, take a breath, acknowledge how you are, accepting and allowing space for conflicting emotions and giving room and space to hold that.

Practise the snow globe for a quiet mind

Nestled high on the cliffs overlooking the sea, Dzogchen Beara is a very special place that allows you to reconnect with yourself and reset. I found myself in a room with floor-to-ceiling windows overlooking the sparkling Beara Peninsula. The meditation was led by a wonderful lady who talked to us about a snow globe. She spoke of how we live our lives, how we get rattled and shook up and feel all over the place, just like the snow globe. Then she asked us to imagine holding the snow globe steady and letting the contents settle. We visualised the snow scattered and pulled in all directions, then beginning to slow down and come down into itself. Breathing in, breathing out, inner contents settling.

Try it now. See all the thoughts whirling around in your head – *I must do that, Did I do that?* – and allow yourself to pause and breathe in and out, let the snowflakes settle.

It's okay if the snow globe gets moving again. In fact, welcome any resistance, any thoughts of *I don't have time for this*. Acknowledge them and bring compassion to how hard it is to quieten when the demands for your attention are real and can't be ignored. For this moment, see them and know that you will come back to them. You can let them settle for now.

Sit there until you feel ready, then connect back to your body in whatever way feels natural to you.

Keep the image of the snow globe in your mind and whenever you feel shook and whirling, picture it settling for a moment, and then go back to your day.

How to stop racing thoughts

Racing thoughts are nasty, firing like an automatic weapon – *bam, bam, bam* – relentless, damaging, and pure exhausting. Here are some simple steps to help you calm them:

1. Acknowledge they are there and give permission. Pushing against having them in the first place will keep you frustrated and stuck.
2. Perform the physiological sigh – two short inhales, one long inhale; repeat as needed.

3. Do a timeline and ask these thoughts if they are from the:

Past	**Present**	**Future**
I keep worrying about what happened …	I am worrying about what's happening …	I am worried that … will happen …

Or a combination of all three? Spend some time getting to the root of them.

4. Notice where they are showing up in your body, for example:

Neck	Shoulders	Shoulder blades
↓	↓	↓
Headache	Head tension	Heaviness in chest
↓	↓	↓
Feeling agitated	Feeling anxious	Uncomfortable

5. What type of movement do the thoughts have? Are they negative and spiralling, jumping from one thing to the next, or catastrophising?

What negative thoughts are present? _____

Naming them takes their power, so name them:

_____

If the thoughts are spiralling, what other bad thoughts, experiences, memories and conversations (past, present and future) are being collected?

_____

And why? _____

Notice how sticky these thoughts are – when did they stick first? Where did those thoughts come from?

_____

Do they carry embarrassment, guilt, shame, fear, worry, fear of judgement? _____

Do a fact-check. Ask: 'Are these thoughts opinions or fact?'

_____

The best way to check this is to ask yourself: If you were asked to defend these questions in court and were given only the option of fact or fiction, pick one.

Distract yourself from racing thoughts by moving

Racing thoughts can come from anxiety, ADHD, OCD and can turn into rumination. Do these exercises with titration in mind, i.e. small doses, and build up as you are ready and/or get support through therapy.

- Skip with a skipping rope, up to one minute if you can, or whatever feels comfortable for you.
- Shake it out (see Toolbox, page 329).
- Choose some cold therapy according to your time limit or capability (see page 264)
- Walk/run.
- Do yoga.
- Dance.
- Do something that needs your close attention, such as cooking or baking.

CHAPTER 11
Healthy coping mechanisms for physiological anxiety

Anxiety is a full-body experience, which I have divided into three aspects to illustrate how it shows up in your body, mind, and emotions. This is intended to help you understand each aspect and how they interact and to show you that because the root problem is not solely mental, the solutions cannot be solely mental either. We have explored how unprocessed emotions, experiences and trauma can get stuck in your body. I hope you understand and feel a sense of comfort from navigating the intricacies of your nervous system.

I think this chapter will resonate with you, because it is one that I know so many people desperately want and need to hear. This is the practical application and the cornerstone of standing up against the push of hyper-productivity and being more by doing less. Resting is revolutionary in a society that ignores, betrays and denies your body's needs, and profits from you overriding yourself. Before your body says no for you, I ask you to choose to say no.

Resting and relaxing

Hands up if you ever heard or were told that the devil makes work for idle hands. So many of our beliefs come from systems that were interwoven into our life that it can be hard to stand back and separate yourself from them. Let's take a moment to think about what that phrase is actually saying. It is powerfully connecting resting or relaxing with sin, in other words suggesting that is it something you should not do. The connection was made in the fearful tone of fire and brimstone that if you weren't busy, that was sinful, that if you were 'doing nothing', that deserved to be called out and punished. Maybe there is irony in the fact that so many women have lived lives in perpetual hell, following the martyr-like promise of eternal rest in death. Maybe that's what is meant by 'Rest in Peace'? Please, I beg of you, don't wait until then to rest or have peace.

I work with many, many clients who find it nigh on impossible to sit down until 'everything is done', and I always ask them the same question: did you see your mother sit and relax regularly? I have put that question to so many people, and it's always met with an immediate answer: 'No, I never saw my mum sit down, she was always on the go.'

Warning! Reading this chapter may make your house messier and your head, heart, and body happier.

I will admit, I am still a couch jumper. This relates right back to childhood when I'd see the car headlights swing into the driveway and if I was watching TV, I would leap off the couch to be found doing whatever it was I 'ought to' have been doing. Suffice to say, watching daytime TV was not okay in my parents' eyes. I'm kind of laughing as I write this because my arrival doesn't inspire my kids to jump off the couch. But I'd totally settle for them to just get off it and put their dishes in the dishwasher. Nothing would have happened to me, no punishment – my parents are lovely – but I knew that sitting down watching TV would be considered 'doing nothing'. My husband laughs at me when he comes in the door and I leap off the couch – still that same feeling that I 'ought to' be doing something. He always laughs and says, 'It's okay, relax.' And yet still I jump up because that old belief is deeply ingrained, rooted in the idea that I mustn't get 'caught' relaxing. Old beliefs die even harder than old habits!

Why is resting and relaxing so hard? Honestly, because there is always more stuff to do. Okay, I am going to say it, there is always too much stuff to do. But how can you be the one person who says no, when 'everyone else is doing it'? The gap between what you want to do and what you have to do seems to just keep growing wider, until bridging it comes to feel like an impossibility. This is a pretty normal state of affairs for most people, I think, but it's made worse when you add in a life lived in survival mode, which creates a need for stress and urgency. And if you have experienced trauma, relaxing can feel deeply unnerving. Your sense of anxiety might benefit from rest and relaxation, but that very sense of anxiety ends up preventing you being able to rest and relax – it's a vicious circle that loops you right back into old behaviours, even though they are unhealthy for you.

I invite you now to come at this from a perspective of building up your rest and relaxation, one small dose at a time, until your body knows that it is safe to relax. This is how you can use titration to build up your daily dose, until you are able to tolerate and enjoy relaxation.

Answer these questions honestly:

Do you allow yourself to relax?

_____

Do you feel guilty if you rest or relax?

_____

Do you feel you have to earn your rest or relaxation?

_____

What negative words do you associate with relaxation/resting?

_____

In the therapy room, I ask clients to explain to me why they can't relax or rest – and here are the words I hear from them: 'Oh, I'd feel guilty.' 'It feels selfish.' 'That's all well and good, Allison, but no one else will do what needs to be done and then I have to come back to it all. Of course I am tired, of course I want to relax, but it's actually not worth it. It isn't worth the hassle it takes before I leave and then coming back to chaos.'

Are you nodding your head as you read those words? If so, you need to assess your own attitude to rest and relaxation. It's vital for your health, but are you allowing yourself that vital time? If you are not, there's nothing wrong with you. If you find rest and relaxing devilishly hard, nothing is wrong with you. I would ask you to ask yourself a different question, not 'What is wrong with me?' but rather: 'What happened to me?' This is the title of a book I love, written by Bruce Perry and Oprah Winfrey. It invites readers to change the *What's wrong with me?* trauma narrative into a much more comprehensive, compassionate and cathartic question: *What happened to me?*

This is a soft and evocative question. Understanding yourself asks for you to question, *Why do I feel I have to do this a certain way?* Getting curious rather than furious with yourself and looking at systems of belief that may need a reassessment asks for you to understand, without judgement, and to bring in historical context, as in what the norm was at the time. This type of work can benefit hugely from speaking with a therapist. When looking back, remember titration and to do it in small doses so as not to flood your nervous system if intense or painful emotions arise. Part of therapy and somatic body work is to gain freedom from the past, to explore your present, and to engage with yourself for a future that feels good to you.

How often do you receive emotional validation? In my humble opinion, not enough. Acknowledgement of what happened to you is so underrated and yet transformative. From my work with trauma, I know the traumatic event(s) had a huge impact upon you. But the second blow comes in the form of you, others and society dismissing or minimising your traumatic experience. If people simply sat and listened, without silver-lining your pain, that would provide a protective gauze over your psychological, emotional and physical injuries. Validate how it felt, how it feels and grieve what it meant to you to go through what you went through.

Here are nine cultural reasons why you find it hard to relax:

1. You may have been living in chronic survival mode, so resting feels anything but relaxing to you. Living in a state of heightened awareness and being in sniper mode, where you are hypervigilant, and then dropping down to burnout and exhaustion can become the norm. Relaxation can feel anxiety-inducing because staying alert made you feel in control and, most important, it is a familiar state.
2. Your sense of self-value is extrinsically linked to what you do or produce. If your self-worth is enmeshed within what you do, relaxing can feel like you are wasting 'valuable' time, leading to whole-body exhaustion and anxiety.
3. Hyper-productive hustle culture is a personal, societal and organisational mindset that glorifies and prioritises constant productivity at the expense of health and life balance. It relentlessly encourages a concept of external success where people work long hours and push beyond their human limits. It is often future-based, which amplifies the anxiety of not being in the present moment, promoting that if–then thinking, e.g. *If I work late, then I can take a break*. Time to throw away the 'Busy' badge.

4. We live in a society where it is easy to fall into striving to outperform your peers in a narrow concept of what success is while constantly comparing what and how you are doing with peers and even with people you don't know. Comparison has widened its lens, largely thanks to social media, leaving many feeling they are always behind, inadequate and not doing enough.
5. How often does your subject line say 'Urgent' – and the more caps and exclamation marks, the more urgent it supposedly is? When everything is urgent, it becomes so difficult to know what to prioritise. Connection is pivotal, but when you are constantly bouncing from one platform to another, from email to WhatsApp to all incoming information, that swamps your nervous system. Knowing all those 'urgent' things need to be responded to interferes with your brain's ability to let go and relax.
6. If a chaotic environment was the norm while you were growing up, that's all your nervous system knows. Relaxing or calmness may feel unsettling and unfamiliar to your nervous system, which is used to being on high alert. Notice if you find calm situations, people, or experiences 'boring', this can be telling.
7. Resting or relaxing was never modelled to you. If you never saw the people around you relax until everything was done, it can feel challenging to allow yourself to relax when you 'should' be doing all the things. Prioritising rest is a behaviour you can model for yourself and others, with life-changing consequences.
8. Perhaps R&R was openly discouraged. You may have implicitly learned that resting was bad if you never saw it, but if it was explicitly labelled as lazy, unproductive and selfish, that laid down a particular belief in cement. Guilt around taking time to rest becomes rigidly internalised.
9. The 'superwoman' myth is encouraged and perpetuated across society. Unless the cape is a fashion accessory, I'm not interested, because we don't have superpowers to make us capable of what is

not humanly possible in a single day or life. This myth perpetuates over-achieving and betraying your own needs at the cost of getting something done.

Resting mustn't be a privilege of the few; wealth should not be a blocker to wellness. If you are managing systemic oppression, socio-economic exclusion, working to survive and worrying how to pay the bills, resting may be the last thing on your list. There are many factors that exclude people. The rest I advocate is usually free, in nature or where you live. Prioritising rest may feel impossible when under huge financial pressure, but this is when I gently suggest you need it most, if even for a few minutes.

Why am I finding this so hard?

_____

Who encourages you to rest?

_____

Who encourages you to relax?

_____

SHE-FAULT MODE

Those seem like simple, reasonable questions, but how can you relax if you are systemically stuck in an endless mode of doing all that *has to* get done? The reality of resting is that it is hard to relax when your brain is pestering you to get up and get back to your full-time adult admin job.

From the therapy room, I know that many women feel that they can't rest or relax if their children are in childcare or in school. The fear of judgement kicks in, so cleaning, cooking or working are acceptable; but even then, someone will have a comment to make.

Another sin-inducing quote I'm sure you are familiar with is 'There's no rest for the wicked', to which I always reply, 'I must be really wicked, then.' I'm not, but we are all wicked tired. Even as I say this, I know that you are likely countering it in your own mind with: *But I don't have time to rest!* Can you see what's happening here? Can you see that our external value has become directly linked to being busy, productive and whatever the narrow, materialistic idea of 'successful' is? I tell you what it is not: it is not sustainable. It needs to change, before your health changes it for you.

Do you recognise your own thinking here? You want to relax but:

- Taking a break can feel not worth it, especially if you come home to a bombsite.
- The structure or support isn't there for you to do it.
- The impact of past trauma has dysregulated your nervous system and you feel on high alert all the time.
- Anxiety leaves you hyper-aware of physiological symptoms, so breathing techniques, becoming aware of your heart or those internal cues can induce dread, and can feel uncomfortable, threatening and triggering, leading back to the vicious cycle of anxiety.
- The clutter and mess around you impact your brain, which makes you feel like you have more to do and you are never 'off'.
- You find it hard to ignore the other stuff that has to get done.
- You get annoyed if you see your partner relaxing when you want to and end up rage-cleaning.
- You are so tired after looking after others that looking after you feels like another thing to do.

From childhood, women are conditioned to think, 'others first'. And even if you feel like your household is an equitable place, I'm going to boldly say that you may still be the Chief Executive Functions Officer. What do I mean by that? Well, who remembers all the stuff in your house – the parties, the presents, filling out the waivers, the wrapping paper, the card, the kit needed every day, the sandwich preferences, the follow-up doctor appointments, the organising and reorganising, and this is only Tuesday and you haven't even started dinner yet? You've probably heard of the 'mental burden' – who's shouldering the mental burden in your household? Why? If it's you, then you are unwittingly the Chief Executive Functions Officer, and you are, according to paediatric psychologist Dr Ann-Louise Lockhart, the 'frontal-lobe' of your family. Your role and responsibilities may include planning, problem-solving, time management, regulation of emotion (meltdowns, anyone?), task initiation, prioritising ... there are more, but that is more than enough. You get the picture. The CEFO is constantly busy, constantly playing catch-up, constantly exhausted – and that leads to anxiety and stress.

In her book *Fair Play*, Eve Rodsky describes 'she-fault' parenting, which is the situation where the lion's share of parenting and managing falls on the woman in the home.[40] We all know about the invisible work that is done but not seen or valued. But knowing it and changing it are two separate things. Rodsky specifically speaks about the CPEs that underpin all the invisible labour, where you have to: **C**onceive, **P**lan and **E**xecute. Every task you do requires you to do CPE. I remember in the early days of being a new parent feeling embarrassed if someone asked me what I had done all day. I could barely tell them, but I knew that I hadn't stopped for a second. This is why your patience may disappear when you're asked *Where is the ...?, What time is ... ?, Have you seen ... ?, What did you do with ... ?, Why isn't there ... ?,* and even *What can I do to help?* Because, and here's the rub, *you* don't ask anyone where stuff is or expect them to have an answer to your every need. The 'she-fault' parent is found across all families and genders, and across stay-at-home, working, hetero, same-sex, co-parenting, blended and single-parent families, where 'she-fault' is the default. The solution is to recognise it for what it is, and then to rebalance the imbalance.

I read a great book when I started my clinic over 20 years ago and I still use its lessons regularly, and in different settings, personal and professional. The book is *The E-Myth Revisited*; it examined why most small businesses fail. [41] In a nutshell, the answer was that while large businesses have departments, such as marketing, accounting, etc., most small business owners work 'in' their business and are also all the departments – and that means they never work 'on' their business. Two things arise from this. First, how often do you work 'on' changing things in your personal relationships in a strategic way? It is exceptionally hard when your head and heart are constantly working 'in' the day-to-day, week-to-week survival race. It is also exceptionally challenging if you are tasked with a very large mental load. This is why you feel a rush of pure irritation when someone says, 'Why don't you just relax or switch off?' Because it's not easy to do that.

Second, another idea I liked from *The E-Myth* is to create a turnkey business. In a turnkey, if someone had to come in when you were out, they would know where everything was and what to do because it's all laid out in the operations manual. Anyone want that home operations manual? Yes, please! But like anything that works, it will require time, effort and a system that everyone buys into. How would you go about doing that? I did this when I set up in practice years ago. I'm also taking inspiration from great houses we've stayed in on holidays. Without embarrassing my kids, one of them did ask me the other day which was the dryer and which was the washing-machine. Suffice to say, they didn't know which programme to run. I'll hold my hands up and say 'my bad' and follow it up with: Why is this 'job' on my shoulders? Maybe even starting with a kitchen operations manual, with the machine basics written out, could inspire autonomy, or at least no excuses? Write out the key areas that cause arguments in your home and keep it in one place so everyone can refer to it by themselves. Start by body doubling, where you do the job together or at least you stand nearby as they do it. To make changes, they need your input to get it rolling. See it as an on-boarding process to facilitate more rest and less resentment.

Going back to *Fair Play*, Rodsky wrote a list called 'Sh*t I Do'. However, she turned the list into the Fair Play game with the intent that it would benefit all. Less nagging, more 'unicorn space' and possibly more sex. This relates to a silent side-effect of being too busy – just as you don't have 'working on' time, the other thing you lose is connection time, and time for pleasure and sex. Research and common sense back this up. It's common for sex to end up feeling like another job you have to do at the end of the day, and if the division of work feels unfair, not only do you have no energy left, that connection of feeling supported and working together in a fairer way is lost, and that impacts the emotional and physical desire that feeds into your sexual connection. Resentment does not make for good foreplay.

Rodsky's answer in *Fair Play* was to create your own 'unicorn space', where you have space to be yourself and do things that make you 'you' and that light you up. This freedom is everything. When I think of luxury, it isn't the unattainable five-star type – which I wouldn't say no to! – it's the practicalities that we can all achieve daily. It's not about needing a holiday from your life, but about bringing the best bits of a holiday into your daily life.

Pause and sit with this:

- Rest doesn't need to be earned.
- Relaxation isn't a privilege, it's a human need.

You need space for your body and mind to think, process and feel. If you don't get that space, you get claustrophobic in yourself, which creates stress and anxiety – even if it takes you years to realise it. This was articulated powerfully by a client of mine, Joanne.

I described to Joanne a scale from 1 to 10, 1 being very low anxiety and 10 being extremely high anxiety.

AK: Where are you at on that scale, Joanne?

Joanne: I'm at nine.

AK: What does that feel like, and where is it showing up in your body?

Joanne: Honestly, I feel so angry and frustrated that I feel like this. I don't like who I am when I'm like this, and I feel like I've been like this for years.

AK: Like what?

Joanne: I am so irritable and exhausted. I know I should rest, but it pisses me off when people tell me to 'just relax'. I feel so alone, and like a failure, like, why can't I relax? I try to be so organised, all I feel I do is prepare and do all the stuff, but it is never enough. I also can't afford to work part-time; by the twentieth of the month I am broke, and yet I feel I work all the time. It feels utterly relentless and thankless. The anxiety is there from the moment I close my eyes until I fall asleep, and then it even wakes me bolt upright in the night as I think of all the things I either forgot to do or was supposed to do. I know I need to rest, but it's a bad combo of not knowing how and seriously not having time to. My husband keeps telling me to go off, but when I do, he looks at me like it is the first time he has ever heard this, and he is annoyed with me. Also, his idea of rest is exercise, but I don't want to run around on my own, that's all I do all day long anyway.

When I do get an hour to myself, I feel quite stressed, like I should be doing something else, and I get hugely triggered if I've been out and when I come back, I have more to do than if I didn't leave. If I am at home, the easiest thing to reach for is my phone, problem solved, I scroll the hour away.

> My husband is a great guy, but he doesn't understand the depth of what I do. To be honest, it's so hard to explain it without it sounding trivial. I get frustrated with myself saying the same thing as his face says, 'I've heard this all before' and he's right, nothing ever f'ing changes. When I'm out it feels like he 'minds' the kids. When I get back, I have to start on dinner, homework and the bombsite. Honestly, that's why I've stopped bothering to take time out because it doesn't feel worth it. Going out is making it worse as I now have to catch up on what I didn't do when I wasn't there.
>
> **AK:** How is this playing out in your relationship?
>
> **Joanne:** I feel less connected to him, and resentful. He has the freedom to walk out the door without ensuring everything is in order. And if I don't have everything done, I get cross phone calls asking basic questions that get my back up, so I then sound narky, and he is annoyed with me because I am out, and he is at home, 'minding the kids'. I just don't feel like myself. I don't know who I am, or what I like and, no joke, I don't know how to relax any more.

Joanne's words have been repeated again and again in similar thoughts and feelings by so many of my clients. The problem is – what do you do about it? How can you change your home life and household to be more equitable in responsibility? It requires open and honest discussion between the key stakeholders – that's you, your partner and, when they are of suitable age, your children. There has to be an acknowledgement of what the norm has been, why that has been the norm, and how the norm makes everyone feel. The prospect of opening up these topics and discussions might be daunting, but here are some tips that might help:

- Coming to the conversation with a growth mindset[42] is so helpful, as it encourages growth and learning to come from setbacks and to learn from failure.
- A collaborative mindset is an approach that values working together towards a common goal(s). It's an open and supportive framework where everyone contributes.
- Set the framework that these will be ongoing conversations, that this is the start of new ways to communicate and trying out new things that will foster real progress by allowing normal life interruptions and hiccups.
- Shift perspectives on gender role expectations. Ask questions about assumptions and play around by trying each other's jobs to gain perspective and build connection.
- Understanding your own unique situation and the needs within your unit (all aspects of health and neurodiversity) and not measuring yourselves against others.
- Try different styles of communication, such as walking while talking. This can garner a lot of unexpected buy-in and it's also time together where you are working on making changes that will benefit all. Changing old conversations that were stuck and going nowhere with movement can free up new perspectives.
- Explore your own gender norms that you saw growing up. This can be a dinner conversation, noting the tone is one of curiosity and wanting to understand each other.
- Noticing and naming when you get stuck, defensive, or triggered. Maturity is an underrated attractive trait in a partnership. It is courageous to say, *This has triggered me, can we take a minute?* and courage is contagious.
- Have a safe word for when the conversation needs a pause to reset (I find humorous words help de-escalate).
- Look at the pressure points for both of you, name them and look at flexible solutions.

- Put daily DEAR time in the calendar (Drop Everything And Rest – see page 299). This is 3–5 minutes of downtime per day.
- Identify unmet needs and look at ways of supporting each other. Conversations that are looking to bring change will unearth unresolved issues and past hurts. Be honest and express why you were upset, what it meant to the relationship and what you hope for going forward. Tolerating temporary distress in a solution-focused space is an opportunity for achieving the desired changes.
- Figure and write out the frustrations – such as tiredness, never feeling 'off', lack of personal freedom, financial worries, lack of fulfilment.

What you can see from the above discussion is how the central problem – lack of time for yourself, for rest and relaxation – branches out into new, associated problems such as resentment, feeling undervalued, exhaustion and burnout, all of which can damage personal relationships. The damage can include a loss of connection and intimacy, which creates a distance between you and your partner, makes you feel disconnected from your true self and makes you feel isolated and lonely, which makes the exhaustion and everything else feel even worse. You're spiralling into anxiety. In the therapy room, it is loss of identity paired with a lack of fulfilling and meaningful time spent developing and creating things that form a big part of the frustration that I see physically with generalised anxiety. Spending all your time doing repetitive, thankless tasks erodes your core self.

This is why time, rest and relaxation are crucial to build into your day and week. So try to move past your own mental obstacles and see them as crucial – and then work on including them in your schedule. Make time to figure out what it is that you like, as you may not have had time to even think about that. Make time to pursue hobbies or activities that light you up. Make time to relax and let your thoughts wander. You can't make extra time – but you can reorganise the time that is available to make it work more in your favour. This is why I said this chapter may make your house messier and head, heart and body happier – you can't do it all.

Micro-moments

Micro-moments are small, fleeting points in your daily life that, while small, can measurably add to the quality of your day, your relationship with yourself and with others. They are moments of observation, experiences and interactions, such as noticing the sound of the wind in the trees, watching a warm interaction between people, or another person's laugh making you smile. They are moments that are personal to you that can positively impact your mood and how you feel in that moment.

I think people can take resting and relaxing way too seriously. Don't forget that having fun is restful, that laughter relaxes your whole system. Laughter is genuinely good for you, and it is an internal workout. Relaxing doesn't have to be all about slow movements and deep work. You have to figure out your own relaxing style, it is as unique as you are. And it also doesn't have to be one thing. One day you may find lying on your bed for 20 minutes the perfect luxury, while another day you might prefer the adrenaline buzz of cycling downhill.

Relaxing can be fast or slow. I think checking in with what state you are in – hyperarousal or hypoarousal – and matching the energy there is super helpful. I have kids' boxing gloves and pads and when my children are in that mobilised, ready-to-fight mode, when asking them to relax really isn't going to work, I say to them, 'Okay, I can see you feel frustrated, and you're angry. I'll get the gloves out and you can hit me.' Even saying this to them breaks the intensity of the high drive of anger, because I am meeting them where they are.

I think we have done an injustice to adults by making us believe that relaxing is the only way. Honouring how you are, rather than how you think you should be, is a much more effective tactic to help you self-regulate. It is also part of the story we carry about 'good' and 'bad' emotions. It is a limited concept that ignores what that emotion is trying to tell you.

Drop the aesthetic idea of what you find relaxing and restful. It may change depending on your mood and what you need. I remember doing a personality questionnaire as part of a job interview when I was in my twenties and I seemed to irritate the person because he said, 'You can't like all these things, they are completely different.' I shrugged my shoulders. Why not? Stop trying to squish yourself into neat boxes.

Some examples of helpful micro-moments:

- DEAR time – drop everything and rest. It could be as little as 3–5 minutes (see opposite).
- Silence – for 30 seconds or 60 seconds.
- Heel drops – go outside, shoes off, stand on grass if possible, go up on your toes and then drop your heels down (see Toolbox, page 330).
- Skipping – movement breaks aren't just for kids, and this one is brilliant if you work from home.
- Shake it out – put on a song to match your mood and shake your body (see Toolbox, page 329).
- A personal favourite, which I have named 'Starfishing' – lie on your bed in the starfish position, feel your body being supported by the bed, and sink.
- A walk around the block – even 10 or 20 minutes. Watch the impact it has as a mood changer.
- Write out how you are feeling – rip up or burn the page afterwards.
- Attend to the basics – Are you hungry? Then eat. Are you tired? Rest. Are you overstimulated? Turn down surrounding sound – use ear plugs if necessary. Are you thirsty? Drink some water.
- Breathe and release.
- Use your senses to calm, rest, invigorate or release through your sense of choice.

DEAR TIME: DROP EVERYTHING AND REST

Start practising daily DEAR moments. I think grounding with either heat or cold in a glass or cup is a good way to signal to your body that you are intentionally taking a few moments. If possible, take your coffee, tea or a cold glass of water and go outside. As you hold the cup, settle yourself with a soft breath or a longer deep release. You may find you stretch your arms up, or just sit and relax for a moment. There is no wrong way to do this, you are just giving yourself time. Be aware of your posture, breathe in some space into your chest and head. I like doing this when my head is busy or hopping to the next thing. I breathe space into what may feel like a noisy and busy room.

Bring your focus to your surroundings and regulate through your senses: What can you see? What can you hear? What can you feel? Can you taste the drink and feel it in your hands?

Breathe in again and release.

Don't be fooled by the simplicity of this daily practice. It can be the beginning of a new relationship where you give yourself permission to come back to your body for a few minutes every day. It is a healing and energising experience, and it releases and breathes some more room and time into a busy day, so that your capacity to be more regulated is there for the more testing moments or times of the day. You connecting to you inevitably benefits everyone around you.

Practices that bring you back to your body are what Deb Dana calls 'befriending your nervous system'.[43] Becoming attuned to what is going on inside your body from a place of compassion and curiosity, rather than it being felt as a threat, allows you to figure out which of the 4 Fs (Flight, Fight, Freeze or Fawn) you are in, or which mixture of them. You can then use your breath, or other somatic techniques, to anchor yourself and to feel safe in your body again – or quite possibly for the first time in your life. This is how you build self-trust.

It's a matter of being able to notice, *Okay, I've gone into survival mode. I feel agitated, like time is speeding up and I don't have enough* of it, I have too many thoughts racing through my mind, what will I do first, I'm very overwhelmed and it's hard to focus. This project does need to get finished, but it is not a matter of life or death. BREATHE ... even though I feel huge pressure and I'm terrified it is going to fail spectacularly, I am safe, I am safe.*

When the anxiety kicks in, anchor yourself with your breath and use your inner SOS to move from survival to safety (see page 43). Repeat to yourself: *I am safe, even though this feels threatening, I am safe.*

When you are addicted to the hit of dopamine that stress provides, it will take time to recognise safe and comforting as something you even like. I think so many people feel full and empty at the same time and this is an extraordinarily uncomfortable experience. It matches the disparity of how high-functioning anxiety looks on the outside and feels on the inside.

GLIMMERS

When you want to feel safe and warm in your body, activate everyday joy. Deb Dana describes glimmers as the opposite of triggers. While triggers set off reactions linked to past traumas or distressing experiences, activating the autonomic nervous system's response to threat, glimmers evoke feelings of safety, warmth and connection, offering hope and emotional regulation.

I love the duality of glimmers: even as you are experiencing distress or difficulty, you can also be engaging in this active process of noticing 'micro-moments' that spark ventral vagal energy or glimmers of joy for you. Little specks and moments of light you notice in the dark.

Remember that you are wired to notice the bad – that's why you are so good at it – which means you have to actively seek out the good and acknowledge it. This is a process I highly recommend. Close your eyes for a moment and think of when you last experienced a glimmer. I had a glimmer the other day, and I'll share it with you to show how these moments are so everyday that you could easily miss them.

'Woooow!' It was my middle child, upstairs, and it was the sound of pure joy and awe. Curious, I went up to see what drew such a response. The bathroom window was fully bathed in pink. It is frosted glass, so it looked incredible. There stood my child, her face lit up with the warmth and hope that sunrises bring. We stood there and looked at it together, and then we went into another room to see it from a different perspective, and then we went outside to see it there. It lasted only a few moments. But the sound of the 'wow' was beautiful, and obviously the sky was as well, but I think it was that shared moment of witnessing it together that brought the warm glow to my heart. Then it ended and we resumed the hectic routine to get out the door and to school and work. I placed that moment in my glimmer bank, allowing me to bring it to mind anytime I need to come back to feeling wonder at the world we live in.

If you grew up in the 1980s, you might remember the Ready Brek ad, with the kid outlined by a glow of warm goodness as he headed out into the cold, wintry morning. This isn't a sad story of walking miles to school; it probably took me 45 seconds to walk around the corner, or less if I snuck under the school fence behind my house. But that is how I see glimmers: you feel warm inside and it protects you from the dark outside. As a child, I wanted to glow like the Ready Brek kid; now I know a way to do it as an adult.

If your nervous system is being tripped and triggered all day long, actively practising the art of noticing the good around you is a way to bring some calm and warmth into your day. Start by identifying what brings you micro-moments of joy that feel good inside your body. It can be helpful to write them down, figuring out what lights you up, and then actively becoming a glimmer-seeker in your everyday life, rooting out daily joy.

How to find everyday glimmers:

- When you notice a warmth in your body in response to someone you love, or a lovely moment, or in nature, savour it. Savouring is the art of acknowledging how you feel.

- To deepen the feeling, you can connect to where you feel it in your body. Where are you drawn to placing your hands? Some find it is located in their heart.
- Begin to practise noticing when you become aware of micro-moments of joy.
- Attend to it with your senses, noting what you can hear or feel or sense.
- Or just give yourself a moment of being completely present in the moment.
- There is no right or wrong way, so be kind to your experience.

The wonderful thing about glimmers is that as you become more aware of them, you can find more of them in your everyday life. A glimmer is a fleeting moment; you are not trying to control or capture it. Decide to become a glimmer-seeker and spread the word to others.

Why you need to strive less and rest more

The perspectives here will create a clearer, compassionate, more nuanced understanding of your life as a 'living landscape painting'. The first time I heard this phrase was when I was gazing out of the most magnificent window in the Nobel Room at Farmleigh House in the Phoenix Park, looking out on to the most incredible garden. The tour guide explained that rather than hanging a beautiful but non-changing painting over the fireplace, a window was placed above the fireplace to create 'a living landscape painting'. The view changed every day, sometimes every hour, as the light and mood moved along with the seasons. It struck me that this applies in our lives as well. The landscape of your life is an ever-changing living landscape painting. The idea of this fills me with joy, and it is the premise of this book and my work. The external environment is alive, living, growing and out of your control. But how you respond to it is within your control and is an ongoing process. The outside affects who you are and how you live your life as you juggle the modern world's demands and complexities.

You have core needs: safety; rest; connection with your body and mind rather than intellectualising; and connection with yourself and others. The power lies in practical application and experiential learning. Knowledge is power, but it remains a fleeting thought until acted upon. By processing stored memories, acknowledging emotions and befriending thoughts, we cultivate essential life skills like regulating the nervous system daily, a challenging yet rewarding endeavour.

The Practical Psychology

These questions aim to uncover beliefs driving behaviours that hinder your rest and relaxation. I hope they provide compassionate understanding and empower you to make necessary changes.

Did you see your parent/s relax as a child?

_____

What was said about relaxing?

_____

What did you learn about being productive or busy?

_____

As a child, did you hear phrases like, 'Why are you just sitting there? What are you doing? Get up, come on, let's get going'? Did you feel it was okay to relax and rest?

_____

If you are reading this thinking, 'I'm connecting with this', how and where does it show up in your life now?

___

If you saw your parent(s) staying in bed a lot of the time, perhaps because they struggled with mental or physical health issues, did this lead you to want to do the opposite?

___

Does this cause issues if you are in a relationship?

___

If you are in a same-sex relationship, is it more equal?

___

If in a heterosexual relationship, are there different gender expectations?

___

This last question leads in part as to why we find it so hard to relax.

What do you find relaxing?

___

What do you find restful?

___

When do you want to do the one you like the most?

___

How are you going to put that plan into place?

_____

Are there some micro-moments that you can interweave into your daily life? What are they?

_____

SHAKING IT OUT

This is a fantastic somatic technique to help regulate physiological anxiety. When you need to get the feelings of overwhelm out, try shaking. This needs to be experienced to prove to yourself how effective it is. I remember reading about a psychologist whose area of expertise was panic attacks. He himself suffered intensely debilitating panic attacks, and he felt extreme shame because his clients thought he was so calm and he helped so many, and yet he was completely stuck having acute day- and night-time panic attacks. He tried many different types of therapy, researched endlessly and tried anything he thought would help, the remedy eventually came from an unexpected source. One night he was watching a nature programme and a lion had just tried to attack a gazelle. The gazelle escaped and as soon as it knew it was out of danger, it started to shake out its legs, head and body. David Attenborough's dulcet tones explained that this was the perfect form of recovery after the gazelle's body had been flooded with survival-activated hormones of adrenaline, norepinephrine and cortisol to mobilise its muscles to run, flee and survive to tell the tale.

Hmm, thought the psychologist on his couch, *what have I got to lose? Makes perfect sense that these stress hormones had to be physically released out of the body.* The gazelle couldn't do a mindfulness meditation, so was this nature's perfect answer? He got off his couch and started to shake his arms, feeling a bit silly at first and looking over his shoulder to make sure no one was about to come into the room. He then started moving his shoulders and neck and head, shaking his arms above his head in a releasing way, and then the same with his legs. Did it look pretty? Probably not. But it felt so good. Shaking like this can be done to music, depending on what you are trying to release.

Emotions get stuck in your body. While we aren't being chased by lions, our bodies can get stuck in survival mode from past trauma and our hyperactive lives and feel they are under threat. This is no less scary in your mind as you survive your everyday life.

Name the demands on your life. Which ones bring the fear for you?

_____

What do you need to shake out of yourself?

_____

You can shake for the length of a song, around three minutes, or whatever feels right for you. You will be pleasantly surprised at how freeing and cathartic it is to let go of what you are holding on to physically that needs to be released.

How to shake it out
For an example, I have a shake-it-out reel on Instagram: go to @thepractical.psychologist.

PART 3

From revival to finding the everyday joy of enough

CHAPTER 12

The new culture of enough

Take a moment to acknowledge all you have overcome. Life is quite the tough experiment, and as you come to understand the function of your emotions and why your nervous system did what was needed to protect, survive and adapt, it's also important to pause, reflect and appreciate that you lived it. Take a deep breath, place your hand on your heart and say, *Hey, that was tough, but you made it*. Before we look forward, take a moment to breathe and recognise how far you've come. A *Reeling in the Years* of sorts, with the good, the bad and the ugly all laid out and ready for a review.

People jokingly refer to their 'villain era', indicating a shift towards prioritising their own needs, albeit indirectly, when they – shock, horror! – decline an unwanted invitation. I might humorously dub my own era 'the age of rage', perhaps emphasising the underlying sentiment behind it. It is ironic that the emotion of anger, the one many women are conditioned to suppress, is the one that may show up quite loudly when your capacity to tolerate a toxic culture becomes undeniably intolerable with age. Maybe it is the wisdom that comes with age, or maybe it is just all too much and you basically get to a point where you call 'enough' on it. I have other non-PC words, but we'll stick with 'enough'.

The words of occupational therapist Dr Brooke Weinstein resonated deeply with me: 'One of the fastest ways to dysregulate your nervous system is to have empathy and compassion for others without boundaries for yourself.'[44]

One of the benefits of ageing is that we have the impetus stemming from anger coupled with the clarity gained through reflection and review. While it's not guaranteed with age, painful experiences can lead to emotional growth and clearer boundaries, in terms of what you will and will not agree with or accept any more. The boundaries we explored become clear lines, communicated with others about decisions to not betray yourself or sacrifice your needs any longer. This awakening is akin to waking a hibernating bear, bringing a realisation of all that had been accepted before now, too glaring to ignore, prompting a deep-seated need for change.

I embraced turning 40, rejecting society's negative stigma, instead finding strength in granting myself and others emotional maturity and space to prioritise our needs. Have you experienced growth in voicing your needs? There is no 'right' age to conduct a life review. For many, they say it comes naturally around 40 and then again at 50, each decade giving more freedom and less ... well, you know what I mean – but it is open to us at any time. The act of looking back, of looking to see where you came from, what that bequeathed to you, how you have managed that, what you have and have not changed: all these questions can lead you to a very strong sense of self. That is a good base from which to review your choices, your current circumstances, your levels of anxiety and your key stressors, the things you would like to change and how to change them. A review such as this can uproot some of the tenacious weeds and help you to get things blooming into the future.

The review process

The review process can come about quite naturally – like a big roundy birthday – or it can come in a more difficult way, via a panic attack or ongoing anxiety that leaves you in the grip of an identity crisis. Among my clients, this is very common. They can be propelled into it in a manner that feels very sudden, but as with the anxiety or panic attack itself, that can be a good outcome of a very challenging situation – being forced to take time to take stock.

This might sound odd, but I love it when I get to work through an existential crisis with a client. It sometimes goes like this: initial presentation is the panic attack that came from nowhere, but as we work though this, we find it did indeed come from somewhere. The identity crisis has in fact been rumbling away under the surface for some time: *Who am I? What do I like? What do I want? Why isn't my life making me feel happy?* Now the anxiety or panic attack ensures it can't be ignored any longer. Your body says, *No more, I've had enough*. When you are in the middle of anxiety or panic attacks, you won't be feeling grateful. You may feel a sense of betrayal, by yourself and your body, and you may have lost confidence and trust because you doubt yourself in situations and places that once felt safe and now feel threatening. The cycle of anxiety is entrenched in avoidance, fear, anticipatory anxiety and withdrawing socially, and fluctuating between Fight and Flight and Freeze and shutdown. All of these feelings and experiences make you question yourself, and who you are, and your ability to cope. It requires a lot of processing to connect the dots from the patterns of the past to the experiences and behaviour of the present. But as those pieces fall into place and you follow the breadcrumb trail back to the source, the ever-dynamic life puzzle begins to make sense. That in turn allows for compassion to land, which leads to a whole new level of understanding of yourself. It can be quite the land.

When the many layers have been explored, you can begin to realise your authentic self, and then the real questions can start to come.

A deeper questioning of yourself: *Oh, so this is who I had to become to survive, to feel good enough, to feel worthy of love, to be accepted.* You land within your body, your mind and soul, you can clearly see where you are, and where you want to be. What you are left with then is a gap between those two things – where you are now, where you want to be. Once you realise that you want more ease and joy, it brings the connected realisation that there must now be change.

This description makes it sound like a straight line from one to other, but obviously life is rarely linear – apart from numerical age. In all other things, we tend to meander and deviate and go down blind alleys, only to do a U-turn and try a new road. There is no right or wrong way, there is only your way and your pace. When you hit an existential crisis, whatever it is prompted by, it asks these deeper questions of you:

- What is important to me?
- What do I value?
- How do I want to live my life?

Let's explore these properly here. While the word 'crisis' has negative connotations, it does also incorporate the inevitability of change, which has positive connotations. Although I'm well aware that even when change is good, it is hard to accept. This is because change is about cracking open aspects of yourself that have restricted you, that don't feel like you, and yet are familiar. It's a mixed experience that naturally raises mixed thoughts and emotions. But don't lose sight of, or faith in, the fact that change is a natural part of life, and can benefit you enormously, one way or another, always reminding you to choose the hard with the better outcome.

What is an existential crisis?

An existential crisis is the combination of a number of factors that throw your sense of self into doubt. The factors work together and can create anxiety and if you keep pushing yourself and ignoring the red flags, it can cause an even deeper sense of loss and disconnection. There are a number of aspects to an existential crisis:

- Identity crisis
- Sense of self and body betrayal
- Self-abandonment of own needs, desires, and joy
- Disillusionment in life and living in a toxic environment
- Being over- and under-stimulated
- Your history (the story of you)
- Lack of connection to self and others.

You can see that we have met each of these facets before as we worked through emotional, psychological and physiological anxiety and defence mechanisms. The truth is, we need to stop trying to keep up with an impossible pace that no one can operate at or sustain. If you do keep this pace for a long period of time, the symptoms of your dysregulated nervous system will impact your sleep, digestion, and your ability to rest, be active and experience joy. Constant busyness allows you to ignore your body's information cues, but all the while your body is becoming more anxious and asking you to listen to it.

Don't let this overwhelm you ... be generous and kind to yourself and see the complexity. Break down what you want to feel, what task you'd like to take on next, and if you don't feel ready for it, ask: *What do I need right now?* Rest is a huge part of the healing process. It's not always 'doing the work' that is part of healing. Sometimes doing nothing is more than enough – this is what I meant when I said less is more. Rather than go for that run, you might need to lie on your bed. We need more stillness, quiet, we need time to think, to review, take stock and figure out what brings joy. These are good and useful things to do for yourself.

When you live inside a maelstrom of constant busyness, in relentless overdrive, you can lose sight of your meaning and your purpose. When that happens, you lose the connection to yourself, past, present and future. That loss creates frustration and anxiety in the mind and the body. The search for meaning and purpose may show up in my clinic as panic attacks, generalised anxiety and a racing mind, stemming from either overwhelm or underwhelm. The self-doubt and the tormented feelings and thoughts of *What is this all about?* hit you hard, and that's the existential crisis – but, maybe, you can also see it as an essential crisis.

Sometimes you do know who you are authentically, but it might not feel safe to show up as yourself. This is where the masks that may have protected you in the past have led you to abandon your own needs. Inhibitory fear may have stopped you making changes you wanted to make, as revealing yourself may be met with criticism and disapproval. From my perspective, as I go through the layers of anxiety as a client begins to unmask and let go of who they think they should be and show up as their true self, I can see that they grant themselves permission to live a life aligned with their core values. And it is within your core values that you find meaning and purpose.

Remember, what may have presented as anxiety may be an existential crisis in disguise.

What is my meaning and purpose?

You can find your *meaning* by reflecting on your values and what brings significance to your life. Identify key areas, such as relationships, work, and your impact on the world.

You can find your *purpose* by reflecting on your 'why' – your strengths, goals, and the decisions that have guided and now guide your life.

When you feel you are living a life that isn't aligned with your purpose and that doesn't feel meaningful, the messages and discomfort become increasingly louder because the inner whisperings, those instinctual feelings, can't be heard above all the external and internal noise.

When the message gets louder, it may show up as panic attacks, generalised anxiety, persistent and excessive worrying and a brain on speed and autopilot. So you need to take the time to ask yourself honestly: *What is my meaning and purpose?* Let's make the time for it now and let me ask you:

What is important to you and why?

_____

Do you feel your life and how you live it are aligned or coherent?

_____

If it is not aligned, why?

_____

What part of your life feels aligned with your authentic self?

_____

What things do you do that don't feel in line with your authentic self?

_____

Why do you do them? (For many, it may be about other people, sense of duty, etc.)

_____

What would a meaningful day look like for you?

_____

Bigger question, what would a meaningful life look like for you?

―――――――――――――――――――――――――――――――――

What parts of your life are in a state of incongruence? (Thinking one way, behaving in another. Leave judgement, guilt, shame out of this, they are not invited to this question session.)

―――――――――――――――――――――――――――――――――

The question of incongruence

From these questions, can you identify any incongruence between your inner self and outer self? Are you living authentically, or are you realising that there are gaps? For example, the meaningful day you described in your answer above – does that correspond to any of your days, or none of your days? If none, why is that? The 'why' is crucial here – what is at the base of the disconnection within you? Because if there are gaps causing a disconnection, they can be a source of constant anxiety.

If you have found some incongruence between how you authentically feel and how you are living your life, please bring the 3 Cs to your exploration into this part of yourself.

Challenge:
What beliefs do you need to challenge to live authentically?

―――――――――――――――――――――――――――――――――

Did you notice a lot of 'shoulding' present?

―――――――――――――――――――――――――――――――――

Compassion:
What was it like to see the frustration of living a life that doesn't feel meaningful for you?

_____

Why has that been occurring?

_____

What are the blockers to living a meaningful life?

_____

Weigh them ... you may have three negatives, but one weighs more than all the others. Which one?

_____

Curiosity:
Has a bit of curiosity arisen about how change could be possible?

_____

What would the next step of this look like in terms of practically adapting it to your life as it is now?

_____

Can you play with the idea of how much time you would need?

_____

What would living a more congruent life look like for you?

_____

These are super difficult and important questions, so please acknowledge how amazing you are for tackling them with honesty. This may be the first time you have ever thought about this, or it may be something you think about all the time but haven't been able to action yet. Either way, be supportive and kind with yourself.

Now I need to ask you:

When did the anxiety and or panic attacks begin?

_____

How long have you felt like your life lacked meaning and purpose?

_____

Did anxiety and panic bring you back to yourself?

_____

Do panic attacks and anxiety stem from a lack of meaning and purpose, or is it the other way round? Our answers may differ. I'd venture to say it's a mix. Loss of identity, major life changes and living on autopilot contribute. When we're constantly doing, we don't pause to question that nagging feeling or gut pain signalling that something's off. Then our adaptable bodies force us to confront these questions, often in challenging ways, after being ignored for too long.

Finding the everyday joy of enough

We have worked from an in-depth understanding of survival mode – which may be the reason you bought this book, through revival mode – where you learned new ways to cope with anxiety; and now, after all that work and all your hard work answering tough questions, we want to take the productive step towards a more authentic and fulfilling life. There was never a promise of ending anxiety – anxiety is necessary, as we found out in earlier chapters – but what you can do is notice your anxiety triggers, identify them clearly, and use healthy coping mechanisms to live alongside them, knowing how to move and adapt when you feel stuck. To do this, you will need to let go of things like perfectionism and constant striving and pleasing others – you will need to take those steps that these chapters have been showing you, to move bit by bit back towards yourself, your needs, your boundaries, your joys in life.

I think most of us long for simplicity amidst the overwhelming barrage of choices. It often seems like marketers aim to dazzle, urging us to constantly pursue more, leaving us feeling inadequate. Yet true joy resides in the small, fleeting and gentle moments, often freely available. Recognising when 'enough is enough' allows us to recalibrate and find joy in sufficiency. Systemic capitalism and consumerism prioritise profit over humanity, often leading to our lifestyles being misaligned with our wellbeing and relationships.

So let us instigate the culture of enough, in all its meanings:

- You have had enough of systemic busyness that causes anxiety.
- You have had enough of ignoring your own body's signals, your feelings, your own desires and wishes.
- You have had enough of coming last on your To Do list.
- You are ready to look at this through another lens, one that sees that:
  - You have enough.
  - You do enough.
  - You are good enough.
  - You are enough.

Through the culture of enough, you can come back to living a life that feels aligned to your inner compass, your meaning and your purpose. It allows you to centre yourself, the people you love, the things that bring you joy. And you know what? You will probably find that those are the simple things. The world keeps telling you that you need so much to find joy, more of everything, but the truth most of us reach in the end is that we need very little – the simple joys, the daily mini-adventures, the sheer, beautiful luxury of time and connection with self and others.

Simplicity is the ultimate sophistication. (Leonardo da Vinci)

In the pursuit of safety, connection and emotional wellbeing, simplicity often emerges as the guiding star. Leonardo da Vinci's timeless wisdom reminds us that sophistication lies not in complexity, but in the embrace of the elegantly uncomplicated. The culture of enough is designed to rekindle the flame of your everyday joy. The exercises throughout the chapters and in the Psychological Toolbox (page 328) may seem deceptively simple, but beneath their surface lies a deep understanding of psychology and neuroscience and how to return to or foster a regulated nervous system. The aim is to connect with the fundamental essence of being human and to feel like yourself once more.

These practices bridge the way home to you, helping you to understand who you have been and why, where you are now and why, and the growth you want to foster into your next phase of life. This journey, much like life itself, can be beautifully messy, simultaneously frustrating and exhilarating, yet always filled with hope.

At its core, anxiety often arises from the uncertainty of what the future holds, coloured by the shadows of our past experiences. As you answered the questions, I hope you unpacked the root of difficult situations for you, or of what you collected from others as a trauma collector. These traumas, Big T and small t, manifested as a weight on your chest and shoulders, a collection of invisible fears that have provoked self-protecting behaviour. This is your invitation to unpack, release and reclaim your breath — to let go of the burdens that were never meant to be yours.

You are here, anchored in the present moment, a pivot point that connects your past, present and the yet-to-be. This is an un-telling of your story, as you let go of the masked selves you have worn in pursuit of the basic human need to belong, to be accepted, to be loved. It is a deep surrender of perfectionism, people-pleasing, busyness and exhaustion. It is an ode to the brave act of being yourself, a sentiment often spoken but rarely truly meant.

Taken as a whole, this book is the map of your personal story, so that you can read and understand it, with practices that can help you to start meeting your own needs, those that resonate with your authentic self. It requires a shift, an ongoing dance of self-assessment as your needs and circumstances evolve to finding space for you and for the glimmers (page 300) that will bring everyday joy. This is why it is called *doing the work*. You will not miraculously ease into your best life overnight. In fact, dropping that expectation will save you a lot of unnecessary heartache. Everything worthwhile requires give and take. Too many of us have been giving for too long. It is time to allow yourself to also experience reciprocity, starting with yourself and your boundaries. Listen to your complaints, hear what you are frustrated about, answer the questions I have asked and if 'it is all too much', then the time to change is now. This is a practical realignment as you develop an inner ability to tune in and know when you can press Pause, Stop and Play, depending on your needs. It brings with it a sense of safety that you have inner control, even when externally you don't.

We live in an age of information overload, where knowledge alone is no longer sufficient. It is the application of that knowledge, the practical integration into our daily lives, that propels us towards real change. As Albert Einstein said, 'Information is not knowledge.' We are so saturated with information that it can create decision paralysis. And that can lead to Freeze, shutdown, immobilisation, and stagnation. Countering this, giving yourself the ability to once again make the best decisions for you, requires you to seek out knowledge, particularly self-knowledge, which becomes embodied only in connection.

> *Knowing is not enough; we must apply.*
> *Willing is not enough; we must do.*
>
> (Johann Wolfgang von Goethe)

What I hope I have given you in these pages is a map to help guide you when you are feeling lost and don't know what to do next. It's not about inundating you with more information, but about empowering you with actionable steps.

As you embark on this journey, remember that growth is a process that unfurls from within, but is shaped by the world around you. Be compassionate with yourself, because the conditions you find yourself in will play a significant role in your healing and growth. This is a gentle beckoning back to yourself. It starts with you, a willingness to take active steps towards the calm, the comfort, and the alignment of head, heart, and body, leading you to be able to answer the most pressing questions:

- Where am I now?
- Where am I going?

In the words of the exquisite dancer Martha Graham: 'The body says what words cannot.' This journey isn't an end. It is a beginning.

You've likely heard of people expressing love through gifts. The words here are a language of safety and connection, guiding you towards integrated living. This is your map, your inner GPS, helping you navigate life's choices and responses authentically. *Where am I going?* is about living a life that feels better for you, that feels like you. It's about finding your way back home, building a space that welcomes and supports you unequivocally.

Let's challenge toxic cultural norms, reassess hyper-productivity, and reclaim our lives from a system that demands more but gives less. Let us look to find personal meaning and purpose, valuing connection, time and ourselves. It's time to burn Superwoman's cape, rebel against unrealistic standards, and make some promises to ourselves: to embrace vulnerability, to grow, to practise self-compassion, and to return home.

Listen to what you complain about because it often holds the key to your needs. Set boundaries, support yourself and celebrate progress, even amidst uncertainty. You have the power to reclaim control, to live authentically, and to connect with yourself on a deeper level. Trust the process and, remember, uncertainty holds its own certainty. Pause, breathe, and start again. Your life control isn't remote, it's within you. You're worthy of love and compassion just as you are. This journey of self-discovery and healing is ongoing. Instead of pursuing an unrealistic ideal of perpetual happiness in adulthood, let us strive for a 'good enough' adulthood, one that embraces life's ups and downs, along with everyday joy.

The Practical Psychology

As noted above, the key takeaway is this: you can now compassionately understand why your nervous system has always supported you. This knowledge that you hold in your hands is your autonomy and your map to reconnect back with yourself. It provides the sense of safety that tells you that you are able to do the work involved in getting to know your anxiety and your physical, mental and emotional reactions to it. You have the autonomy and the ability to do this – and there are many supports to help you. This knowledge then allows you to choose how to manage your anxiety – and, again, there are many ways you can do this:

- Use the 3 Cs – Challenge with Curiosity and Compassion – to identify what is triggering the issue.
- Get support. You do not have to do this alone. Therapy can be one of the most transformative experiences in life.

- Set your expectations. It will not be easy or linear; it can feel very challenging to explore what is going on for you.
- Anxiety responds very well to therapy – CBT (see page 276) helps with the issues you are experiencing now while looking at changing your thought patterns.
- ACT – acceptance and commitment therapy helps you work towards accepting the situation as it is, as you commit to doing things that are helpful. This is very useful in tackling the frustration of having anxiety.
- EFT – emotion-focused therapy helps identify, process and understand the functions of your emotions.
- Psychodynamic therapy looks at your family of origin and relationships and how those aspects shows up in your present life.
- CFT – compassion-focused therapy works wonders as you learn how to bring compassion into play, and often with the harshest critic of them all: yourself.
- A trauma-informed therapist will be able to understand why certain behaviours are present and someone who understands polyvagal therapy and takes a holistic somatic approach will also be very helpful. Anxiety can increase if you try to ignore, suppress or numb it, but it responds so well to therapy.
- Work through the questions in this book and start practising the techniques that work for you.
- Identify the roots of the issue – this may need to be done in therapy as it might be a difficult deep-dive into past experiences.
- Allow room for mistakes, reframe it to a new normality that growth happens in the hard moments (the really hard moments) as you pause and choose to move towards safety.
- Carry out a life review. What can you control? What can you not control? What can you change? What can you not change? Make adjustments from your answers.

- Name it – because knowing that you are experiencing excessive and generalised anxiety can help you to reach out for the support you need.
- You cannot stop anxiety, but you can reset the alarm by regulating your nervous system. Think of this as resetting your emotional temperature to adjust to the internal and external conditions.
- You can control your reactions to your responses, and you can grow.
- You may come away from this book recognising that the anxiety has been protecting you, but that now, as an adult, that's no longer what you need, and that you now have the tools to adapt to and make the changes you would like to make.

Your psychological contract

As a final note, I would like to thank you for reading this book. Thank you for all you have done to this point, for all the work you have put into making changes, for the sweat, blood, and tears. As you move forward, remember to be patient, kind, and encouraging to yourself. Each step you take towards safety and connection empowers others to do the same.

It's time to create a new value system – one that prioritises your health, vitality and joy. No more feeling overwhelmed or as if you're falling short. This is your path home.

I invite you to make a promise to yourself, to overthrow the *It's all too much* regime. Sign your psychological contract, bound by your words and actions:

I promise to myself to:

_____

_____

_____

My psychological contract, bound by my own words and put into action in my deeds:

_____

_____

_____

_____

Signed:

_____

Thank you for being here and showing up for yourself. Your commitment to growth and change is commendable. Embrace hope, follow the plan, and seek out everyday joy as you journey towards becoming your true self.

I leave you with hope, a plan, and joy to get lost and found as you become who you know you are and live your life the way you want to live it.

Welcome home,

Allison x

Your psychological toolbox

There are plenty of helpful practices for you here, but don't feel you have to do this alone. Consider reaching out to your GP and/or a mental health professional, such as a psychologist, psychotherapist or psychiatrist, and get the specific support you need. Additionally, you may seek nutritional advice, explore somatic body-based therapy and spend time in nature. Nature knows how to soothe your nervous system and this therapy is free. To view demonstrations of these exercises, go to my Instagram page, @thepractical.psychologist. Remember, every person and situation is unique, so tailor your approach to fit your needs. I recommend trying these therapeutic interventions gradually, using a titration method similar to adjusting medication dosages.

A note on actual medications: Never come off medication without consulting your GP or healthcare provider.

Tool	**The practical pause** ⏸
What is it?	When you need a calm moment before reacting or responding.
How to apply it	• Remember this before you say yes or no to any decision or before the anger or words are about to spill out of your mouth, words that would be better if they stayed in. • Breathe in and say: PAUSE. • Practise pressing PAUSE in non-stressful situations, then you'll be ready for the stressful ones.
Tool	**The physiological sigh**
What is it?	When you need to hit the nervous system reset button. This works as a habit circuit-breaker. Trust me with this exercise; don't be fooled by its simplicity. This may be my favourite everyday breath. Exceptionally powerful to move you from Fight or Flight to feeling centred, more in control and calmer.
How to apply it	• Two short breaths in. • One long breath out.
Tool	**Shake it out**
What is it?	This is an incredibly effective technique for reducing anxiety in the body.
How to apply it	It is easiest to explain this with a visual demonstration, which you can find on Instagram: @thepractical.psychologist (see also page 305)

Tool	Ear pulls
What is it?	This is a vagus-stimulating ear massage, and it feels like a secret everyone needs to know. I feel a sense of warmth and safety even when thinking of this exercise. My youngest sister did this, with no understanding of vagus nerve. She'd sit beside my dad on his chair, a lovely big sage green sofa chair with marshmallow softness. Sitting on the arm of the chair, she'd suck her thumb and rub her nose with her index finger as she rubbed my dad's earlobe with her other hand. It was her version of a 'calm' story. And even sitting alongside her when she was doing it was comforting.
How to apply it	This one works best as a visual, so you can find a demonstration on Instagram: @thepractical.psychologist
Tool	**Heel drops**
What is it?	When you need to get out of your head and back into your body.
How to apply it	A great morning exercise that you can do in 20 seconds: • Go outside. • Stand barefoot on the grass. • Breathe in and exhale. • It can be nice as you breathe in to raise your arms and circle them slowly. • When you feel grounded, go up on your toes (comfortably) and then thump down on your heels. This is a great exercise to start the day and to connect and come into your body. For a

	demonstration, see @thepractical.psychologist on Instagram.
Tool	**DEAR moments**
What is it?	- Drop
- Everything
- And
- Rest
How to apply it	- This can be 3–5 minutes, or longer. Whatever feels right for you.
- That's it, no further instructions, just stop and rest.

Again, don't be misled by its simplicity; this is an essential in your psychological toolkit. |
| **Tool** | **Movement and music** |
| **What is it?** | When you want to change your mood or vagal state, this is a fun way to do it. |
| **How to apply it** | Dancing.

Like choosing your coffee strength, pick the tempo for what you need in that moment. Choose the music to match the mood and change the state.

For example, when I'm:
- *angry:* I listen to 'The Uprising' by Muse
- *needing confidence:* 'Anseo' by Denise Chaila and Jafaris
- *needing a mental holiday:* 'Juliet' by Avalon
- *needing self-compassion:* 'Human' by Rag'n'Bone Man

Make your own emotion and mood playlist. |

Tool	Humming, singing, chanting, gargling
What is it?	A little secret. You know how important I think finding your voice is? Well, you can self-regulate by humming, singing, chanting, and yes, by chanting I do mean OMMMMMM. Try it before you knock it. Likewise, try gargling after you have brushed your teeth.
How to apply it	- Hum your favourite song. - Sing along in the car, shower, house, wherever you like. - Chanting – you could start with 'OM' – try this in a group setting, like yoga or meditation, and you will be amazed at the impact upon you and as a connector. - Gargling – who doesn't love double-jobbing? Fresh breath and vagal tone? Yes, please! - I have noticed a lot of my clients are in choirs, and I nearly knew before they told me because it was like there was a space in their throat that they knew was a powerful tool to connect to themselves and others. The practice of singing had made a noticeable difference. You can practise anytime, anywhere.
Tool	Shoulder-to-shoulder talks
What is it?	When you need to have or start a hard conversation. Sometimes eye contact can get in the way of talking honestly. Some people respond really well to shoulder-to-shoulder talks – you can do this in the car or out walking, for some effective talking-and-walking therapy.

How to apply it	- Reflect on what you need to talk about.
- Write out beforehand how it is impacting you and what you'd like to get out of the conversation.
- Pull out your key thoughts.
- Frame it from a place of compassion and wanting to understand and be understood.
- Go for the walk and have the talk.
- It doesn't all have to get sorted then and there; starting is the hard part.
Tool	**Nature**
What is it?	Do you remember going on a nature walk as a kid armed with your nature sheet and pencil? Looking for the treasures of conkers, acorns, leaves, sticks and rocks? We had much more fun To Do lists back in those days.

    Anyone who walks with a child will have a mindful walk, whether they want to or not.

    I'm not asking you to stop every few steps to examine every rock or leaf you pass, but I wonder what senses you habitually block out or forget when you go for a walk?

    Does it end up being a multitasking 'opportunity'? You can find out by asking yourself if on your last walk you:

- Phoned a friend
- Listened to a podcast
- Blasted your favourite music
- Talked so much you barely drew breath?

If you did, you probably weren't fully present for the walk bit – and it benefits you hugely to be fully present, all senses engaged. |

How to apply it	- There is an everyday prize in nature, and it doesn't pay the bills but it will support you with the incessant physical, mental and cognitive demands placed upon you. Let your senses roam and take in every detail of the scene around you: the bird flying overhead; how the light dapples through the tree leaves and branches; the shadows moving; the crunch of the leaves or the cool green grass or soft sand beneath your feet. Be fully present as you walk.
- Going for a walk like this is a deeply effective way to soothe, release and regulate your nervous system.
- If you like, the first part of the walk can be more of a stomp, an angry internal muttering that compassionately acknowledges why it all feels too much. Then, when you're ready, do a releasing breath, and come fully into the space you are walking in.
- The pathway to down-regulating and soothing your nervous system can be induced by noticing patterns in nature, such as fractals (see page 335).
- If the rant-walk is needed first, embrace it, because openly acknowledging and validating how you feel heals more than you know. Trust me and keep trying it: angry walk first, stomp, stomp, stomp, then follow nature to get to feeling more connected and back in your body.

Tool	Fractals
What is it?	Fractals are natural geometric shapes with repeating patterns, known as the 'fingerprints of nature'. When you look at a leaf pattern or a snail shell, you are looking at fractals. Studies involving fMRI research have found that fractals have a therapeutic impact on our brains and that looking at them can reduce stress by 60 per cent, helping to regulate our emotions and promote feelings of relaxation and wellbeing. If you were like me at school, your copybooks and schoolbooks were probably decorated in strings of repeating patterns – that was your brain seeking solace in fractals. How does it work? When you look at fractals, there is a response inside your eye that increases alpha waves in your frontal lobe, which in turn delivers the body–mind feel-good factor. I think we all know this on an instinctive level. When I get bogged down at the PC, with all the tabs shouting for my attention, I take a break and go out to the garden and my attention always falls on one giant fern in particular. I just know that when I focus on its green shapes and patterns, I feel calmer. It soothes my frazzled mind. Sitting in my garden staring at plants to relax makes me definitely feeling middle-aged!
How to apply it	If you need to increase concentration, reduce stress, and feel calmer, one quick and easy way to achieve this is to go outside and take a fractal walk.

	- Look up fractals online, so you know exactly what you are seeking, then go for a walk with your eyes peeled for them and see how many fractals you can spot. - Look at the patterns and notice what impact they have on your body and mind. - Look for the 'Y' patterns in the branches of the trees – the reason behind this is that the sunlight can travel from the top of the trees all the way down to the bottom branches. - Notice your internal reactions: does it settle you, or change your breathing, or reduce irritation? - To add to it, take in some breaths, stretch, yawn, sigh. - Check in again. Did you notice a reduction in what may have felt like a pervasive sense of urgency? - Take a picture. Almost all my Instagram posts are nature shots, as I find they instantly calm and soothe me. You can create your own fractal gallery for when you need to rest your mind.
Tool	**Silence**
What is it?	A good friend of mine, Laura Carr, who is a lifelong meditation practitioner, always ends our walks by sitting facing the sea and inviting me to spend a few moments in silence. Sharing silence with someone is a powerful and infrequent experience. Let's challenge our notion of 'uncomfortable silence' and see it as a silent salve in our noisy world.

How to apply it	• Holding silence – 30 seconds. • Start with 30 seconds and notice what occurs. • You are not practising to become a monk, so expect a lot of mental monkeys jumping around from one thought branch to another, and acknowledge them. Even give them a wave – 'Hi, Monkey Mind, I see you.' • Then return to your breath, the moment and the ultimate luxury of momentary silence. • Intentionally spend time in silence.
Tool	**The breath of joy**

What is it?	When you need the energy of a cup of coffee in a breath.
	    This breath is a beauty. I tested this one hard. Right as I was about to grab another coffee straight after the first one, I knew I needed something with the same kick and energy of a coffee, but without the coffee. I can verify that I love this breath and how effective it is.
	    Please note: Not recommended if you have high blood pressure or eye issues, such as glaucoma, or eye injuries.

How to apply it	• Stand straight, feet shoulder distance apart, knees slightly bent. • Take three sharp inhales through your nose. • Inhale and raise your arms, swinging them up to your shoulders, palms facing up, and back down again. • Inhale again, swinging your arms parallel to your body and back down. • Inhale and swing your arms in front of your body, palms facing each other.

	- One long exhale with a 'ha' breath. - Bend your knees deeply as you exhale, swing your arms past your knees and up behind you. This fills your system with oxygen. Stop if you feel dizzy. Do it for three minutes, or what you feel works best for you. This may sound more complicated than it is: it is simply three sharp inhales, with one long 'ha' exhale, combined with the arm movements. If you, like me, can't follow instructions to save your life, you can find a full demonstration at: @thepractical.psychologist. This breath is hugely energetic and it invigorates and wakes up your system. Great for a quick movement break or when you feel stuck, sluggish, or not in a good mood.
Tool	**Grounding**
What is it?	When you need to come out of your head and feel centred in your body with a calm, energised recharge. It's the same principle as plugging in your phone to recharge the battery. You might think it sounds woo woo, but it's not – it's free and it works, so I give it a big thumbs-up.
How to apply it	- Take off your socks and stand your two lovely feet on the grass. - Take a deep breath in and as you release it, close your eyes. - Deepen the breathing by imagining roots coming from your feet, like a tree, and planting into the ground.

	- Straighten up through your spine and shoulders, easing out the creases and knots. Imagine a line the whole way through the centre of your body and gently pulling up towards the sky. - Feel yourself connected from beneath your feet to the top of your head. You are rooted and strong. - Take a lovely filling breath and feel life course through you. - Tune into your heart. - Listen to the sounds around you. - Feel the breeze on your hands or arms. - Feel energised, calm and centred. - And when the time feels right for you, thank yourself for the moment, for you, thank nature for sharing that moment and return to your day.
Tool	**Butterfly hug**
What is it?	This is an EMDR technique created by Lucy Atigas when helping survivors of hurricane Paulina in 1998. (EMDR, eye movement desensitisation and reprocessing, is a technique used in psychotherapy to promote healing from emotional distress.)
How to apply it	- Cross arms in an X at chest height – think of a sleeping Dracula pose. - You can lock your thumbs together to be like a butterfly. - Middle fingers under your collarbone. - Tap your hands alternately, flapping like a butterfly.

	• Do this for around 30 seconds, or until you feel a sense of relief.
Tool	**Pat down**
What is it?	Think of this as a friendly frisk to reduce anxiety. This type of proprioception (sensing where your body is in space) brings you back into your body and can feel grounding and calming.
How to apply it	• You can do this sitting, or lying down if someone does it for you. • Tap down your shoulders, chest, torso, thighs all the way to your feet. • Keep your hands flat • Do it twice, or as many times as you feel you need. • Breathe in and release.

Elemental Psychology

I have always felt grounded and connected to the four elements and have found the blend of nature and psychology transformative within my everyday life. The connection and interaction for your body, mind, emotions and soul create a richness that is invaluable – and free! I invite you to bring the cathartic energy of the fire element; the expansive transformative power of air to your breath; the soothing, invigorating, rebirthing experience of water to cleanse, clear and feel; and the grounding presence and stability of the earth.

Let's explore how you can bring the four elements into your everyday life.

FIRE

When you need to change and want to transform, purge the old ways and renew.

- Fire is transformative. It has great power, warmth and intensity. It draws people in for connection. It is the hearth and heart of a home.
- If you have a fireplace or stove, light it. If you don't, light a candle.
- You may have written down some of the things we have discussed thus far, answering the questions I have put to you, or you may wish to now write down the things you need to let go of, the things that are causing you anxiety, things you would like to stop doing. Write them down. Then burn the paper you wrote them on. It might sound a bit witchy, but the act of burning your list can be a deeply cathartic and releasing experience.
- Safety first, please! If using a candle, use a fireproof bowl and perhaps do it outside.

AIR

When you feel heavy and need to feel lighter in yourself, body, and soul.

- Practise intentional breathwork (see box breathing, page 118).
- Slow your breathing down, notice what speeds it up. Don't worry or judge – just notice.
- Listen to the rhythms of your breaths.
- Notice how different states elicit different breaths.
- Use this information to intentionally move from a state of Fight or Flight to rest and digest.
- Use your breath to create inner space in your mind and body. When your mind is full, use your breath to create some space, clarity and focus.
- Begin to trust your breath as an exceptionally powerful resource.

- If you have experienced panic attacks, I won't have to persuade you how powerful your breath it is; use it to feel good as well.
- Experiment with becoming familiar with what comforts you and slowly learn how to tolerate breaths that have previously brought feelings of angst, anxiety, and panic.
- If you feel uncomfortable or uneasy, place your hands on your chest and stomach. Breathe into your chest and into your belly, and then slowly exhale. Practise this slowly and mindfully.

WATER

When you feel stuck and need things to move, use water to bring in more flow.

- Intentionally increase your water intake if you do not drink enough.
- Look at water – the sea, rivers, lakes, fountains, garden water features, whatever soothes you.
- Listen to sea sounds, whether in real life or via your phone.
- Be in water, fully immersed or just to your neck, whatever you enjoy.
- If you feel anxious or stressed, splash your face with water, splash your hands beyond your wrists, take a cold shower, go swimming.

EARTH

When you need to feel a sense of solid ground, stability and reliability.

- Walk barefoot on grass or sand or go barefoot at home.
- Gardening – go outside, breathe, observe, and get your hands dirty.
- If you enjoy earth-based experiences, you could try a clay/pottery class. Hand-based art/craft is regulating, bringing you into the present moment. It is also deeply satisfying in part because it feels good to start and finish a project – an antidote to our task-driven lives.

- Lie on the ground. This gives great proprioceptive feedback and can bring feelings of safety. Proprioceptive feedback is the information from the sensory receptors in your muscles lying on the ground that send messages to your brain saying where your body is; it's like its own inner GPS. Now you know why toddlers lie down on the ground when they are feeling overwhelmed.

ETHER, WHICH HOLDS ALL FOUR ELEMENTS

When you need physical space and know you need to hold emotional space for yourself. You do this by creating a supportive and nurturing environment within yourself where you can process your emotions, thoughts and experiences free of judgement and criticism, allowing for self-awareness, self-compassion, and self-acceptance.

- Think of ways of actively creating space for yourself.
- Practise silence.
- Sit in silence.
- Notice when there is not enough space for you and change this, stating clear boundaries by expressing clearly what you need.

It is calming to know that the spaces in-between can become an integral part of your everyday joy to bring what you need to yourself ... even if this is just a few moments of silence and returning to your breath. (See page 297 for micro-moments.)

- Which element are you most drawn to and why?
- How is each different from the others?
- Which is most soothing, comforting, invigorating, refreshing?
- Why?

Write it out

We have mentioned before that writing down thoughts and feelings can be very therapeutic and can help to put them in context and understand them better. If this approach resonates with you, here are some writing prompts to use when you are in a tough or challenging moment or situation. This will help you to name the root of the issue, and then to name the steps you could take to resolve the issue. I recommend that you rip up your page into pieces after you've done this – for the emotional release, and for the privacy.

When I need to let go of (e.g. frustration):

_____

What I can do to repair (e.g. accept how I am feeling):

_____

The words I keep inside:

_____

What I can do to repair:

_____

Who I can share with:

_____

The parts of me I struggle with:

_____

What I can do to repair:

_____

It hurt me when you said:
_____

How I will repair:
_____

What I wanted to say was:
_____

How I could repair:
_____

Acknowledgements

I might start with a simple and deeply felt thank you. It takes support to do hard things and acknowledging this is important, as I didn't do it on my own.

So much of this book is about radical honesty and compassion bearing witness to the truth that modern life feels too much for too many. While this book is non-fiction, I have a wish that the reality of everyday life could be easier for everyone, and that is why I wrote it. Writing this, at times, felt like a psychological suspense thriller, as I ventured through the nervous system for answers. But the truth is, we must each ask ourselves what sacrifices are being made to continue living a pace of life that is untenable. I'd prefer a rom-com pace of life and my hope is that this book connects you back to yourself and others.

There are many people whose unwavering support helped me so much in what at times felt like too much.

When Sarah Liddy, senior commissioning editor at Gill Books, reached out to me after listening to the Joe Duffy *Liveline* show on anxiety and panic attacks, it opened the floodgates. People shared their struggles of managing frenetic lives, overwhelmed by anxiety. As Sarah and I sat chatting, she proposed the idea of a book on this topic. In my mind, I thought, *Of course*, but also wondered how I'd manage amidst my busy life. The 'how' is thanks to all of you.

I owe this accomplishment to the incredible people I love deeply. None of this would have been possible without the support of my family. Throughout the writing process, I received invaluable time, understanding, and countless hugs – essential ingredients in book-making. My husband, Thomas, took the girls on trips to Ballaghaderreen so I could write and did many a shop run, school run and his own runs to be able to help with our very busy household; also managing me and my bold brain that was permanently switched to book mode, with many a midnight chat as I excitedly shared my fascinating polyvagal research, with much laughter and 'Go to sleep, Allison, switch off your brain.' So a huge thank you to my amazing husband, whom I love so much.

To our beautiful three girls, thank you for being my heart, soul and everything that matters.

Thank you, Alannah, for your kindness and chats, you are one in a million and have a heart of gold.

Thank you, Hayley, as you'd dance into the room and we'd dance up and down the kitchen, providing much-needed movement breaks, and the surprise coffees that brought warmth and support.

Thank you, Brooke, for the beautiful cards and words of encouragement, laughter and constant hugs and letting me 'do my work'. I truly appreciate what you all did.

I know I went over my word count, so there isn't enough room to give enough thanks due here to my amazing family. They know how much I love them, and I know how lucky I am.

To my mum and dad, Mary and Val, constant sources of inspiration and hands-on support. Thank you for listening to me talk about the book and holding space for me with unconditional love and warmth. I appreciate you both so much.

To my sisters, thank you: Barbara, for dragging me out for quick walks and talks, and roast dinners on a plate served with a warm heart and ear; Carol Ann, when your *'you got this'* mug arrived at my front door and filled me up so much and got me across the finish line;

Sarah-Jane, thank you for always being there as you endured my epic rants, my constant pal as I poured out my heart, to be met with kindness and comfort, always managing to make me laugh.

A special thanks for the many days spent working at M-Space, Barbara and Carol Ann's workspace hub, which provided me with room to think and to work uninterrupted. Except hopefully when I wasn't interrupting my writing buddy Cecelia Ahern next door. Thanks for all the chats and encouragement, as always.

To Tommy and Ogie, my wonderful in-laws, and to all my nieces and nephews on both sides, I love you all so much.

To my psychologist buddies, you know who you are. Deborah Mulvany, from our days in Maud's café, thank you always for your friendship and so much laughter and love.

Sinead Brady, I loved our voice-note podcasts, thank you for being the soundest sounding-board in every aspect of the word.

Niamh Fitzpatrick, as I think about it, I have basically friendship voice-noted all these amazing people, and Niamh, your kindness, wisdom and cheering me on helped so much. There were so many unexpected doorstop drops; they meant a lot. Despite not seeing many of you for a while, I felt deeply connected and supported by all of you amazing people. Thank you.

To Laura Carr and Victoria Jones, amidst our laughter, walks and supportive talks, I know how lucky I am to have found myself some truly amazing spicy soul-sisters.

To the book club, Paint, and schoolgirls, my voice-note ladies from Carol and Karen and many more, my lovely neighbours and friends, thank you.

Thank you, Sarah Liddy, for inviting me to write this book, my second book with Gill. I'm deeply passionate about aiding clients in transforming their relationship with anxiety and life. I'm grateful for the opportunity to extend this mission to reach as many people as possible, fulfilling a profoundly meaningful purpose in my life.

Aoibheann Molumby, editorial manager at Gill, thank you for everything. I loved our brainstorming sessions together, where you helped me see not only from a psychologist's perspective but also how to effectively translate session experiences to the reader.

Rachel Pierce, my wonderful editor, thank you so much for your guidance and hard work on book number two together. I felt very supported by you, your expert guidance and kind support. Thank you immensely.

To the superb team at Gill, thank you Jane Rogers for the copy-editing, publicist Kristen Olson, Charlie Lawlor and everyone who works incredibly hard to make a book transform from something in my mind to a bookshelf, and into readers' hands. It is hugely important work.

To Faith O'Grady, my literary agent, thank you for believing in me and championing my work once again.

To my inspirational clients who teach me every day and inspire me that the human spirit can overcome, grow and become more beautiful every day. This book is for each and every one of you.

To all of you who have felt exhausted, lost and like it was only you. I wrote this book to show you the way back home to you. To change one nervous system at a time, to collectively change how we live our lives with compassion, integrity, and humanity.

With much love and thanks,

Allison x

Notes

1. *Anxiety and Depression Association of America. (n.d.). Anxiety disorders – Facts and statistics.* Retrieved September 7, 2023, from https://adaa.org/understanding-anxiety/facts-statistics.
2. Deborah Dana is a clinician and founding member of the Polyvagal Institute. This section is adapted from her *Polyvagal Practices: Anchoring the Self in Safety* (2023). W.W. Norton & Co.
3. Adapted from Stephen Porges (1995). 'Orienting in a defensive world: Mammalian modifications of our evolutionary heritage: A polyvagal theory', *Psychophysiology* 32:301–318, https://pubmed.ncbi.nlm.nih.gov/7652107.
4. Siegel, D. (1999). *The Developing Mind: How Relationships and the Brain Interact to Shape Who We Are.* Guilford Press.
5. van der Kolk, B. (2014). *The Body Keeps the Score: Brain, Mind, and Body in Healing of Trauma.* Penguin Random House.
6. Levine, P.A. (1997). *Waking the tiger: Healing trauma: The innate capacity to transform overwhelming experiences.* North Atlantic Books.
7. Menakem, R. (2017). *My Grandmother's Hands: Racialised Trauma and the Pathway to Mending Our Hearts and Bodies.* Central Recovery Press.
8. Brown, B. (2021). *Atlas of the Heart: Mapping Meaningful Connection and the Language of Human Experience.* Penguin Random House.

9   Shinn, F.S. (1978). *The Game of Life and How to Play It.* DeVorss & Co.
10   Keating, A. (2018). *The Secret Lives of Adults.* Gill Books.
11   World Health Organization. (n.d.). Anxiety disorders. Retrieved from https://www.who.int/news-room/fact-sheets/detail/anxiety-disorders.
12   Dyson, B. (1996, September 6). Speech presented at Georgia Tech.
13   Otten, D., Tibubos, A. N., Schomerus, G., Brähler, E., Binder, H., Kruse, J., Ladwig, K. H., Wild, P. S., Grabe, H. J., & Beutel, M. E. (2021, February 5). 'Similarities and differences of mental health in women and men: A systematic review of findings in three large German cohorts, *Frontiers in Public Health*, 9, 5 February, https://doi.org/10.3389/fpubh.2021.553071.
14   News-Medical.net. (2022). The gender gap in mental health. Retrieved from https://www.news-medical.net/health/The-Gender-Gap-in-Mental-Health.aspx.
15   Garnett, M.F., & Curtin, S.C. (2023). 'Suicide mortality in the United States, 2001–2021', NCHS Data Brief no. 464. Hyattsville, MD: National Center for Health Statistics, https://dx.doi.org/10.15620/cdc:125705.
16   Hochschild, A. R. (1983). *The Managed Heart: Commercialisation of Human Feeling.* University of California Press.
17   Wingfield, A. H. (2016, January 26). 'How "Service with a Smile" takes a toll on women', *The Atlantic*, https://www.theatlantic.com/business/archive/2016/01/gender-emotional-labor/427083/.
18   Lee, L., & Madera, J. (2019). 'Faking it or feeling it: The emotional displays of surface and deep acting on stress and engagement', *International Journal of Contemporary Hospitality Management*, 31(10), 1108, IJCHM-05-2018-0405.
19   Zvobgo, V., Abraham, R., & Sabharwal, M. (2022). 'Faking versus feeling emotions: Does personality–job fit make a difference?', *Public Personnel Management* 51(1), 125–148, https://doi.org/10.1177/00910260211034213.
20   Emma. (2018). *The Mental Load: A Feminist Comic.* Seven Stories Press.
21   Wittchen, H. U., Jacobi, F., Rehm, J., Gustavsson, A., Svensson, M., Jönsson, B., Olesen, J., Allgulander, C., Alonso, J., Faravelli, C.,

Fratiglioni, L., Jennum, P., Lieb, R., Maercker, A., van Os, J., Preisig, M., Salvador-Carulla, L., Simon, R., & Steinhausen, H. C. (2011). 'The size and burden of mental disorders and other disorders of the brain in Europe 2010', *European Neuropsychopharmacology* 21(9), 655–679, https://doi.org/10.1016/j.euroneuro.2011.07.018

22 Borysenko, J. (1998). *A Woman's Book of Life: The Biology, Psychology, and Spirituality of the Feminine Life Cycle.* Riverhead Trade.

23 Maté, G. (2011). *When the Body Says No: Exploring the Stress–Disease Connection.* Trade Paper Press.

24 Woody, C.A., Ferrari, A., Siskind, D., Whiteford. H., & Harris M.A. (2017). 'A systematic review and meta-regression of the prevalence and incidence of perinatal depression', *Journal of Affective Disorders* 219: 86–92.

25 Mughal, S., Azhar, Y., & Siddiqui, W. 'Postpartum Depression'. [Updated 2022 Oct 7]. In: StatPearls [Internet]. Treasure Island (FL): StatPearls Publishing; 2024 Jan. Available from: https://www.ncbi.nlm.nih.gov/books/NBK519070/

26 Cleveland Clinic. (n.d.). Postpartum anxiety. Retrieved from https://my.clevelandclinic.org/health/diseases/22693-postpartum-anxiety

27 Nillni, Y. I., Mehralizade, A., Mayer, L., & Milanovic, S. (2018). 'Treatment of depression, anxiety, and trauma-related disorders during the perinatal period: A systematic review', *Clinical Psychology Review* 66: 136–148, https://doi.org/10.1016/j.cpr.2018.06.004.

28 Bindeman, J. (2024). 'Postpartum anxiety can't happen to me'. Retrieved from https://www.anxiety.org/postpartum-anxiety-risk-factors.

29 Ali, E. (2018). 'Women's experiences with postpartum anxiety disorders: A narrative literature review', *International Journal of Women's Health* 10: 237–249, https://doi.org/10.2147/IJWH.S158621.

30 Levine, P.A. (2010). *In an Unspoken Voice: How the Body Releases Trauma and Restores Goodness.* Berkeley, CA: North Atlantic Books.

31 Levine, P.A. (1997). *Waking the Tiger: Healing Trauma: The Innate Capacity to Transform Overwhelming Experiences.* Berkeley, CA, North Atlantic Books.

32 Hari, J. (2023). *Stolen Focus: Why You Can't Pay Attention*. Bloomsbury.

33 Lembke, A. (2021). *Dopamine Nation: Finding Balance in the Age of Indulgence*. Penguin Random House.

34 Diener, E., & R. Biswas-Diener, R. (2008). *Happiness: Unlocking the Mysteries of Psychological Wealth*. Blackwell Publishing.

35 Van der Kolk, B. (2006). 'Clinical implications of neuroscience research in PTSD', *Annals of the New York Academy of Sciences* 1071, 277–293, 10.1196/annals.1364.022.

36 Kanaya, Y., & Kawai, N. (2024). 'Anger is eliminated with the disposal of a paper written because of provocation', *Scientific Reports* 14(1), doi: 10.1038/s41598-024-57916-z.

37 Attributed to Anne Lamott, among others.

38 Linehan, M.M. (1993). *Cognitive-Behavioral Treatment of Borderline Personality Disorder*. New York: Guilford Press.

39 Anderson, B. O., Berdzuli, N., Ilbawi, A., Kestel, D., Kluge, H. P., Krech, R., Mikkelsen, B., Neufeld, M., Poznyak, V., Rekve, D., Slama, S., Tello, J., & Ferreira-Borges, C. (2023). 'Health and cancer risks associated with low levels of alcohol consumption', *Lancet Public Health*, January 8(1):e6-e7, doi: 10.1016/S2468-2667(22)00317-6. PMID: 36603913; PMCID: PMC9831798.

40 Rodsky, E. (2021). *Fair Play: Share the Mental Load, Rebalance your Relationship and Transform your Life*. Quercus Publishing.

41 Gerber, M. E. (1995). *The E-Myth Revisited: Why Most Small Businesses Don't Work and What To Do About It*. Collins Business.

42 Dweck, C.S. (2008). *Mindset: The New Psychology of Success*. Ballantine Books.

43 Dana. D. (2020). *Befriending Your Nervous System: Looking Through the Lens of Polyvagal Theory*, audiobook. Sounds True.

44 Weinstein, B. [brookeweinst]. (2024, June 20). Instagram. https://www.instagram.com/brookeweinst/p/C6r1pdVIrRo/

Bibliography

Abe, K., & Nakashima, K. (2022). 'Excessive reassurance-seeking and mental health: Interpersonal networks for emotion regulation', *Current Psychology* 41(7), 4711–4721, https://doi.org/10.1007/s12144-020-00955-2.

Ali, E. (2018). 'Women's experiences with postpartum anxiety disorders: A narrative literature review', *International Journal of Women's Health* 10, 237–249. https://doi.org/10.2147/IJWH.S158621.

American Psychiatric Association (APA) (2013). *Diagnostic and Statistical Manual of Mental Disorders* (5th edn). Washington, DC: APA.

Anderson, B.O., Berdzuli, N., Ilbawi, A., Kestel, D., Kluge, H.P., Krech, R., Mikkelsen, B., Neufeld, M., Poznyak, V., Rekve, D., Slama, S., Tello, J., & Ferreira-Borges C. (2023). 'Health and cancer risks associated with low levels of alcohol consumption', *Lancet Public Health* 8(1), e6-e7, https://doi.org/10.1016/S2468-2667(22)00317-6.

Angum, F., Khan, T., Kaler, J., Siddiqui, L., & Hussain, A. (2020). 'The prevalence of autoimmune disorders in women: A narrative review', *Cureus* 12(5): e8094, https://doi.org/10.7759/cureus.8094.

Baldwin, J. (1962). 'As much truth as one can bear', *New York Times*, https://www.nytimes.com.

Bandelow, B., Boerner, J.R., Kasper, S., Linden, M., Wittchen, H.U., & Möller, H.J. (2013). 'The diagnosis and treatment of generalised anxiety disorder', *Deutsches Ärzteblatt International* 110(17): 300–310, https://doi.org/10.3238/arztebl.2013.0300.

Berman, M., Jonides, J., & Kaplan, S. (2009). 'The cognitive benefits of interacting with nature', *Psychological Science* 19: 1207–1212, https://doi.org/10.1111/j.1467-9280.2008.02225.x.

Brown, B. (2010). *The Gifts of Imperfection*. Hazelden Information and Educational Services.

Brown, R. M. (1983). *Sudden Death*. Bantam Books.

Carlson, D.L., Miller, A.J., Sassler, S., & Hanson, S. (2016). 'The gendered division of housework and couples' sexual relationships: A reexamination', *Journal of Marriage and Family* 78(4): 975–995, https://doi.org/10.1111/jomf.12313.

Claxton, G. (2016). *Intelligence in the Flesh: Why Your Mind Needs Your Body Much More Than It Thinks*. Yale University Press.

Cronise, R.J., Sinclair, D.A., & Bremer, A.A. (2014). 'The "metabolic winter" hypothesis: A cause of the current epidemics of obesity and cardiometabolic disease', *Metabolic Syndrome and Related Disorders* 12(7): 355–361, https://doi.org/10.1089/met.2014.0027.

Dana, D. (2018). *The Polyvagal Theory in Therapy: Engaging the Rhythm of Regulation*. Guilford Press.

Dana, D. (2020). *Befriending Your Nervous System: Looking Through the Lens of Polyvagal Theory*, audiobook. Sounds True.

Dana, D. (2020). *Polyvagal Exercises for Safety and Connection: 50 Client-centered Practices*. W. W. Norton & Company.

Dana, D. (2021). *Anchored: How to Befriend your Nervous System using Polyvagal Theory*, audiobook. Sounds True.

Diener, E., & Biswas-Diener, R. (2008). *Happiness: Unlocking the Mysteries of Psychological Wealth*. Blackwell Publishing.

Dunbar, R.I.M. (2010). *How many Friends does One Person Need? Dunbar's Number and other Evolutionary Quirks*. Faber and Faber.

Dweck, C.S. (2008). *Mindset*. Ballantine Books.

Eisenberger, N.I., Lieberman, M.D., & Williams, K.D. (2003). 'Does rejection hurt? An FMRI study of social exclusion', *Science* 302(5643): 290–292, https://doi.org/10.1126/science.1089134.

Esperland, D., de Weerd, L., & Mercer, J.B. (2022). 'Health effects of voluntary exposure to cold water: A continuing subject of debate', *International Journal of Circumpolar Health*, 81(1): 2111789, https://doi.org/10.1080/22423982.2022.2111789.

Estés, C.P. (1992). *Women who Run with the Wolves: Myths and Stories of the Wild Woman Archetype.* Ballantine Books.

Fuchs, M., Sinclair, D., & Lembke, A. (2022). 'Are ice-cold showers good for you? I tried it for two months', *Washington Post*, 10 March.

Gerber, M.E. (1995). *The E-myth Revisited: Why Most Small Businesses Don't Work and What To Do About It.* Collins Business.

Golding, K. (2015). 'Connection before correction: Supporting parents to meet the challenges of parenting children who have been traumatised within their early parenting environments', *Children Australia* 40: 1-8, https://doi.org/10.1017/cha.2015.9.

González, V. M., & Mark, G. (2004). '"Constant, constant, multi-tasking craziness": Managing multiple working spheres', *Proceedings of the SIGCHI Conference on Human Factors in Computing Systems*, pp. 113–120). ACM.

Hagerhall, C.M., Laike, T., Küller, M., Marcheschi, E., Boydston, C., & Taylor, R.P. (2015). 'Human physiological benefits of viewing nature: EEG responses to exact and statistical fractal patterns', *Nonlinear Dynamics, Psychology, and Life Sciences* 19(1): 1–12.

Hari, J. (2023). *Stolen Focus: Why You Can't Pay Attention – And how to Think Deeply Again.* Bloomsbury.

Harvard Health Publishing. (2020). 'Understanding the stress response'. Retrieved from https://www.health.harvard.edu/staying-healthy/understanding-the-stress-response.

Hochschild, A.R. (1983). *The Managed Heart: Commercialisation of Human Feeling.* University of California Press.

Howes, R. (2009). 'The definition of insanity: Perseverance versus perseveration', *Psychology Today*, https://www.psychologytoday.com/ie/blog/in-therapy/200907/the-definition-insanity.

Jarero, I., & Artigas, L. (2012). 'The EMDR integrative group treatment protocol: EMDR group treatment for early intervention following critical incidents', *Revue Européenne de Psychologie Appliquée* 62: 219–222, https://doi.org/10.1016/j.erap.2012.04.004.

Kanaya, Y., & Kawai, N. (2024). 'Anger is eliminated with the disposal of a paper written because of provocation', *Scientific Reports* 14(1), doi: 10.1038/s41598-024-57916-z.

Lembke, A. (2021). *Dopamine Nation: Finding Balance in the Age of Indulgence*. Dutton.

LePera, N. (2021). *How to do the Work: Recognize Your Patterns, Heal from Your Past and Create Your Self*. HarperCollins.

Levine, P.A. (1997). *Waking the Tiger: Healing Trauma : The Innate Capacity to Transform Overwhelming Experiences*. North Atlantic Books.

Levine, P. (2010). *In an Unspoken Voice: How the Body Releases Trauma and Restores Goodness*. North Atlantic Books.

Linehan, M.M. (1993). *Cognitive-Behavioral Treatment of Borderline Personality Disorder*. New York: Guilford Press.

Lisle, D.J., & Goldhamer, A. (2003). *The Pleasure Trap: Mastering the Hidden Force that Undermines Health and Happiness*. Healthy Living.

Lorenz-Spreen, P., Mønsted, B.M., Hövel, P. & Lehmann, S. (2019). 'Accelerating dynamics of collective attention', *Nature Communications*, 1–9, https://doi.org/10.1038/s41467-019-09311-w.

Mandelbrot, B. (1990). 'Fractals – a geometry of nature: Fractal geometry plays two', *New Scientist*, https://www.newscientist.com/article/mg12717343-900-fractals-a-geometry-of-nature-fractal-geometry-plays-two/.

Mark, G., Gonzalez, V.M., & Harris, J. (2005). 'No task left behind? Examining the nature of fragmented work', *Proceedings of the SIGCHI Conference on Human Factors in Computing Systems*, pp. 321–330). ACM, https://doi.org/10.1145/1054972.1055017.

Mark, G., Iqbal, S.T., Czerwinski, M., & Johns. P. (2015). 'Focused, Aroused, but so Distractible: Temporal Perspectives on Multitasking and Communications', in D. Cosley, A. Forte, L. Ciolfi and D. McDonald (eds.), *Proceedings of the 18th ACM Conference on Computer Supported Cooperative Work and Social Computing*, CSCW 2015, Vancouver, BC, Canada, March 14–18 (pp. 903–916).

Maté, G. (2003). *When the Body Says No: The Cost of Hidden Stress*. A.A. Knopf.

Maté, G., & Maté, D. (2022). *The Myth of Normal: Trauma, Illness and Healing in a Toxic Culture*. Avery.

Muscara, C. (Instagram post) https://www.instagram.com/p/CpSqt-HvqtN/.

Nillni, Y.I., Mehralizade, A., Mayer, L., & Milanovic, S. (2018). 'Treatment of depression, anxiety, and trauma-related disorders during the perinatal period: A systematic review', *Clinical Psychology Review* 66: 136–148, https://doi.org/10.1016/j.cpr.2018.06.004.

Perry, B.D., & Winfrey, O. (2021). *What Happened to You? Conversations on Trauma, Resilience and Healing*. Flatiron Press.

Pert, C. B. (1999). *Molecules of Emotion: Why You Feel the Way You Feel*. Touchstone.

Porges, S.W. (1995). 'Orienting in a defensive world: Mammalian modifications of our evolutionary heritage. A polyvagal theory', *Psychophysiology* 32(4): 301–318, https://doi.org/10.1111/j.1469-8986.1995.tb01213.x.

Porges, S.W. (2022). 'Polyvagal theory: A science of safety', *Frontiers in Integrative Neuroscience* 16: 871227, https://doi.org/10.3389/fnint.2022.871227.

Porges, S.W., Doussard-Roosevelt, J.A., & Maiti, A.K. (1994). 'Vagal tone and the physiological regulation of emotion', *Monographs of the Society for Research in Child Development* 59(2/3): 167–186, https://doi.org/10.2307/1166144.

Rodsky, E. (2019). *Fair Play: A Game-Changing Solution for when you have too much to do (And more Life to Live)*. Random House.

Santin, M., & Kelly, B. (2017). 'The Managed Heart revisited: Exploring the effect of institutional norms on the emotional labor of flight attendants post 9/11', *Journal of Contemporary Ethnography* 46(5): 519–543, https://doi.org/10.1177/0891241615619991.

Sher, B. (1998). *It's Only Too Late if You Don't Start Now: How to Create Your Second Life after Forty*. Delacorte Press.

Sherrington, C.S. (2007). *The Integrative Action of the Nervous System*. Yale University Press.

Shinn, F.S. (1925). *The Game of Life and How to Play It*. DeVorss.

Substance Abuse and Mental Health Services Administration. (2016). *DSM-5 Changes: Implications for Child Serious Emotional Disturbance*. Substance Abuse and Mental Health Services Administration.

Thoreau, H.D. (1971). *Walden*, ed. J. Lyndon Shanley. Princeton University Press.

van der Kolk, B.A. (2006). 'Clinical implications of neuroscience research in PTSD', *Annals of the New York Academy of Sciences* 1071: 277–293, https://doi.org/10.1196/annals.1364.022.

van der Kolk, B.A. (2014). *The Body Keeps the Score: Brain, Mind, and Body in the Healing of Trauma*. Viking.

Wingfield, H.A. (2016). 'How "service with a smile" takes a toll on women', *The Atlantic*, https://www.theatlantic.com/business/archive/2016/01/gender-emotional-labor/427083/.

Wittchen, H.U., Jacobi, F., Rehm, J., Gustavsson, A., Svensson, M., Jönsson, B., Olesen, J., Allgulander, C., Alonso, J., Faravelli, C., Fratiglioni, L., Jennum, P., Lieb, R., Maercker, A., van Os, J., Preisig, M., Salvador-Carulla, L., Simon, R. & Steinhausen, H.C. (2011). 'The size and burden of mental disorders and other disorders of the brain in Europe 2010', *European Neuropsychopharmacology* 21(9): 655–679, https://doi.org/10.1016/j.euroneuro.2011.07.018.

Woody, C.A., Ferrari, A., Siskind, D., Whiteford, H., & Harris, M. (2017). 'A systematic review and meta-regression of the prevalence and incidence of perinatal depression', *Journal of Affective Disorders* 219: 86–92, https://doi.org/10.1016/j.jad.2017.05.003.

Zvobgo, V., Abraham, R., & Sabharwal, M. (2022). 'Faking versus feeling emotions: Does personality–job fit make a difference?', *Public Personnel Management* 51(1): 125–148, https://doi.org/10.1177/00910260211034213.